D1083035

Against Mechanism

AGAINST MECHANISM

Protecting Economics from Science

PHILIP MIROWSKI
Tufts University

ROWMAN & LITTLEFIELD
Publishers

ROWMAN & LITTLEFIELD

Published in the United States of America in 1988
by Rowman & Littlefield, Publishers
(a division of Littlefield, Adams & Company)
81 Adams Drive, Totowa, New Jersey 07512

Library of Congress Cataloging-in-Publication Data

Mirowski, Philip, 1951–
  Against mechanism: protecting economics from science /
Philip Mirowski.
  Bibliography: p. 233
  Includes index.
  ISBN 0-8476-7436-3
  1. Economics—History. 2. Science—History. I. Title.
HB71.M635 1987
330′.09—dc19

90 89 88
4 3 2 1

Printed in the United States of America

This one's for Pam:
being married to an economist is not
everyone's idea of fun

Contents

Acknowledgments

I have been lucky for someone who never really was terrifically enamored of joining the Economists' Club, in that a number of economists have been willing to listen to some of my wilder ideas and taken them seriously enough to criticize them. The parade of open-minded economists began with my thesis advisor, Gavin Wright, although I still wonder what he really makes of all of it. Chapters 1 and 6 were improved immeasurably by discussions and correspondence with Larry Samuelson. The participants in seminars at Harvard, University of Massachusetts–Amherst, Yale, Wellesley, Stanford, Duke, Syracuse, and the Princeton Program in the History of Science all contributed to clarification of ideas herein. An invitation to participate in a conference on the Rhetoric of Economics at Wellesley College in April 1986 prompted me to write Chapter 8: I hold this experience as my own personal proof that events and circumstances influence our research agenda much more than we might like to admit. A preliminary draft of Chapter 10 was written during a stay in London in 1977; I owe much gratitude to Dawn and Eddie Finn for providing the warmth and comfort that made it possible.

I would like to acknowledge the comments and express thanks to (in no particular order): Roy Weintraub, Geoff Harcourt, Bob Coats, David Weiman, Carol Heim, Avi Cohen, Alex Field, Martin O'Connor, Warren Samuels, Norton Wise, Theodore Porter, Don Katzner, Randall Bausor, Barry Eichengreen, Edward Norton, Bob Wolfson, Samuel Hollander, Bruce Caldwell, William Parker, Arjo Klamer, Neil de Marchi, Michael Bernstein, William Darity, Craufurd Goodwin and Paul Wendt. Curiously enough, Duncan Foley started me down this road, even though he has no idea that he was the catalyst. I am grateful to my brother Paul for providing lawyerly and other sorts of advice. Also, thanks to John Pepper for helping with the index, and to Tufts and IBM for the personal computer: how did anyone revise without it?

I would also like to thank the following for permission to reprint all or parts of the following which have appeared elsewhere: Chapters 1 and 12, Academic Press; Chapter 3, the *Journal of Economic History;* Chapters 4, 7, and 9, the *Journal of Economic Issues;* Chapter 5, Kluwer-Nijhoff Publishers; Chapter 6, *Philosophy of the Social Sciences;* and Chapter 11, *History of Political Economy* and Duke University Press.

Against Mechanism

Introduction

How to Protect Economics
from Science

> The economic laws aimed at and formulated under the guidance of this preconception are laws of what takes place "naturally" or "normally," and it is of the essence of things so conceived that in the natural or normal course there is no wasted or misdirected effort . . . the resulting economic theory is formulated as an analysis of the "natural" course of the life of the community, the ultimate theoretical postulate of which might, not unfairly, be stated as some sort of law of the conservation of economic energy . . . there prevails an equivalence of expenditure and returns, an equilibrium of flux and reflux, which is not broken over in the normal course of things. So it is, by implication, assumed that the product which results from any given industrial process or operation is, in some sense or unspecified aspect, the equivalent of the expenditure of forces, or the effort, or what not, that has gone into the process out of which the product emerges.
>
> —Thorstein Veblen, *Industrial and Pecuniary Employments,* 1900

I am a teacher, and one thing I have learned is that the preponderance of teaching consists of bold assertions in the face of ignorance, solipsistic skepticism, and contentious disbelief. One of the tricks of teaching is to deflect this dialectic by presenting knowledge as a pragmatic sequence of "how to" exercises, where techniques and answers lead to others in an insistent and satisfying lockstep. Yet even here one cannot readily avoid the chicken-or-egg problem. At the very beginning of a course of study in a new discipline, the "why" questions are difficult to avoid, at least initially. When the "whys" are unavoidable, the most frequent recourse is to the putative "laws" of the phenomenon: laws of nature, laws of behavior, laws of thought, laws of regularity.

I have always been a little uneasy and perhaps even ambivalent about this curious appeal to laws. The very metaphor itself embodies a contradiction. Laws are conventions constructed by human beings, yet often they are invested with legitimacy through appeals to overarching principles or rules that are not the handiwork of humans. Particularly in the disciplines that seek to explain human society, the concept of law is frequently used, but not without a certain defensiveness. "We have laws, too," the social "scientists" maintain, with a nervous glance in the direction of their colleagues, the physical scientists.

In my capacity as an economist, I have often felt that tingle of embarrassment, that vertigo. One must begin an inquiry somewhere, and an appeal to law is as good as any other authoritarian ploy. But what was it about that ritual obeisance in the direction of science that made me uneasy? I found this an extremely elusive problem, although one that had also troubled a few economists before me. For instance, I discovered this concern, and hence an instinctive empathy with the American Institutionalist school of economists and, in particular, with the work of Thorstein Veblen, because he also appeared to be driven to question the relationship of an understanding of economic activities to "science." But the answers of the institutionalists seemed diffuse, and I must admit that initially I did not comprehend the depth of Veblen's critique. To try to clarify the issues in my own mind, I then decided to look to my counterparts in the physical sciences to see how they responded to this conundrum.

One of the places I started was a popularized account of natural law by one of the most flamboyant and articulate physicists of our time, Richard Feynman. In his *The Character of Physical Law* (1965), he chose to begin his series of lectures with the Newtonian gravitational law. The gravitational law is a perennial favorite of the pedagogue because it is reassuringly simple, seemingly familiar, and appears to be universal. Feynman is careful not to overdraw this portrait, reminding us that even though Newtonian gravitation can claim the status of a "law," it has been modified in the theory of relativity and by quantum theory, and we have still to get it exactly right. A fine balance is struck: there are laws, but we only approach their truth content.

What is fascinating about these lectures is that Feynman does not long maintain this balance. In the next lecture, instead of tendering another equally satisfying example of a physical law, we are told that "mathematics is a deep way of expressing nature, and any attempt to express nature in philosophical principle, or in seat-of-the-pants mechanical feelings, is not an efficient way" (ibid., 57). What has all this to do with law? Feynman himself apparently was not sure, since in the space of the same lecture he claimed that "nature" is intrinsically mathematical, but also appealed to the supposedly inductive observation that nonmathematical reasoning in physics has not been very fruitful. Matters are further clouded by the admission that there exists no unique mathematical expression of any physical principle. Feynman then purveys yet a third way of looking at mathematics and law: "mathematics is not just another language. Mathematics is language plus reasoning; it is like a language plus logic . . . if you do not appreciate mathematics, you cannot see, among the great variety of facts, that logic permits you to go from one to another" (ibid., 41). At this juncture, I realized that I had heard this all before in the context of methodological discussions in economics. Frankly, it hadn't been very persuasive in that context, and it wasn't any more compelling when it came out of the mouths of physicists.[1]

In Feynman's third lecture, he surveyed a class of physical laws called "conservation laws." "The physicist uses ordinary words in a peculiar manner. To him a conservation law means that there is a number which you can calculate at one moment, then as nature undergoes its multitude of changes, if you calculate this quantity again at a later time it will be the same as it was before; the number does not change" (ibid., 59). Feynman proffers examples such as the conservation of energy, the conservation of angular momentum, the conservation of electric charge, and so on. For a while it seems we have hit upon another set of simple and universal laws, but then we are brought up short: Feynman allows that conservation laws might not really be physical laws at all, but rather *characteristics* or *rules* which govern the format or expression of physical laws. For instance, physicists once believed that mass was conserved, and later believed that energy was conserved, but Einstein's infamous equation $E = mc^2$ collapsed them both into a more general principle. A hint of a suspicion arises, which Feynman does not openly refute, that all of these conservation principles are merely artifacts of our attempts to describe formally things that undergo change. Most interesting to an economist, Feynman compares such relationships between horsepower hours, foot pounds, electron volts, and calories to the relationships between dollars and cents, shillings and pounds (ibid., 74). It seemed to me that, at least for economists, the institution of money was the paradigm of the conventional, and the farthest thing from that talisman of the lawlike, the physical. The curious status of conservation laws in physics prompted me to investigate the history of physics in greater detail, and what I discovered there directly resulted in the ideas contained in Part I of this volume. Those historical connections in turn led me to read more deeply in the literatures of philosophy and philosophical anthropology, especially the works of the early pragmatists, such as Charles Sanders Peirce, and others such as Richard Rorty, Mary Hesse, and Émile Meyerson, as well as the works of Durkheim, Mauss, and Mary Douglas. The first fruits of that endeavor may be found below in Chapters 7 and 8, which explicitly discuss the process of the reification of social law through projection of natural law, as well as the giddy reflections of our own visage in the mirror of nature.

But back to Feynman. What is happening to those nice simple laws, those physical (and therefore independent) touchstones of our understanding? By the time he reaches quantum mechanics, even Feynman has to admit that his survey of the notion of physical law is genteelly coming apart at the seams. Provocatively, Feynman suggests that all of the "characteristics" of physical laws that he has discussed—symmetry, probability, and conservation principles in classical mechanics, thermodynamics, quantum mechanics, and relativity—if imposed simultaneously as a joint law, give inconsistent and unacceptable results. What *has* happened to physical law? This end-product of physical research, our heritage of physical law, is self-contradictory; one or more of its "characteristics" must be jettisoned. "The question is, what to throw away, and what to keep. If you throw it all away that is going a little far, and then you have not much to work with. After all, the conservation of energy looks good, and it is nice, and I do not want to throw it away. To guess what to keep and what to throw away takes considerable skill" (ibid., 166).

Now, we would not wish to accept a loose-jointed popular lecture as an adequate discussion of either physics or of the philosophy of physical law, but that is not the point. We are concerned now with my original chicken-and-egg problem—how does one initiate a convincing research program? Economists begin by appealing to "laws," as if everyone understood what was meant by such an appeal. When pressed on the issue, these economists then tend to pass the buck to "physics" and their image of science as the lender of credibility of last resort. Yet here is an eminent physicist who is unwilling to accept the debased currency; and indeed, a more profound acquaintance with the history and philosophy of physics only further encourages skepticism with respect to an explicit scientific law and scientific method.[2] Of course, all of this could be written off as pragmatic storytelling, something on the order of "Lies My Teachers Told Me," except that its consequences are particularly insidious and all-pervasive when one thinks about social and economic processes. In other words, appeals to physical law are not just pedagogic devices in the context of economics; they hide and obscure one of the fundamental "unobtrusive postulates" of social theory in the West.

I have not chosen the Feynman lectures at random. Not only do they display the rather imprecise notions of physical law to be found among practicing physicists; they also display the rather incongruous attitudes of scientists toward their colleagues in the "social sciences." Even though Feynman effectively lays bare the uncertain status of physical law in his own discipline, with nary a pause nor a hesitation he simultaneously insists that the study of human society should be reduced to the study of individual psychology, and thence to biology, then chemistry, and finally, to physical law (ibid., 125). This clarion call for the reduction of all social theory to physical law actually receives a relatively muted statement in the Feynman lecture: this sequence of reductionism is a veritable cliché in most quarters. Elsewhere Feynman reveals a boisterous contempt for those who might entertain the notion that there is any legitimate knowledge outside of physics.[3] It is this contempt that greets the economist when he or she actually turns to the physical sciences to glean some guidance concerning the nature of physical law. One objective of the research contained in this volume is to reveal that contempt as a symptom of a baseless prejudice that all economics needs is a good dose of scientific method as a prescription to ameliorate all its ills.

The curious juxtaposition of the uncertain status of physical law in the twentieth century with the imperative to "make economics a science" prompted the research collected in this volume. Six years ago I set out to try to make sense of the interplay of economics and science, which I rapidly came to understand was really the interplay between economics and physics. This was also the objective of Thorstein Veblen eighty-six years ago, as witnessed by the epigraph of this chapter.

I now have come to believe that Veblen was on the right track, as is argued in Chapter 6 below, but that various historical conditions militated against a full comprehension of the significance of the fundamental question "Why is economics not an evolutionary science?" Veblen himself was an indifferent mathematician and was not very interested in the mathematical formalisms of physics; and, as is argued below in Part I, it is impossible to understand neoclassical economics without understanding physics in its mathematical incarnation. Further, it was only later in the twentieth century, with the advent of the theory of relativity and quantum mechanics, that the earlier consensus on the meaning of physical law broke down within physics. This is not the appropriate place to discuss the history of physics, but I do think it germane at least to indicate that the main reason this book can exist in 1987 but not in 1900 is that our culture's conception of the nature of physical reality has been profoundly shaken only in the era of recent memory. Once that had happened, it became much more possible to see orthodox economic theory for what it really was: a bowlderized imitation of nineteenth-century physics.

Hence the essays collected in this volume represent an attempt to revive what I view to be the spirit of the institutionalist economics of Thorstein Veblen, John R. Commons, and Wesley Clair Mitchell. Their project was to confront and disarm the mechanistic structure of economics that had been blithely appropriated from the physicists of the nineteenth century and turned into an orthodoxy of "scientific economics." The major theme that resonated among their otherwise disparate writings was that they were all united "against mechanism." Their project faltered because it failed to take into account the actual structure and practices of physics, and because it ultimately misunderstood the dangers of trying to appropriate the legitimacy of science, as I argue in Chapter 7 below.

Contrary to popular preconceptions, I shall claim that economics needs protection from science, and especially from scientists such as Richard Feynman, or any other physicist who thinks he knows just what is needed for economists to clean up their act. Economics needs protection from the scientists in its midst, the Paul Samuelsons and the Tjalling Koopmans and all the others who took their training in the physical sciences and parlayed it into easy victories among their less technically inclined colleagues. And worst of all, economics needs protection from itself. For years economics has enjoyed an impression of superiority over all the other "social sciences" in rigor, precision, and technical expertise. The reason it has been able to assume this mantle is that economics has consistently striven to be the nearest thing to social physics in the constellation of human knowledge. There are many rewards and pressures tied to being the paradigm of social physics in Western culture, and it would be foolish to think that the economics profession could be weaned from them rapidly or effortlessly.

So who or what will protect economics from science? I have no magic nostrums to retail, but I do believe this book provides some limited answers. One principle adhered to throughout this volume is that the discipline of historical research is one of the more effective antidotes to appeals to "science" and "natural law." Indeed, one way to resist the sirens with their ubiquitous paeans to a "scientific economics" is simply to juxtapose the histories of physics and economics. The essays in Part I of this volume demonstrate that a familiarity with the history of physics can explicate the origins and content of orthodox neoclassical theory, including the previously mysterious "simultaneous discovery" of marginal utility theory. Chapters 2 and 3 demonstrate that it was not so much the *methods* of science that were appropriated by the early neoclassicals as it was the *appearances* of science, for the early neoclassicals possessed a singularily inept understanding of the physics that they so admired. Chapters 1 and 2 also introduce the crucial concept of economic conservation principles, perhaps the most neglected and yet most significant clue to the scientific pretensions of neoclassical economic theory.

Another antidote to the widespread ailment of scientism in economics is an examination of the various philosophical preconceptions that are freighted in as part of an unthinking acquiescence to "mathematical rigor." In Part 2 the relationship of the first institutionalist program in economics to mathematical models is examined from various angles and aspects. First, the assertion that there is a "New Institutional Economics" of an orthodox cast is evaluated in Chapters 4 and 5. Basically, the argument there is that neoclassical economists have tried to preempt the questions of the institutionalist school by attempting to reduce all social institutions such as money, property rights, and the market itself to epiphenomena of individual constrained optimization calculations. All these attempts have failed, despite their supposed dependence upon mathematical rigor, because they always inadvertently assume what they aim to deduce. Second, the importance of conservation principles is discussed in Chapter 6. Conservation principles are the key to the understanding of a mathematical formalization of any phenomenon, and it has been there that neoclassicals have been woefully negligent. Third, the notion that the image of man in any given school of economics is directly a function of that school's conception of science is broached in Chapter 7, and is put to work in differentiating neoclassical theory from its institutionalist counterpart.

A third method for protecting economics from science is to detail explicitly how neoclassical economic theory uses certain images of "science" to discipline and defeat any rival research programs. In Chapter 8 we discuss the entertaining example of the recent flap over Donald McCloskey's renunciation of science in favor of "Rhetoric" as a defense of neoclassical theory. Because this tactic was inherently self-defeating, it reveals all the more starkly the dependence of the orthodoxy upon a very specific conception of science. Also

in Chapter 8, the role of metaphors as generators of scientific research programs is given explicit consideration. Chapter 9 then shifts to a metaphoric
rival to neoclassical theory, namely, the biological-evolutionary metaphor.
Because this metaphor was very important to the first generation of institutionalists in their opposition to neoclassicism, it is all the more important to
understand the failure of two neoclassical theorists, Sidney Winter and
Richard Nelson, to try to appropriate the biological metaphor and to subordinate it to the neoclassical research program. Those convinced that biology is
well on its way to being reduced to physics should definitely take note.
Finally, Chapter 10 considers one prominent attempt to render Marxian
economics more scientific and thus to absorb it into the neoclassical research
program.

Part 4 is intended to end this volume on an optimistic and propitious note.
Once one becomes convinced that physics has been the dog wagging the
economics tail for quite some time now, there still remains the nagging question: Does this realization lead anywhere other than to critique? In other
words, is it possible to do institutionalist economics in such a way as to give
substantively novel answers to questions of interest? I do believe that this is a
possibility, and have attempted to document the existence of an independent
neo-institutionalist economic theory in a companion volume called *The Reconstruction of Economic Theory* (1986). Here Chapters 11 and 12 are intended
to demonstrate that one can also do historical and empirical research within
the neo-institutionalist framework. Chapter 11 argues that the scientistic bent
has precluded the examination of certain classes of empirical data such as firm
accounts, and that, incidentally, this aversion to certain forms of empiricism
dates back to Adam Smith. Chapter 12 argues that the notion of hysteresis is
central to a historically based economics; hence a Laplacean conception of a
time-independent natural law must inevitably clash with a temporally dependent explanation of prices.

There is one more suggestion as to how to protect economics from science.
The reader will notice that the essays collected in this volume are written in a
style and tone not often found in economics journals. While I might try to
avoid responsibility for this idiosyncratic trait by claiming the devil made me
do it, I do think there is some cause to try and prepare the reader for the
spectacle of an economist indulging in personal asides, writing in the first person, reveling in wordplay (however pedestrian), and even venturing a joke or
two. Many of these pieces were originally written for economics journals,
but I soon learned to my chagrin that editors of economics journals will resist
deviance from the flat style of the colorless observation report right down to
the wire. Once one peruses the articles in this volume, I hope it will become
apparent that there is a reason for this recalcitrance: form is content, and a
discipline made to imitate physics must also imitate the deadly style of *Physical Reviews A*. If this be so, then it behooves economists who repudiate the
slavish imitation of physics to rediscover their literary and philosophical

roots, and to write as if they had quirks, opinions, and personalities. In this, as in much else, I take my cue from Thorstein Veblen, who managed to develop the most circumambulatory, antipodal, autacoid, lucubratious, and flexuous styles of prose in the entire English language.

Notes

1. These issues are discussed in detail in my "Mathematical Formalism and Economic Explanation," in Mirowski, ed., *The Reconstruction of Economic Theory*.

2. There has been a veritable outpouring of work on the history and philosophy of science in the last two decades. A good place for the novice to start, if only to see just how tumultuous things have gotten, is Paul Feyerabend's "How to Protect Society from Science," which can be found in Ian Hacking, ed., *Scientific Revolutions* (1982).

3. Here are some examples from *Surely You're Joking, Mr. Feynman*, (1985), 279-83:

> In the early fifties I suffered temporarily from a disease of middle age: I used to give philosophical talks about science . . .
>
> So here comes this wonderful list of books. I start down the first page: I haven't read a single one of the books, and I feel very uneasy—I hardly belong. I look at the second page: I haven't read a single one. I found out, after looking through the whole list, that I haven't read *any* of the books. I must be an idiot, an illiterate! There were wonderful books there, like Thomas Jefferson *On Freedom,* or something like that, and there were a few *authors* I had read. There was a book by Heisenberg, and one by Einstein, but they were something like Einstein, *My Later Years,* and Schrödinger, *What Is Life?*—different from what I had read . . .
>
> Finally I said, "What is the *ethical* problem associated with the fragmentation of knowledge?" He would only answer me with great clouds of fog, and I'd say, "I don't understand," and everybody else would say that they did understand, and *they* tried to explain it to me, but they couldn't explain it to me!
>
> . . . I started to say that the idea of distributing everything evenly is based on a *theory* that there's only X amount of stuff in the world, that somehow we took it away from the poorer countries in the first place, and therefore we should give it back to them. But this theory doesn't take into account the *real* reason for the differences between countries—that is, the development of new techniques for growing food, the development of machinery to grow food and to do other things, and the fact that all this machinery requires the concentration of capital. It isn't the *stuff,* but the power to *make* the stuff, that is important. But I realize now that these people were not in science; they didn't understand it. They didn't understand technology; they didn't understand their time.

Part I

Scientism in Neoclassical Economic Theory

1

Physics and the "Marginalist Revolution"

The mathematician is an inventor, not a discoverer.—Wittgenstein (1978, I. 168)

Internal *versus* External Histories of Science

Interest in the origins of neoclassical theory has a number of motivations. The first is antiquarian: it is concerned with tracing the intellectual antecedents of a given innovation. The second is epistemological: the methods of great discoverers are held to provide an exemplar for currently accepted methods of research. The third is ontological: the occurrence of independent simultaneous discovery is used to suggest the substantiality and reality of the phenomenon identified. William Stanley Jevons, for instance, wrote that, "The theory in question has in fact been independently discovered three or four times over and must be true" (Jevons 1972, IV, 278). The fourth is practical: it provides a reservoir of metaphors and theoretical suggestions which might serve to prompt novel contemporary lines of inquiry which are obscured or slighted by modern theory. Confusion or doubt over the origins of modern neoclassical economic theory would introduce the possibility of serious historical, epistemological, ontological and practical confusions in its exposition.

At present, the most popular textbook of the history of economic thought attempts to dispose of the issue by absolving itself of any responsibility for discussing origins:

> Therefore, to try to explain the origin of the marginal utility revolution in the 1870's is doomed to failure: it was not a marginal utility revolution; it was not an abrupt change, but only a gradual transformation in which the old ideas were never definitively rejected; and it did not happen in the 1870s. [Blaug 1978, 322]

This text denies that there was any unified and self-conscious movement. In its stead, it portrays a haphazard and fragmented agglomeration of economic theorists, whose only common denominators were the twin notions of diminishing marginal utility and utility-determined prices. Since neither notion was particularly novel in the 1870s, it follows from this portrayal that there was no discontinuity in the economic thought of the period, and the economic theory has embodied one continuous discipline from Adam Smith until the present (see Bowley 1973, ch. 4).

The thesis that innovations in economic theory in the 1870s and 1880s were unexceptional and merely a continuation of the unbroken threads of economic discourse in the preceding half century meets a number of difficulties. The first problem is that not all the major protagonists would have agreed with such an assessment. One cannot read the letters and published works of Stanley Jevons, Léon Walras, Francis Edgeworth, Irving Fisher, Vilfredo Pareto and others without repeatedly encountering assertions that their work represented a fundamental break with the economics of their time. Much of their professional lives was spent promoting the works of this small self-identified côterie. The second impediment to the gradualist view is the fact that the most discontinuous aspect of the "marginalist revolution" was not the postulate of a utilitarian theory of value, but rather something no historian of economic thought has ever discussed in detail: the successful penetration of mathematical discourse into economic theory. In both their correspondence and in their published work, the early neoclassical economists recognized each other as *mathematical theorists* first and foremost; and when they proselytized for their works, it took the form of defending the "mathematical method" in the context of economic theory. The third impediment to the gradualist view is the fact that all the major protagonists were concerned to differentiate their handiwork from previous political economy on the explicit ground that it was of a scientific character. While the claim that one's theory is "scientific" (and therefore deserves respect) echoes throughout the last three centuries of social theory, in the case of Jevons *et al.* this claim assumes a very specific and narrow form, shared by all the principals. An understanding of these three points will lead inexorably to a reevaluation of the significance of the rise of neoclassical economic theory.

The gradualist view of the genesis of neoclassical theory has generally been prefaced with some methodological remarks on the contrast between "internalist" and "externalist" intellectual histories (Blaug 1978; Black, Coats, and Goodwin 1973). The internalist version, the one presently favored by neoclassicals, assumes that all ideas are merely reactions to previous developments internal to the discipline under consideration. The job of an intellectual historian is to trace the descent of ideas from scientist to scientist through time, revealing how error was rooted out by the internal criticism of logical deduction and empirical testing, while scientific truths were preserved and nurtured. New insights and concepts are pioneered by key individuals, but the sources of those insignts are not an important part of the historian's narrative (Popper 1965). The historian may use sociological and other external considerations to explain adherence to superseded theories; but adherence to the successful theory is felt to need no other explanation other than its *prima facie* success (Bloor 1976).

This view is in contrast to externalist intellectual history, which seeks the determinants of successful theories in the political, philosophical and/or social currents of the time. The externalist historian is satisfied to identify the link between an historical interlude and the construction and acceptance of a successful theory, without expending undue effort to trace the intellectual pedigree of its precursors within the science. Undoubtedly, much of the hostility of neoclassical economists to externalist explanations of the "marginalist revolution" stems from the weak and unconvincing nature of the few attempts: Bukharin (1927) associated it with the rise of a new class of *rentiers* in *fin-de-siècle* Europe; whereas Stark (1944) saw it as a reflection of some general Kantian influences in conjunction with the assertion that the economy of mid-nineteenth century Europe was actually characterized by atomistic competition. It has been observed repeatedly that these portrayals are not historically accurate; nor do they describe correctly the milieu of the major protagonists (Blaug 1978; Kauder 1965).

The internalist–externalist dichotomy has itself impeded the understanding of the rise of neoclassical economic theory. It forces the student of history to choose between a tautology and a disdain for theory, which has rendered the history trivial for all present purposes. Further, recent philosophers of science have severely undermined the distinction (Bloor 1976; Kuhn 1970). It is particularly necessary for social theorists to be aware of both the social and intellectual parameters of their own practices.

An Alternative Thesis

Our first thesis may be stated simply and directly: there was a readily identifiable discontinuity in economic thought in the 1870s and 1880s which was the genesis of neoclassical theory; and both its timing and intellectual content can be explained by parallel developments in physics in the mid-nineteenth century. The evidence is drawn from (i) the published works of the first neoclassicists; (ii) an example from the physics of the time which reveals the parallels; and (iii), biographical information about the principals.

All the major protagonists of the "marginalist revolution" explicitly stated in their *published* works the sources of the inspiration for their novel economic theories. Jevons (1970, 144–147) wrote that his equation of exchange does "... not differ in general character from those which are really treated in many branches of physical science." He then proceeds to compare the equality of the ratios of marginal utility of two goods and their inverted trading ratio to the law of the lever, where in equilibrium the point masses at each end are inversely proportional to the ratio of their respective distances from the fulcrum. Note at this stage that Jevons' exposition does not adequately support his statements in the text: since he does not derive the equilibrium of the lever from considerations of potential and kinetic energy, he fails to justify the parallel between the expression for physical equilibrium and his use of differential equations in his own equations of exchange.

Far from being an isolated and insignificant metaphor, this invocation of the physical realm is always present in Jevons' writings on price theory. For example, in his defence of the mathematical method before the Manchester Statistical Society, he insists that

> Utility only exists when there is on the one side the person wanting, and on the other the thing wanted... Just as the gravitating force of a material body depends not alone on the mass of that body, but upon the masses and relative positions and distances of the surrounding material bodies, so utility is an attraction between a wanting being and what is wanted. [Jevons 1981, VII, 80]

When one observes that more than half of Jevons' published work concerns the logic and philosophy of science, one begins to see that the metaphor of physical science was the unifying principle, and not merely a rhetorical flourish. In his major book, *The Principles of Science,* he suggests that the notion of the hierarchy of the sciences justifies "... a calculus of moral effects, a kind of physical astronomy investigating the mutual perturbations of individuals" (1905, 759–760). The reduction of social processes to simple utilitarian considerations is compared to the reduction of meteorology to chemistry and thence to physics, implying that there is only one scientific methodology and one mode of explanation—that of physics—in all human experience.

Léon Walras was equally explicit concerning the motivation behind his published work. In his *Elements of Pure Economics* he claims that, "the pure theory of economics is a science which resembles the physico-mathematical sciences in every respect" (1969, 71). Walras explains in great detail his occupation with "pure economics" in Lessons One to Four of the *Elements*. In his opinion, a pure science is only concerned with the relationships among things, the "play of the blind and ineluctible forces of nature" which are independent of all human will. Walras insists that there exists a limited subset of economic phenomena which could be the objects of a pure scientific inquiry: they are the configurations of prices in a regime of "perfect competition" (for further elaboration see chapter 4 below). Such "pure" relationships justify and indeed, for Walras, *demand* the application of the *same* mathematical techniques as those deployed in mid-nineteenth century physics; other social phenomena tainted by the influence of human will would be relegated to studies employing nonscientific rhetorical techniques.

The proposed unity of technique in physics and economics is fully revealed in Walras's article of 1909, "Économique et Mécanique" (reprinted in Walras 1960). In this article he develops the two favorite metaphors of the early neoclassical economists, the rational mechanics of the equilibrium of the lever and the mathematical relations between celestial bodies; he also asserts that the "physico-mathematical science" of his *Elements* uses *precisely* the identical mathematical formulae. He then proceeds to scold physicists who had expressed scepticism about the application of mathematics to utilitarian social theories on the ground that utility is not a measurable quantum; Walras retorts that the physicists themselves have been vague in their quantification of such basic terms as "mass" and "force." The proposed connections between the terms of the sciences could not have been made more manifest: "Aussi a-t-on déjà signalé celles des *forces* et des *raretés* comme *vecteurs,* d'une part, et celles des *énergies* et des *utilités* comme *quantités scalaires,* d'autre part" (Walras 1960, 7).

Francis Ysidro Edgeworth was a third partisan of "mathematical psychics" who was quite explicit about the wellsprings of the neoclassical movement. If only because of his extravagant and florid writing style, he is worth quoting directly:

> The application of mathematics to the world of the soul is countenanced by the hypothesis (agreeable to the general hypothesis that every psychical phenomenon is the concomitant, and in some sense the other side of a physical phenomenon), the particular hypothesis adopted in these pages, that Pleasure is the concomitant of Energy. *Energy* may be regarded as the central idea of Mathematical Physics: *maximum energy* the object of the principal investigations in that science... 'Mécanique Sociale' may one day take her place along with 'Mécanique Celeste,' throned each upon the double-sided height of one maximum principle, the supreme pinnacle of moral as of physical science. As the movements of each particle, constrained or loose, in a material cosmos are continually subordinated to one maximum sub-total of accumulated energy, so the movements of each soul whether selfishly isolated or linked sympathetically, may continually be realising the maximum of pleasure. [Edgeworth 1881, 9, 12]

Vilfredo Pareto, a fourth confederate of the marginalist cadre, adopted a much more pugnacious but essentially identical position:

> Strange disputes about predestination, about the efficacy of grace, etc., and in our day incoherent ramblings on solidarity show that men have not freed themselves from these daydreams which people have gotten rid of in the physical sciences, but which still burden the social sciences... Thanks to the use of mathematics, this entire theory, as we develop it in the Appendix, rests on no more than a fact of experience, that is, on the determination of the quantities of goods which constitute combinations between which the individual is indifferent. The theory of economic science thus acquires the rigor of rational mechanics. [Pareto 1971B, 36, 113].

In some ways, Pareto was the most ruthless proponent of the physical metaphor, and because of this, found himself the first of the neoclassicals to have to defend himself from attacks by mathematicians and physicists (Volterra, in Chipman et al., 1971, 356–96).

Once one recognizes these passages for the manifestos that they are, one sees that they are ubiquitous in the writings of early neoclassical economists. They can be found in Fisher (1892), Antonelli (1886), Laundhardt (1885) and Auspitz and Lieben (1889). In fact, the explicit appropriation of this specific physical metaphor is present in every major innovator of the marginalist revolution, with the single exception (discussed later) of the Austrian school of Carl Menger. The adoption of the "energetics" metaphor and framework of mid-nineteenth century physics is the birthmark of neoclassical economics, the

Ariadne's thread which ties the protagonists, and which can lead us to the fundamental meaning of the neoclassical research program.

Physics and Economics

Historians of economic thought, and many other economists as well, have long been aware that there are some close familial resemblances between physical concepts and neoclassical economic theory (see Sebba 1953; Lowe 1951; Knight 1956; Weisskopf 1979; Samuelson 1972; Thoben 1982). The reason why these observations have passed without notice is that the extent and significance of the linkage has not been chronicled from the viewpoint of physics. For example, it has become a cliché to refer to neoclassical economics as being "Newtonian," perhaps bolstered by some offhand assertions that both are atomistic, both have resort to the language of frictions and equilibrium, and, depending upon the disposition of the commentator, perhaps inclusion of a pejorative comment that both are "mechanistic." Indeed, if those observations exhausted the sum total of the analogy, then it would merit no further serious consideration. However, recourse to the history of mathematics and physics shows that the characterization of neoclassical economics as "Newtonian" is both inept and misleading.

Historians of science are increasingly sceptical of the conventional wisdom that the history of physics consists of two discrete periods: one, stretching from the sequence Galileo-Descartes-Newton to roughly 1895, called "Classical Physics"; and the second, a twentieth century phenomenon based on quantum mechanics and relativity. To quote a recent textbook:

> The term "Newtonian" as applied to 18th and 19th century physics implicitly conflates Newton's natural philosophy and the physics of this later period, and is hence a misleading description. The developments in theoretical mechanics in the 18th century show a significant departure from the mechanical and mathematical assumptions of Newton's natural philosophy; and the physics of imponderable 'fluids', active substances and the anomalous forms of matter current in the 18th century contrasts with Newton's theory of nature... Despite the dominance of the program of mechanical explanation... the term 'Newtonian' is misleading when applied to physics in the 19th century. The conceptual innovations of 19th century physics—energy conservation, the theory of the physical field, the theory of light as vibrations of an electromagnetic ether, and the concept of entropy—cannot be meaningfully be described as "Newtonian." [Harman 1982, 10–11]

In point of fact, the word "physics" was not generally used in English until the middle of the nineteenth century to refer to the united study of mechanics, light, heat, etc., both because of its Aristotelian connections (Cannon 1978, 113, *et seq.*) and because there was no consensus on a unified theory of these phenomena until the rise of energetics in the middle of the century. Problems with Newtonian concepts in the nineteenth century with respect to light, heat and electricity led to the proliferation of types of postulated matter and their associated separate attractions and repulsions, which in turn led to contradictions inherent in the idea of more than one Newtonian force (Agassi 1971; Harman 1982). Energetics as a unifying principle was created by Helmholtz's famous 1847 paper "On the Conservation of Force" (Kahl 1971), drawing upon earlier study of the conceptualization of *vis viva* (or 'living force') and the interconvertability of heat and mechanical work. This innovation induced substantial revision of many previous physical doctrines, and created the discipline of physics as the unified study of phenomena linked by energetic principles.

This watershed in physics altered not only the subject matter but the techniques of research and methodological prescriptions as well. It was linked to the mathematical supersession by French analytical methods and Leibniz's notation for the calculus of the English use of the Newtonian calculus of fluxions and the English fondness for geometrical argument (Bos 1980). It was accompanied by changes in the acceptable standards of theory formation: these included an increasing refusal to specify the underlying nature of phenomena described mathematically; fewer concessions made to intuitive plausibility; increasing imperatives to measure quantitatively without being precise as to what it was that was being measured; and a predisposition to accept the "usefulness" of a model as a form of proof (Heidelberger, in Jahnke and Otte 1981; Harman 1982).

Crucial in this revolution in thought concerning physical processes was the transformation of vague "forces" into a Protean, unique, and yet ontologically undefined "energy," which could only be discussed cogently through the intermediary of its mathematical eidolon. In this guise, energy did not characterize Newtonian particles, but rather processes. It shifted the description of motion itself away from vectors such as momentum and towards scalars encompassing the new "energy." Its divergence from Newtonian concepts became apparent when the conservation law was enunciated, because the conservation law provided the only means by which to identify an energetic system as in some sense the "same" as it underwent various changes and transformations (Theobald 1966; Meyerson 1962).

Some familiarity with the history of physics, even one as sketchy as that provided above, is necessary for an understanding of the fact that neoclassical economics was not prompted by a Newtonian analogy. Classical economists made reference to the Newtonian analogy in nonessential contexts (see Blaug 1980, 57–58); but they could not reconcile the inverse square law, the calculus of fluxions and other Newtonian techniques with their overall conception of social processes. The rise of energetics in physical theory induced the invention of neoclassical economic theory, by providing the metaphor, the mathematical techniques, and the new attitudes toward theory construction. Neoclassical economic theory was appropriated wholesale from mid-nineteenth century physics; utility was redefined so as to be identical with energy.

An example may make this clearer for the modern reader. Consider a point-mass displaced a distance from point A to point B in a three-dimensional plane by a force vector F. This force vector can be decomposed into its perpendicular components, $F = iF_x + jF_y + kF_z$, where the notation i,j,k represents unit vectors along the three axes. In the same manner, the vector of displacement dq can also be decomposed into its perpendicular components, $dq = idx + jdy + kdz$. The work accomplished (that is, the product of the force and the infinitesimal displacements) is defined as the integral of the force times the displacements, or:

$$T = \int_A^B (F_x dx + F_y dy + F_z dz) = \frac{1}{2}mv^2 \bigg|_B - \frac{1}{2}mv^2 \bigg|_A$$

Energetics redefined the change in mv^2 (previously called *vis viva*) to be conceptualized as the change in kinetic energy of the particle. The vector formalization could then be rewritten as a single-valued scalar function, with T representing the change in kinetic energy. In the eighteenth century, there had been much controversy over whether *vis viva* was conserved in motion; energetics clarified the issue in the following manner. Suppose that the expression $(F_x dx + F_y dy + F_z dz)$ is an exact differential, or in other words, there exists a function $U(x,y,z)$ such that:

$$F_x = -\partial U/\partial x;\ F_y = -\partial U/\partial y;\ F_z = -\partial U/\partial z.$$

This uniquely identified scalar function U was interpreted as the unobserved potential energy of the particle. Then it is the *total* energy of the particle, $T + U$, which is conserved through any motion of the particle. The postulate that total energy is conserved was significant, because it allows a rigorous specification of the "principle of least action." This principle, in its various forms, dated back to Maupertuis in the eighteenth century, who noted that the actual paths of motion traversed in many mechanical phenomena could be described mathematically as evincing the minimum of the particle's 'action.' William Hamilton in the 1830s pioneered "the central conception of all modern theory in physics" (Schrödinger, quoted in Crowe 1967, 17) by defining the action integral over time of the path of a particle as:

$$\int_{t_1,A}^{t_2,B} (T - U)dt.$$

The Hamiltonian principle of "least action" asserts that the actual path of the particle from A to B will be the one which makes the action integral stationary. The path may be calculated by finding the constrained extrema, employing techniques of Lagrangean constrained maximization/minimization or, in more complicated cases, using directly the calculus of variations. In a conservative system, where $T + U = $ a constant, action is a function of position only, which implies that all motion is fully reversible, and exhibits no hysteresis (Kline 1972, ch.30).

To summarize: in the 1820s theoretical treatises in mechanics began to stress the work integral and its mathematical relationship to *vis viva* (Harman 1982, 36). In the 1830s, Hamilton linked this framework to the mathematics of constrained extrema (Hankins, 1980). Starting in the 1840s, the interconvertability of mechanical energy and other energetic phenomena was postulated; by the 1860s, the mathematics of unobservable potentials and constrained extrema were extended to all physical phenomena.

Walras insisted that his *rareté* equations resembled those of the physical sciences in every respect. We may see now that he was very nearly correct. Simply redefine the variables of the earlier equations: let $\mathbf{F}$ be the vector of prices of a set of traded goods, and let q be the vector of the quantities of those goods purchased. The integral $\int\mathbf{F}\cdot dq = T$ is then defined as the total expenditure on these goods. If the expression to be integrated is an exact differential, then it is possible to define a scalar function of the goods x and y of the form $U = U(x,y,z)$, which can then be interpreted as the "utilities" of those goods. In exact parallel to the original concept of potential energy, these utilities are unobservable, and can only be inferred from theoretical linkage to other observable variables. Relative prices are equal to the ratios of the marginal utilities of the goods by construction: the "potential field" of utility is defined as the locus of the set of constrained extrema, although the early marginalists reversed this logic in their expositions of the principle. Instead of treating utility as a derived phenomenon, they postulated the utility field as the fundamental exogenous data to which market transactions adjusted. The mathematics, however, are the same in both instances.

There *is* one major difference, however, between the mathematics of energetics and its transplanted version in neoclassical economics. The conservation principle in energetics does not translate directly into neoclassical theory: the sum of income and utility is not conserved, and is meaningless in the context of economic theory. Does this mean that neoclassical economics has managed to dispense with the artifice of a conservation principle? This may appear to be the case, because neither the progenitors of neoclassicism nor any of its modern adherents have ever seriously discussed this aspect of the physical metaphor (see chapter 6 below). Yet to cast any problem in a constrained maximization framework, the analyst *must* assume some sort of conservation principle. In physics, it is widely understood that the conservation principle is the means by which the system being considered retains its analytical identity.

In other words, the adoption of the energetics metaphor in economics has imposed an analytical regimen, the rigors of which have hitherto gone unnoticed. Neoclassical theorists, from the 1870s onwards, have surreptitiously assumed some form of conservation principle in their economic models. In the period of our present concern, the principle took two forms: (a) the income or endowment to be traded is given exogenously and, further, is assumed to be fully spent or traded; thus, for practical purposes, T is conserved; and/or (b) the transactors' estimation of the utility of the various goods is a datum not altered by the sequence of purchase, nor any other aspect of the trading or consuming process (or, as Marshall sheepishly admitted, desire was equated with satisfaction by *assumption*); so in effect the utility field U is conserved (see chapter 6). In this case, the analogy between physics and economics would be as if physical theory had managed to preserve what has proved to be an anachronistic element: as if Hamilton had somehow managed to preserve the conservation of *vis viva* (kinetic energy) within the new mathematics of energetic extrema.

Once the parallels between mid-nineteenth-century physics and neoclassical economic theory are outlined, and it is acknowledged that the progenitors themselves openly admitted them in their published writings, most would accept the thesis that the "marginalist revolution" should be renamed the "marginalist annexation." Should doubts linger, however, the thesis should be clinched by an examination of the biographical particulars of the protagonists.

The most obvious and straightforward case is that of the most respected of neoclassical progenitors, Léon Walras. In his first effort to mathematicize his father's concept of *rareté,* Walras attempted to implement a Newtonian model of market relations, postulating that "the price of things is in inverse ratio to the quantity offered and in direct ratio to the quantity demanded" (Walras 1965, I, 216–17). Dissatisfied with this model, Walras tinkered with various formulations, but none involved the constrained maximization of utility until the late autumn of 1872. At that time, a professor of mechanics at the Academy of Lausanne, Antoine Paul Piccard, wrote a memo to Walras sketching the mathematics of the optimization of an unobserved *quantité de besoin* (Walras 1965, I, 308–11) along the lines outlined above. Although Walras trained originally as an engineer at the École des Mines, he did not possess a deep understanding of the new energetics: this can be observed in his reactions to the letters of Hermann Laurent (Walras 1965, III, 417–20) correcting his errors of interpretation and mathematical representation. While these letters did prompt him to write "Économique et Mécanique," they did not prompt him to revise his *Elements* significantly. This suggests that Walras did not comprehend the real thrust of these letters, which question the appropriateness of various aspects of the physical metaphor. It was left for his successors Antonelli and Pareto to explore some of the *social* implications of the mathematics of energetics.

It is significant that all the earliest members of the Lausanne school were trained as engineers. Giovanni Antonelli was an Italian civil engineer whose monograph *On the Mathematical Theory of Political Economy* explicitly discusses utility theory in the manner described above (pp. 366–68) (Antonelli 1886). He is now considered a pioneer in the problem of integrability, which here we interpret as an acknowledgement and extrapolation of the implications of conservation principles. The significance of this problem did not receive widespread attention until well into the twentieth century (Samuelson 1950). Vilfredo Pareto was also trained as an engineer, and this expertise enabled him to explore the implications of the path-independence of the realization of utility, a direct extrapolation of the path-independence of equilibrium energy states in rational mechanics and thermodynamics (Pareto 1971A). This work was consigned to oblivion partly because Pareto and Antonelli gave up economic theory in later life, and partly because no one outside a very limited circle of engineers who had a working knowledge of the new economic theory could read it. The English-speaking world had to wait until the 1930s when an influx of physicists—and engineers—manqués into economics led to the revival of their work.

The biographical evidence in the case of Jevons is not as direct, but is substantial. Prompted by his father to become an engineer, Jevons studied chemistry and mathematics in London. He attended some of Michael Faraday's renowned public lectures at the Royal Institution, at which Faraday claimed that magnetic forces did not obey the Newtonian force rule (Jevons 1972, I, 82). This is significant because in the land of Newton in the 1850s Faraday was one of the very few partisans of field theories and energetics: indeed, Jevons' letters make clear his enormous respect for Faraday. We also have evidence that Jevons was familiar with the writings of Thomson and Joule on the interconvertibility of heat and mechanical work, writings which led to the enunciation of the theory of the conservation of energy (Jevons 1905a, 465). Later in his life Jevons remained conversant with the field of energetics, and even wrote to James Clerk Maxwell arguing a point of controversy in Fourier's theory of heat (Jevons 1972, IV, 207–8).

If there was a difference between Jevons and Walras, it was this: Walras did not evince any deep understanding of mid-nineteenth-century physics, and applied the mathematical techniques and the metaphor in a mechanical and unimaginative manner, leaving it for others to draw out the logical and connotative implications of the physical metaphor. Jevons, on the other hand, was even less of a mathematician than Walras, but did dedicate his life's work to drawing out the meaning of the metaphor of energetics for the sphere of the economy. This point is not readily apparent, because Jevons' work is rarely considered as a whole. His major achievements were the *Theory of Political Economy, The Coal Question,* his work on sunspots and the business cycle, and *The Principles of Science.* The connection between the four can best be summarized in Jevons' own words, from his paper "The Solar Influence on Commerce" (Jevons 1972, VII, 97): "Long ago George Stevenson acutely anticipated the results of subsequent scientific inquiry when he said that coal was sunshine bottled up; now it is among the mere commonplaces of science that all motions and energies of life... are directly or indirectly derived from the sun." The maximization of utility, the prediction that England was rapidly exhausting energy stocks in the form of coal, and the lifelong theme that economic crises must be caused by energy fluctuations exogenous to the social operation of the economy, are all direct extrapolations from the energetic movement of the mid-nineteenth century (chapter 3 below). The last point gains credibility when one notes that Jevons recorded in his journal that Faraday explicitly discussed the periodicity of sunspots in his lectures of 1853 (Jevons 1972, I, 82). As for the *Principles of Science,* it can be read as a plea for the unity of methodology in all sciences, in the face of the serious upheavals and discontinuities which erupted both in subject matter and in research methods in mid-nineteenth century physics. The fact that his own conception of scientific endeavor was highly colored by the rise of energetics can be observed in the *Principles'* definition of science: "Science is the detection of identity, and classification is the placing together, either in thought or in the proximity of space, those objects between which identity has been detected" (Jevons 1905, 673–74).

The Austrians Were Not Neoclassicals

Those familiar with conventional histories of neoclassical economic theory must, by this point, be impatient to object: what about Menger and the Austrians? Do they fit the thesis which links the rise of neoclassical theory to the rise of energetics in physics?

Although it has become conventional wisdom to cite the triumvirate of the marginal revolution as Jevons, Walras, and Menger, these three actors themselves did not accept this regimentation. Jevons did not mention Menger once in all his writings: a curious reticence in one so determined in later life to uncover all predecessors and fellow revolutionaries. Walras did correspond with Menger, but only to discover to his amazement that Menger did not recognize his contribution on account of its mathematical nature. This was sufficient for Walras to deny Menger's role in the revolution, writing in a letter to Bortkiewicz in 1887 that Menger's and Böhm-Bawerk's efforts to describe the theory of "Grenznuten" in "ordinary language" was unsuccessful, and even painful (Walras 1965, II, 232). Walras viewed Menger's 1871 *Principles* as merely an attempt at *translation* of marginalist ideas into ordinary language, and a failed one at that: there was nothing novel or original there; he thus denied Menger any status as an equal. (Interestingly enough, this opinion seems to be shared by many modern neoclassical economists. In this regard, see Samuelson 1952, 61.) Menger did not conform to Walras's main criteria for a neoclassical theorist: he was not mathematical, he did not adhere to the norms of physical science, and therefore he was not "scientific."

In contrast, historians of economic thought are persistently perplexed by Menger's recalcitrance at being elevated to membership in the triumvirate. Howey, the most careful of these writers, notes:

... although Menger talked about the Austrian school, no one would gather from his words in any of his publications after 1871 down to his death that the Austrian School had the slightest connection with the Marginal Utility School. He either did not admit the connection, or wished to minimise it, or took it for granted. Menger never publicly admitted any kinship with Walras or with Jevons. [Howey 1960, 142]

There is much more here than petty squabbles over precedence or methodology, or personality clashes, or nationalistic insularity. There is the possibility that the Austrians, or at the very least Menger, were not part of the fledgling movement of neoclassical economic theory. This possibility has already been suggested by some Austrian economists, notably by Erich Streissler in a centenary collection of essays on the marginalist revolution (Black, Coats, and Goodwin 1973, 160–75). Streissler points out that Menger's scales of successive marginal satisfaction, introduced in the middle of his *Grundsätze* (Menger 1981, 127), were not at all central to his conception of economic theory. This contention is indirectly supported by Kauder (1965, 76), who reports that Menger crossed out this table in his author's copy of the book. Howey (1960, 40) notes that Menger's "importance of satisfactions" cannot easily be translated into the language of utility because it did not vary in *quantity*. "Satisfaction" never varied, but its subjective importance could be altered in a regular manner. Streissler maintains that Menger's major concerns—uncertainty, changes in the quality of goods, the absence of a notion of equilibrium, and hostility to the "law of one price"—were motivated so fundamentally by his radical subjectivism that he could not be considered as promoting the same theory as Jevons and Walras. From our present perspective, we can find support for Streissler's thesis by examining Menger's relationship to physical theory.

After a personal visit, Bortkiewicz wrote to Walras that Menger did not have the least idea of mathematical analysis (Walras 1965, II, 519). Perusal of his major works indicates that he was also unfamiliar with the physics of his time. Yet despite these inadequacies, Menger launched a scathing attack upon the German historicist school in his *Untersuchungen über die Methode*, mainly consisting of the contention that his opponents did not understand the nature of "exact science" (Menger 1963). In sharp contrast with Jevons' *Principles of Science*, Menger's weak and unconvincing claims that he was promoting the methods of "exact research of a Newton, Lavoisier or Helmholtz" reveal an ignorance hastily camouflaged by bombast. He attempted to extend his radical subjectivism to physics without giving a single example from the physical sciences. He denigrated empiricism without being specific about the practices to which he objected. His conception of science was severely Aristotelian and he never addressed the fact that the scientists of his day had rejected this. He rather appropriated their names for credibility.

Menger cannot be considered a neoclassical economist because he rejected two basic pillars of that theory: the law of one price, which states that all generic goods in a market (however defined) must trade at the same price in equilibrium (see Dennis 1982; Bausor 1986); and the concept that traded goods in some sense are related as equivalents in equilibrium (Menger 1981, 191–94). Absence of the first subverts any deterministic notion of equilibrium. Absence of the second explains Menger's hostility towards quantification. Absence of both effectively prevented the introduction of the physics analogy into economic theory. The mere postulation of a diminishing marginal utility is not sufficient to generate a neoclassical theory of price. In this respect Menger is no different from Dupuit (1952), who also recognized diminishing marginal utility, but also repudiated a single equilibrium price. Were it not for three historical accidents—first the *Grundsätze* was first published in 1871; second, Menger's illustrious student Wieser promoted his claim to be a founder of neoclassical theory (and himself *did* adopt the new marginalist techniques from Laundhardt and Auspitz and Lieben); and third, Menger's works were largely unavailable outside the German-speaking world—Menger would not today be considered as one of the marginalist revolutionaries.

There has been much disagreement as to what constitutes the "hard core" of neoclassical economic theory: the fundamental basis of the research program which, if altered, would signal the substantive development of a non-neoclassical economic theory (Latsis 1976; Boland 1982). The core is not simply methodological individualism, nor is it utilitarianism, because both were active research strategies in social theory well before the rise of neoclassical theory, and because the Austrian and certain sociological research programs also hold them as tenets. It is the second thesis of this paper that the hard core of neoclassical economic theory is the adoption of mid-nineteenth-century physics as a rigid paradigm, a hard core it has preserved and nourished throughout the twentieth century, even after physics has moved onwards to new metaphors and new techniques. This thesis explains a number of issues which have eluded other attempts at locating the hard core of neoclassical theory.

First, it explains why neoclassical theory and mathematical formalism have been indissolubly wedded since the 1870s, even though a cogent defense of the necessity of the link has been notable by its absence. Second, it explains the success of neoclassicism in preempting other research programs in economics by means of the forceful claim that it is scientific, even though standards of scientific discourse in the larger culture have changed periodically during the last hundred years. Third, it explains the preference for techniques of constrained maximization over any other analytical techniques, which include output—output matrices, game theory, Markov chains, and a myriad of other techniques proposed over the last century (Samuelson 1972). Fourth, it explains the persistent use of an unobservable and unmeasurable value determinant—utility—in textbooks and in applied research, despite protestations that utility is not "needed" for neoclassical results (Wong 1978).

Fifth, it explains the modern controversy over the necessity for a "microfoundation for macroeconomics," which can be interpreted as a complaint that Keynesian economics has not conformed to the hard core research strategy, and is therefore somehow illegitimate (Weintraub 1979; Lucas 1981). Sixth, it explains why neoclassicism links certain economic variables to particular exogenous variables, which are themselves "naturally" determined and therefore analytically immutable and outside of the scope of economic theory. All these characteristics are borrowed from nineteenth-century energetics.

Physical Metaphors, Organic Metaphors and the Role of Marshall

It is not unusual for a science to adopt the metaphors and/or analytical techniques of another discipline. The story of Darwin's appropriation of the concept of population pressure on resources from Malthus's *Essay on Population* is but one example of a pervasive phenomenon. Indeed, some historians of science attempt to explain the rise of energetics by the influence of German *Naturphilosophie* in mid-nineteenth-century culture (Kuhn 1977). What is unusual and noteworthy about the rise to preeminence of neoclassical economic theory is the lack of consciousness, and therefore the concomitant lack of any assessment or critique, of the sources of its analytical and technical inspiration. Newtonian action-at-a-distance came under severe scrutiny and criticism from philosophical perspectives in the eighteenth and nineteenth centuries. Darwinian natural selection has repeatedly been reconsidered at the level of the fundamental organizing metaphor. The list could be extended indefinitely: many of the basic organizing principles of physics have undergone criticism and revision over the past two hundred years. All these episodes reveal a willingness to reconsider theory at the level of the "hard core," as opposed to revision of the "protective belt." In effect, the strength of physics lies in its openness to fundamental revision, and not, as the naïve conception has it, in its unwavering preservation of eternal verities.

Neoclassical economists, on the other hand, have often appealed to the dignity of the scientific endeavor, without understanding what it entails, or why they felt justified in claiming privileged scientific status for their paradigm. Until Georgescu-Roegen (1971), the extent of the dependence of modern neoclassical theory upon the physical metaphor had not even been surveyed seriously. What is still missing is a preliminary balance sheet of the gains and losses from adherence to this research strategy.

For early neoclassical theory, one can compile a condensed set of accounts. On the credit side, the main object of the early marginalists has been achieved: the abolition of the *anomie* and the lack of systematic theory of mid-nineteenth-century political economy, and the creation in its place of a shared research program with shared goals, as well as a well-defined set of research techniques. Attention moved away from broad and ill-defined growth and development issues to a much narrower set of concerns tethered to the notion of short-period equilibrium price (Garegnani 1976). Systematic empiricism was encouraged by a shift in focus to certain easily quantifiable variables. The discipline of economics was divided up into a set of subfields, both theoretical and applied, which could provide researchers with a clearly defined expertise and thus identity. This played an important part in the growing professionalization of economics in the later nineteenth century, guaranteeing it a secure place in the academic environment (Checkland 1951a). In other words, the appropriation of the physical metaphor effectively appropriated credibility for economics as a respected science.

The debit side of the account is more subtle, and so more contentious. Perhaps the major debit entry is the fact that the early neoclassicals themselves did not adequately understand the physical metaphor and the constraints which it imposed upon social theory. For example, Jevons did not explicitly derive the equilibrium of the lever from energetics principles in his *Theory of Political Economy,* thus leaving him open to ridicule by Marshall, who jeeringly suggested in a bold review that he try to integrate his equation of exchange (Jevons 1981, VII, 145). With the single exception of Marshall, all the early neoclassicals used the energetics metaphor; no other economists understood enough physics to discuss its implications and flaws.

Yet consider a short impressionistic list of these flaws. First, all energetics before the second law of thermodynamics (the entropy law) presumed that all phenomena were perfectly reversible, and thus equilibrium could not be time-dependent. In pre-entropy physics, history does not matter. The conservation principle is crucial in this respect, because it defines identity through time. When this metaphor is imported into the social sphere, it implies that in equilibrium bygones are bygones; thus one could practically ignore how a market actually functions in real time, paying attention only to putative "eventual" outcomes. Hicks (1979) and Shackle (1967) are the latest in a long line of illustrious figures to complain about this issue; but their complaints have not made any substantive headway because they have not seen how deeply rooted this principle is in neoclassical techniques. Second, something must be conserved in order to apply the techniques of constrained extrema, the "maximum principle." When the physical metaphor is imported into the social sphere, neoclassicists were not at all precise about what the conserved entity was, and they have not yet been able to settle this issue. If utility is conserved, then surprise and regret as psychological phenomena have analytically been ruled out of court. If income or endowments are conserved, then Say's Law is implicitly invoked, and there is no theory of output other than a psychological notion of "virtual" production (Clower 1970). Third, in energetics, all physical phenomena are fully and reversibly transformable into any other phenomena. When this idea is transported into the context of the economy, then all goods become fully and reversibly transformable into all other goods through trades. There is no requirement for a specific money commodity or set of financial institutions, because they would be redundant. The analogue of energetics is the barter economy. Fourth, equilibrium is identified with extremum principles in physics because they provide a concise method of summarizing the actual path of particles in empirical experience. When the metaphor is imported into economics, the use of extremum principles is claimed to "prove" the superior efficacy of a particular kind of economic organization. Physics long ago renounced this teleological interpretation; economics has come to embrace it.

If contemporaries had understood what kind of economy the energetics metaphor described, then neoclassicism would have met substantial logical opposition. We may infer this from the fact that when the physics metaphor was explicitly introduced into the social sphere in other contexts, it met with strenuous opposition (Sorokin 1956, ch. 1). But this is where economics is the anomaly in the history of social theory: because the "inventors" did not understand energetics or the social metaphor with any great depth or subtlety, they rarely discussed the merits or demerits of the application of physical techniques and metaphors to social theory. No other economist understood enough physics to see its implications; nor were they induced to study physics by any of the writings of the early marginalists. Effectively, neoclassical economic theory was a *fait accompli* whose origins and fundamental bases were buried by historical accident, to the extent that the sources of inspiration of Jevons, Walras, Pareto, *et al.* could appear as a puzzle to their posterity.

It should not appear from my summary that the entire economics profession were sleepwalkers, stumbling unwittingly into a maze of energetics. Alfred Marshall, for one, certainly discussed some aspects of the adoption of physical metaphors (Marshall 1898); and he clearly had some reservations. However, the case of Marshall is actually illuminated by an understanding of energetics.

Marshall's place in the history of economic thought has always been a curious one. He hinted, both privately and in print, that many of Jevons' ideas had been "familiar truths" to him when they were published, thus intimating that somehow he also deserved "discoverer" status. Since much of what appears in introductory and intermediate microeconomics texts as the theory of supply and demand is, in fact, the handiwork of Marshall, there is a grain of truth in his claim. However, once the actual sequence of events is uncovered, it appears that Marshall's major service in the marginalist revolution was as a popularizer; and, like other popularizers, he altered the material which he promoted.

Recent study of Marshall's early unpublished writings, especially by Bharadwaj (1978), reveals that his early work was on the equilibrium of a supply curve with a phenomenological demand curve: he did not much care what lay behind his demand schedule. Implicitly, movements along the demand curve came from variations in the number of buyers, rather than a posited constrained maximization by an individual buyer. 'The word "utility" itself was used only once in relation to Adam Smith, and not approvingly' (Bharadwaj 1978, 367).

The saga of the journey between Marshall's early *Essay* and his *Principles* is the story of a decision to incorporate the innovations of the marginalist revolutionaries in order to shore up the foundations of the demand blade of the "scissors," while preserving his original concerns with the underlying theories of the supply schedule. Unhappily, the superficial parallels between diminishing returns and diminishing marginal utility could not obscure the fact that the result was more like paper and stone rather than scissors. For example, much of Marshall's typology of markets involved altering of the timeframe of analysis and deriving its resulting effects upon the supply schedule. This method produced some embarrassment when applied to the demand side, either because the underlying demand determinants remained constant over time, revealing that the fundamental cause of price was an exogenous posited psychology, as Jevons had maintained, or because the demand curve would also be shifted in relatively arbitrary ways, undermining any claim that an equilibrium of demand and supply had been identified. Perhaps it was predictable that the attack would be pressed against the part of the system which Marshall originated (Sraffa 1926), and that the ensuing retreat would vindicate Jevons' position.

Marshall sensed that his concerns could be overwhelmed by the zeal of his marginalist allies, and this partly explains why he does not conform in style to the characteristics of the marginalist cadre identified above. Witness his defense of Ricardo vis-à-vis Jevons; his soft-pedalling of the mathematical method; his insistence on the basic continuity of economics from Adam Smith to his time; his persistent praise of organic metaphors: all these activities are attempts to incorporate energetics into economics while controlling or perhaps altering some of its more objectionable aspects. Many wave as a banner Marshall's claim that, "The Mecca of the economist lies in economic biology," but few bother to quote the next sentence: "But biological conceptions are more complex than those of mechanics; a volume on Foundations must therefore give a relatively large place to mechanical analogies...." (Marshall 1920, xiv). However much he might protest, the fact remains that Marshall did render the energetics metaphor palatable for an English audience which would probably have resisted the brash revolution of a Jevons. Further, he fostered the illusion that "The new doctrines have supplanted the older... but very seldom have subverted them" (Marshall 1920, v).

It is important to appreciate that Marshall thought that the physical interpretation could be separated from the mathematical technique, and that his reservations lay in the interpretation rather than the technique. Those who happily quote Marshall's dictum to 'burn the mathematics' should read carefully the preface to the eighth edition of the *Principles:*

The new analysis is endeavoring gradually and tentatively to bring over into economics, as far as the widely different nature of the material will allow, those methods of the science of small increments (commonly called the differential calculus) to which man owes directly or indirectly the greater part of the control that he has obtained in recent times over physical nature. It is still in its infancy; it has no dogmas, and no standard of orthodoxy... there is a remarkable harmony and agreement on essentials among those who are working constructively by the new method; and especially among such of them as have served an apprenticeship in the simpler and more definite, and therefore more advanced, problems of physics. [Marshall 1920, xvi–xvii]

But of course there was dogma and a standard of orthodoxy: that was why agreement had been achieved relatively quickly by the mathematical workers; the standards and ideas had been appropriated during their apprenticeship in physics. The *Principles* is a book that touts the mathematical method while attempting to deny that the method could influence the content of what was being expressed. The clearest manifestation of this tension occurs in the Appendix to the *Principles,* where, in the midst of a series of abstruse notes concerning the application of constrained maximization to utility, there is an incongruous discussion of the applications of Taylor's Theorem to the webbing between a duck's appendages (Marshall 1920, 841–42). The purpose of the digression is to suggest that the calculus was being borrowed from an organic evolutionary metaphor, rather than from physics. Not only did Taylor's Theorem have nothing to do with the duck's webbing in Marshall's actual example; but the calculus of constrained maximization was not employed by evolutionary theorists in Marshall's day.

The Meaning of the "Marginalist Revolution"

The energetics metaphor can be found in every major neoclassical theorist of the nineteenth century and can be used to explain some controversies in the history of economic thought. It is a very neat pattern; perhaps too neat. Is it being too wise after the event in defining neoclassicism tautologically as coextensive with the introduction of the physics metaphor into social theory, and then brushing other authors aside? I do not think so. This chapter merely points out what has been there for all to see in published writings, biographies, and the history of science.

This chapter has *not* specified why the energetics metaphor was so attractive to nineteenth-century economic theorists, or discussed why the economics tail still is or is not wagged by the physics dog. Such omissions are due to the fact that such a discussion requires a much larger original content and a grounding in the philosophies of science and theory choice. The philosophy of science is so important because it indicates where to begin searching for acceptable explanations of the adoption of the physics metaphor (see chapter 8 below). Should we look to the level of personal motivation or structural tendencies? Should we look to empirical inadequacies or logical flaws, or some less rigid intellectual influences? These questions give rise to a research project, which could be carried out at many different levels: the level of individual desires (e.g., Jevons' personal motivations) that of individual influences (e.g. Edgeworth's family were friends of Hamilton), that of class interests, that of the sociology of professions (here the location of economists in universities), that of the cannons of empiricism (the rise of quantification as a preferred empirical technique), that of the status of alternative competing research programs (say, the dilution of the Ricardian program by Mill and the retreat of the labor theory of value), and that of metaphysical predispositions in the larger culture [e.g., the western tendency to see social relations as rooted in "natural" processes (Levine 1977)].

Another reason why modern philosophy of science is important is that it has highlighted the significance of the history of science. Discussion of the above issue can be cogently prosecuted only in conjunction with the study of the actual (as opposed to mythical) history of mathematics, physics, etc. Only then would we be able to extend the inquiries into the twentieth century with questions like: what is the relation between the penetration of input—output methods into economics and the preceding rise of matrix methods in quantum mechanics? What is the link between Niels Bohr's "Correspondence Principle" and that of Paul Samuelson? Another question of interest concerns the relation of mathematical technique to model content. Did mathematical economic theorists before 1870 "fail" because they were inept, or for other more profound reasons?

Finally, we can clarify the issues broached at the outset. The antiquarian question has been settled: neoclassical economic theory is bowdlerized nineteenth-century physics. The epistemological issue has been illuminated: present research techniques may be favored *because* they were appropriated from physics. The ontological issue has been reinterpreted: neoclassicism was not "simultaneously discovered" because it was "true," as Jevons and others would have it; instead, the timing of its genesis is explained by the timing of the energetics revolution in physics, and by the fact that scientifically trained individuals in different Western European countries at that time had access to the same body of knowledge and techniques. The practical issue, however, has scarcely been addressed. One cannot predict where new theories will come from, but one can venture a broad inductive generalization from past patterns: that a substantial nonneoclassical economic theory will distinguish itself by consciously repudiating the energetics metaphor.

2

The Sciences Were Never at War?

Some Early Skirmishes Between Physicists and Economists

I

The most profound fact about the history of neoclassical economics is also one of the least well known facts concerning its sources of inspiration, and therefore its logical structure: the neoclassical theory of the maximization of utility was derived directly from the immediately preceding innovations in physics in the 1840s through 1860s. This fact should not be interpreted as suggesting that there are some vague metaphorical and/or mathematical similarities between the two research traditions. Instead, as we have seen in Chapter 1, neoclassical economics was a simple appropriation and bowdlerization of the theory of energy (which we shall dub "energetics," although this risks some confusion with a late nineteenth-century movement within physics); to put it bluntly, the progenitors of neoclassicism copied down the physical equations and just changed the names attached to the variables. The lack of familiarity with this fact is doubly puzzling, given that most of the progenitors of neoclassicism admitted as much in their published writings. There can be no clearer admission than that found in Irving Fisher's doctoral dissertation, which Paul Samuelson has called "the best of all doctoral dissertations in economics" (1950, 254). In Fisher (1926, 85–86) there is a dictionary and concordance of translations of variables in "mechanics" into those of "economics"; the most pertinent for our present purposes is the entry admitting that "energy" in physics corresponds to "utility" in the newfangled economics.

The intention of this chapter is *not* to attempt to convince the reader of this profound and farreaching fact. Instead, in an era in which economists regularly must suffer the slings and arrows of ridicule, the author proposes that it might be both entertaining and instructive to summarize the early reactions of physicists to this presumptive poaching upon their territory. The modern interest in this episode should not arise simply because of the esteem which is generally accorded physicists in the unspoken hierarchy of the sciences, but also because some of the insights of those early critics are still relevant today, especially in three crucial areas: (a) the role of mathematics in the content of economic theory; (b) the perennial complaint that neoclassical theory is "static" and not "dynamic"; and (c) the often-heard opinion that utility is expendable in the larger scheme of neoclassical economics.

II

The second most remarkable fact about the appropriation of the physical model by the progenitors of neoclassicism is that the original progenitors found themselves unwilling or incapable of implementing the energetics metaphor to its full extent. Although most social theorists did not have a clue as to what the marginalists were doing, those trained in the physics of the day understood it quite well, and immediately recognized what aspects were included and what was left out without comment or justification. A few of these scientifically trained individuals made the effort to summon these lacunae to the attention of the early neoclassicals, to the acute embarrassment of the latter.

We conjecture that the first time this happened was probably with Fisher's thesis in 1892. His thesis advisor, J. Willard Gibbs, undoubtedly asked Fisher why his indifference points should be able to be integrated into utility surfaces. Far from being a minor technical complaint, Gibbs made Fisher aware that the absence of integrability would necessarily mean that there could exist no such quantity as total utility. Fisher, with his usual bravado, admitted such a possibility in his thesis, and then proceeded to obfuscate the entire issue with the following bizarre statement:

> Even if the integration were possible there would still be an arbitrary constant. We could even claim that total disutility exceeds total utility and all man can do is minimize the disagreeable instead of maximize the agreeable. In other words, if we embrace hedonism, there is nothing in economic investigation to cause us to choose between optimism and pessimism. [Fisher 1926, 89]

Of course this was a red herring, and a smelly one to boot, since that was not at all the thrust of Gibbs's query. Gibbs did not care if utility could be comparably scaled to disutility. He wanted to know why Fisher did not explore integrability as the next logical step toward a dynamic theory of optimization: Hamiltonians are solved for conservative integrable systems. Fisher, uncomprehending, instead went on to say (on the same page) that he did not need integrability for his theory, and indeed, he did not need utility, period. It is from this point that we can date the collective neoclassical amnesia with regard to the physics metaphor.

The second instance of a scientist harassing the new "economic science" came close on the heels of the first, in 1898. Hermann Laurent, a mathematician at the École Polytechnique and the author of a textbook on rational mechanics (1870), wrote to Walras about some things, as he put it, "ce qui choquera un peu moins les mathématiciens purs" (Walras 1965, vol 3, 116). Laurent queried Walras as to the appropriate unit of value (ibid., letter 1,374). Walras, after trying to fob him off with compliments, responded with a repetition of the thesis in his *Elements* that it is not proper to speak of a unit of value, only an arbitrary *numeraire* (ibid., letter 1,377). Laurent, a little perturbed at being patronized, wrote back that he was asking about *dynamics* and the essential role of time, but that Walras had only responded with a static argument (ibid., letter 1,378). Walras, getting a little flustered, then accused Laurent of conceptualizing value as an absolute magnitude, in analogy with certain physical magnitudes such as length, weight, and force. He wrote, "A vrai dire, vous tendez à identifier purement et simplement la valeur et la force an prenant pour unité de valeur la valeur de l'unité de force" (ibid., vol. 3, 47–48). Walras then went on to say that he thought of value as a magnitude *sui generis,* and did not expect that there existed any unit of value that was constant over time and space. Laurent, by this time, was beginning to wonder whether Walras was just playing dumb, being obstreperous, or perhaps simply did not understand the physics involved (ibid., letter 1,380). As might be expected, the correspondence then cooled for a while, but after a friendly letter from Walras a year later, Laurent decided to try one more time. This letter of 13 May 1900 (ibid., letter 1,452) is a miracle of compression and lucidity. Laurent wrote (my translation):

Let $dq_1, dq_2, \ldots, dq_N$ be quantities of merchandise $A_1, A_2, \ldots, A_N$ consumed during time dt. Their total price is

$$p_1 dq_1 + p_2 dq_2 + \cdots + p_N dq_N \tag{1}$$

where p_i designates the price of a unit of q_i. If one accepts that there is a standard of measure for utility, then one must also accept that expression (1) is integrable after having multiplied by a factor μ, if it is an exact differential. Then one posits

$$d\Phi = \mu[p_1 dq_1 + p_2 dq_2 + \cdots] \tag{2}$$

$$\frac{d\Phi}{dq_1} = \mu p_1, \quad \frac{d\Phi}{dq_2} = \mu p_2, \cdots$$

and hence the derivatives are proportional to the prices, such that one would be able to call the *raretés* of $A_1, A_2, \cdots$ the partial integrals.

$$\int \frac{d\Phi}{dq_1}, \cdots$$

which will be the utilities. But there is one difficulty: the measure of rarete depends on the factor μ. One could respond that it is just a matter of definition, but that does not mean it is any less interesting to interpret the significance of the factors of integration.

If the differential equation (1) is null then the function Φ is constant, and after our hypothesis, will there exist *one* relationship between prices and the quantities consumed?

This again threw Walras into a tizzy. First he compared his work to that of the early progenitors of the calculus, who knew their techniques worked, although they were unsure of its principles. Then, in a statement that would be ironic if Walras had possessed a little more savoir faire, he insisted that there are other economists who are also good mathematicians, such as Bort-kiewich, Pareto, and Barone, who also start from the same point of departure without quibbling about these issues: such consensus is rare. (He seemed to be implying that there was safety in numbers.) He then proceeded to reveal his thorough confusion with regard to the mathematics by suggesting that the integrating factor is equal to the ratios of marginal utility to price, and to rewrite Laurent's equation (1) as a system of individual demand and supply equations. Finally, he reiterated that he did not see any need for a standard or measure of utility (ibid., letter 1,454). It is amazing that Laurent doggedly tried one more time, writing that Walras still had not answered his question. Patiently he asked: why is equation (1) an exact differential, and what is the economic interpretation of the factor of integration? (ibid., letter 1,455). In exhaustion, Walras ignored the question about the exact differential entirely, and responded by shifting his premises to insist instead that the integrating factor is the marginal utility of the numeraire; he claimed that this was similar to Marshall's discussion of the marginal utility of money (ibid., letter 1,456). Both sides then returned to nurse their bruised egos, never to correspond again concerning this issue.

Laurent should be considered one of the unsung heroes of economic theory, because of his avid devotion to getting the content of the physical metaphor correctly specified. Just when the Walras correspondence looked to him as if it were going nowhere, he decided to try one of the neoclassicals who might possess a little better comprehension of the issues involved. In an effort clearly above and beyond the call of duty, early in 1899 he composed a number of letters to Vilfredo Pareto, essentially posing the same queries.[1] Pareto's first response was to praise Laurent's mathematical textbooks and to insist that it gave him great pleasure—in his words, "for the first time"—to discuss these questions with a person well versed in mathematics. He then tendered his stock answer: it was not a question of utility being numerically measurable; it was only a rank ordering of greater or less. In the next para-graph, there appeared a jolting non sequitur, in which he stated that the "gen-eral economic problem" is to take the prices in question (1) as variables and not as constants. If this is the case, pleasure or utility will depend upon the order of consumption. But, he concludes, we can usually ignore this case (Chipman 1976, 47).

Laurent must have been perplexed by this further indication of erratic behavior on the part of the avatars of economic mechanics and rational economic man. Not only was Pareto's letter internally inconsistent; it resem-bled Walras's responses in its cavalier assertions that the problem was insignificant. Yet their respective understandings of the problem had no rela-tion one to another, and worse, neither had a connection to the obvious phy-sics metaphor. Laurent chose to press the inquiry with greater insistence, to which Pareto replied with a wholly different defense.

Pareto began by agreeing with Laurent that one can only measure that which is susceptible to being added and equalized. Pareto then admitted that pleasure was not susceptible to addition or equalization. This was not a crippling admission, he suggested, since all the sciences pretended to measure what was not measurable in their early stages. Then followed a thoroughly awkward comparison of economics with geometry (ibid., 48). Realizing belatedly that this analogy wanders into a cul de sac, Pareto then committed another of his characteristic non sequiturs. Peripatetically, he decided that Laurent had mistakenly attempted to derive equilibrium from the single equation (1), whereas both equations (1) and (2) were required to locate equilibrium.

At this point, we are at a loss as to why Laurent wanted to pursue the matter further, but, as Pareto would undoubtedly say, *chacun à son goût*. Pareto's next letter is more than a little testy, and at one stage he writes, "What you say about the habits of pure mathematics doesn't bother me" (ibid., 56), perhaps reevaluating the joys of a friendly chat with relentlessly logical mathematicians. (We remind the reader that at this same time, Pareto was attempting to intimidate other social theorists, such as Croce, with the supposed precision of his mathematical science.) In the last letter, Pareto tangles himself up further by (a) taking the position that there is no reason to integrate equation (1), since it is merely a budget constraint; and by (b) denying that the integral of equation (2) is what he meant by utility (or, in his redundant terminology,"*ophelimité*"). He then tried to drive this point home by an illustration of the derivation of prices in a two-good system. Laurent must have thrown up his hands in disgust at this, since both statements are obviously false; and furthermore, since the integrability problem does not arise in a two-good world, his example was simply irrelevant.[2] As a reaction to the dearth of satisfactory answers to his questions, Laurent published a *Petit traité d'économie politique mathématique* in 1902, but its critique provoked no interest or attention.

The third instance of a scientist taking a neoclassical economist to task was Vito Volterra's 1906 review of Pareto's *Manuale di economia politica* (in Chipman et al. 1971, 365–69). The complaint was the same: mathematics should be used in economics only with caution. Volterra warned that when there are more than two goods, Pareto's expression (identical to that of (1) above) would not necessarily be integrable. By 1906 this must have seemed like a déjà vu to Pareto. Moreover, by that time he must have reconsidered his retorts to Laurent, since he relinquished all his later defenses and returned to his immediate reaction to Laurent's first inquiry: all the fuss must be about the problem of utility depending upon the order in which goods are consumed. This was the gist of his article on "Open and Closed Cycles of Ophelimity" in the *Giornale degli Economisti* in 1906, which was intended as a public reply to Volterra's gentle criticism (in ibid., 370–85).

The terminology of open and closed cycles reveals that Pareto had begun to grasp what was at issue, although we shall see that he never completely understood or felt comfortable with the critics' concerns or his own replies. The terminology of open and closed cycles, which has appeared so incomprehensible to Pareto's later partisans (see ibid., 324), was intended to evoke the open and closed cycles of the work integral, and thus directly to admit the analogy of energy and utility. In a closed cycle the initial and final states of a system are independent of path; in mechanics, this is isomorphic to a statement of the conservation of energy. One recognizes that a mechanical system can be brought around a closed cycle by the fact that the expression

$$\sum F_x dx + F_y dy + F_z dz + \cdots$$

is integrable and is an exact differential; hence the continual badgering questions about the integrability of equation (1). It is not to Pareto's credit that he took the metaphor of a path too literally, and associated it with the effect of the temporal order of consumption or the utility experienced. His example of the order of consumption of soup and roast beef made the problem sound trivial, an opinion he himself expressed in the first page of the paper. The triviality of the problem derived from Pareto's interpretation, however, and not from the intrinsic character of the problem. In a field theory of value, the actual act of consumption is supposed to be irrelevant to the magnitude of the utility derived from the good, since it is a virtual notion. Hence, consideration of temporal problems of the sequence of consumption is rendered meaningless. Further, we have already observed that neoclassical equilibrium was, of necessity, a static conception, which ruled the passage of time out of consideration. This was well understood by the more sophisticated neoclassicals at the turn of the century. Fisher, for instance, wrote that "total utility is not an experience in time but the sum of increments of utility substitutionally successive...the marginal utility to a given individual of a given commodity is the same at all instants at which he buys or consumes it or sells or produces it" (1926, 19). Hence, in the eyes of most of his contemporaries, Pareto was discussing a nonproblem. It did not help matters that he spent most of his time on a two-good example, when the integrability problem mathematically arises only with three or more goods.

III

The history of the integrability problem in neoclassical economics is an extremely peculiar interlude. Around the turn of the century, these major figures in neoclassical thought were challenged by some even bigger luminaries in the scientific community; to a man, they acquitted themselves abysmally. It should have been all the more humiliating since two obscure Italian engineers—Giovanni Antonelli and Pasquale Boninsegni—had already got the technical mathematics right, although they did not actually contribute anything to the elaboration of the economic theory (for Antonelli's 1886 work see Chipman, et al, 1971, 333–63; for Boninsegni's, see Boninsegni 1902).

Yet Antonelli and Boninsegni, and indeed, all the embarrassing inquisitions by natural scientists, were forgotten at least until the 1930s: it was as if it all had never happened. The discussion of the revival of interest in this problem in the 1930s and its attendant causes must await another day; but for now, our concern is simply to relate this odd fact to the adoption of a field theory of value.

What happened around the turn of the century was really quite simple. A number of mathematicians and scientists stumbled upon some of the writings of the early neoclassicals and immediately apprehended what was going on: these economists were calling energy "utility." Their reaction was to try and see if these economists were merely using the physical mathematics to browbeat and hoodwink their colleagues, or if there actually were legitimate parallels in the two traditions. With their background in the physical sciences, they knew what the really critical attributes of the energy concept were: Was it conserved in a closed system? Was it a variable of state, which would then suggest various procedures for its empirical examination? These are the questions they asked, but they phrased them in shorthand terms, as would one mathematician to another: Why is equation (1) above an exact differential? Why should we expect utility to be integrable, and what is the interpretation of the integrating factor? As we have observed, these questions were met with defensiveness or incomprehension. The fact was that all the progenitors of neoclassical economics had been trained as engineers, but that their grasp of the physics was shallow and superficial. And these were the same individuals who insisted that economics must become a mathematical science in order to instill some discipline and clarity of thought.

The problem of integrability, far from being merely an arcane game played by a small coterie of mathematicians, was (and still is) the key to the understanding and evaluation of the neoclassical cooptation of the physics metaphor. The early progenitors of neoclassicism liked the analogy of utility as energy, but could not be bothered to examine the analogy in sufficient detail to evaluate rationally its strengths and drawbacks. One facet of the analogy from which they persistently averted their gaze was the principle of the conservation of energy, even though that principle was the single most important unifying concept in physics in the third quarter of the nineteenth century. The reason they shunned the concept (when they understood it) is that, as we have seen, the metaphor implied that the sum of utility (the potential energy) and expenditure (the kinetic energy) should remain a constant. Not only was this repugnant and absurd on the face of it, but it also harbored a deeper meaning that could potentially undermine the entire neoclassical research program. The overall thrust of the emulation of physics by economics throughout its history has been to discover the hidden fundamental natural determinants of value that lay behind the veil of everyday phenomena of money prices and incomes. Utility as a field of vector potentials fit that pattern quite nicely, but the physics apparatus did not stop there. A potential field should be coupled with a well-defined set of transformation algorithms into kinetic forces, because the field and the forces are just two aspects of the same ontological thing. The analogy, strictly and logically interpreted, would thus suggest that money and utility were the same ontological thing. Even worse, since most newcomers to neoclassicism found it difficult to believe that utility actually exists, would it not have seemed superfluous and redundant to have based a new theory of value upon an intangible and unobservable eidolon, when the other legitimate metric of value was reassuringly tangible, nestled in everyone's pockets?

The temptation here is to cite Santayana's dictum that those who are ignorant of history are doomed to repeat it. At the turn of the century and subsequently, many economists who did not know that neoclassicism was reprocessed physics felt that they could assume that money and/or income possessed a "constant marginal utility" (Marshall 1920, 842). Little did they realize that they were simply completing the original physical metaphor by imposing the "conservation of energy," through the condition that money and utility were identical. Some pointed out that this assumption imposed stringent restrictions on the utility function (Samuelson 1942), but what they did not add is that it rendered the whole contraption of the utility function redundant, since money provided the unique and sufficient direct cardinal measure of utility in that regime. The same comment applies to the habit of interpreting the integrating factor of the differential equation (1) as the marginal utility of money. This explains why the natural science critics of early neoclassicism were so insistent upon specification of the interpretation of the integrating factor: if there existed some such constant, then the empirical implementation of the physical metaphor would hold some promise, because that aspect of value would have some empirical regularity and stability. Of course, those scientists had no way of knowing that they were prodding a sore spot of the appropriated physics model: if money was a sufficient and credible measure of value, then the whole project of a science-based value theory, which aimed to uncover the fundamental lawlike reality obscured by the blooming buzzing phenomenological diversity, was pointless.

The question of the extension of the physics metaphor to encompass Hamiltonian dynamics merged all the critical issues of time, process, conservation principles, and integrability into a single, seemingly technical issue. A genuinely rigorous response to this question would, by its very nature, need to incorporate an evaluation of the suitability of the energetics metaphor to describe social processes. For whatever reasons, this extension and its attendant evaluation have been avoided whenever possible by neoclassicals. Instead, they have gone out of their way to concoct other bizarre scenarios of dynamic movements between the static equilibria identified by the physics model. Jevons invented a black box called a "trading body," which performed all the dynamic functions of coordination in an unspecified manner (Jevons 1970, 135–38). Walras posited his famous "auctioneer," who prevented all trading activity while potential transactors resorted to hypothetical questions about their utility fields. Others attempted a pseudo-dynamics predicated upon the difference between demand and supply functions, piling one Rube Goldberg contraption atop another. The purpose of all these contrived schemes was to circumvent the dynamics constructed by the physicists within the logic of the physics model.

What would the suppressed neoclassical Hamiltonian dynamics have looked like? There would first be the problem that the Hamiltonian formalism is expressed in the format of generalized coordinates. A system with S individuals and N commodities has SN degrees of freedom, which can be reduced to $SN - k$ by the explicit incorporation of the k constraints into the coordinate system. Hence the variables expressing the quantities q_i of the N commodities would be rewritten as functions of the new, artificial coordinates $\alpha_1, \alpha_2, \ldots, \alpha_{N-k}$ and time:

$$q_1 = q_1(\alpha_1, \alpha_2, \ldots, \alpha_{N-k}, t)$$

$$q_2 = q_2(\alpha_1, \alpha_2, \ldots, \alpha_{N-k}, t) \tag{3}$$

$$q_N = q_N(\alpha_1, \alpha_2, \ldots, \alpha_{N-k}, t)$$

These generalized commodity coordinates are somewhat opaque, in that they have no immediate intuitive interpretation; that is, their dimensions are no longer the physical amounts of any particular commodity.[3] Their primary purpose is to make it easier to write down the Hamiltonian equation:

$$H = E(\beta_1, \beta_2, \ldots, \beta_{N-k}) + V(\alpha_1, \alpha_2, \ldots, \alpha_{N-k}) \tag{4}$$

Here the βs can be interpreted as "generalized prices" associated with the αs the generalized commodity coordinates. (The analogies with the physics are: the αs are generalized spatial coordinates, and the βs are generalized momenta). Knowledge of the Hamiltonian equation in the most general sense is knowledge of the future evolution of the system. The laws of dynamics are expressed by Hamilton's equations:

$$\frac{d\beta_i}{dt} = -\frac{\partial H}{\partial \alpha_i} \quad \text{and} \quad \frac{d\alpha_i}{dt} = \frac{\partial H}{\partial \beta_i} \tag{5}$$

$$i = 1, \ldots, N-k$$

At this juncture, considerations of conservation principles and integrability would enter the picture in a decisive fashion. In physics, the purpose of rewriting the coordinates in a generalized format is so that the Hamiltonian equation (4) can be written in the two separate parts $E + V$. If energy is conserved in the system, the first part, E, is interpreted as the kinetic energy, depending only on momenta; and the second part, the V, is the potential energy, depending only upon position. Hence the Hamiltonian is equal to the total energy of the system, which is a constant. A major obstacle to the importation of the Hamiltonian into neoclassical economics is that the parallel conservation of expenditure plus utility would be blatantly obvious whenever anyone wrote out equation (4).

The issue of integrability also becomes much simpler in the Hamiltonian framework. If one desires to model the evolution of some arbitrary function f of a position and momentum through time, one employs the mathematical technique of the Poisson bracket. If the function is invariant, the Poisson bracket $[f,H] = O$. (See Prigogine 1980, 23; or Goldstein 1950, 250–258.) Importing this method into neoclassical economics, one might similarly wish to model the evolution of some function of generalized prices and commodity coordinates through time, and search for invariants. If the sum of expenditure and utility is conserved, then the Poisson bracket of the Hamiltonian with itself is:

$$[H,H] = O \tag{6}$$

It comes as somewhat of a surprise to find that the "Antonelli conditions" for integrability, frequently cited in the twentieth-century literature (Samuelson 1950; Chipman et al, 1971, 347) are nothing more than equation (6) above. In other words, under the guise of a "merely technical" mathematical condition, the assumption of integrability is a surreptitious reimposition of the conservation of expenditure plus utility, as well as the imposition of the conditions for a Hamiltonian dynamics *over and above* any other postulated mechanism for the convergence of prices to equilibrium over time. So much for the bracing influence of mathematical formalism upon the communication of assumptions.

IV

It may seem harsh and unfair to criticize the first generation of neoclassicals for not hewing more closely to their adopted physics model. After all, was it not just a metaphor, and as such, merely meant to suggest certain novel lines of inquiry, rather than to bind the economists blithely to do exactly what the physicists were doing?

This was the attitude of Pareto when challenged by Croce to defend his mechanism. His defense ran:

> Evidently it is not a case of identity but of resemblance... mechanics can be studied leaving aside the concept of forces. In reality all this does not matter much. If there is anyone who does not come to hear mechanics mentioned, very well, let us disregard the similarity and let us talk directly about our equations. We shall only

have to face the drawback that in certain cases we shall have to labor greatly in order to deduce from those equations certain consequences that we would have perceived at once had we kept in mind the fact that mechanics had already deduced them from its own equations, which are similar to ours. [Pareto 1953, 185]

Yet another irony of the situation was that it was precisely the consequences of the mechanical equations that were a major source of the objections to the neoclassical research program; and that these objections were circumvented precisely by suppressing any further discussion of mechanics, and later reinventing the wheel under a different (and more obscure) rubric. It is certainly true that one need not be obsessed with the exact duplication of all aspects of a metaphor when such a pattern is transferred from one area of inquiry to another. Nevertheless, one of the main attractions of analogic reasoning is that it provides a shortcut in the exploration of the implications and structures of a given explanatory configuration, precisely because those implications and structures have undergone appreciable development elsewhere. Pareto's response to Croce said, in effect, that it does not matter that our mathematical model came from rational mechanics, since we can pick and choose whatever aspects we like and disregard the rest. Pareto's error, as well as that of the other neoclassicals, was his obliviousness to the fact that some parts of the metaphor were not freely disposable. It is this which is the gist of our criticism.

The essence of the neoclassical analysis is the appropriation of the physical concept of the field. While the notion of a field is a very flexible concept, it does possess a certain amount of regularity and structure, which, if absent, would undermine its logical integrity. The history of physics reveals that the primary indispensable element of a field is the imposition of some conservation principle or principles. In prosaic or intuitive terms, the field can be a very nebulous thing. In order to endow it with the stability of causal explanation, there must be certain regularities with regard to its interaction with other theoretical entities. It is the function of conservation principles to define the identity of the system as it undergoes its various phenomenal transformations, as well as to define the interaction of discrete systems. This function is particularly relevant in physical field theories, where fields can pervade what appears to be empty space.

The epistemological necessity of conservation principles in field theories is mirrored in their mathematics. As we have repeatedly observed, variational principles are always linked to conservation principles. There is no such thing as a mathematics of extrema without some correspondingly conserved entities or quantities. Neoclassical economists, out of neglect or ignorance, refused to learn this lesson from the history of physics, and acted as though they could appropriate the variational principle and ignore issues of conservation. Various natural scientists tried to remind them of this, but they were met with incomprehension. Lack of comprehension, however, did not mean the absence of conservation principles in neoclassical economic theory: the physical metaphor was completed absentmindedly and surreptitiously, and generally under the guise of mere technical or mathematical issues. Through the mathematics, the physical metaphor took on a life of its own, which compelled neoclassical theory to conform to the structure of a field explanation.

Conservation principles were imposed haphazardly. The mathematics of the physical metaphor required that the sum of potential and kinetic energy—which in the neoclassical version translated into the sum of utility and expenditure—be conserved in a closed system. In a higgledy-piggledy fashion, neoclassical economists imposed the conservation of one, the other, or their sum, depending on the context; sometimes they imposed all three in the same model, which was redundant. The three categories of possibilities in a pure exchange model were: (a) conserve utility; (b) conserve income and/or expenditure; (c) conserve the sum of utility and expenditure.

The conservation of utility is often misunderstood. It does not mean that the sum of utility is constant before and after a trade: obviously, a major tenet of neoclassicism is that trade increases the sum of utilities *realized*. The conservation of utility means that the utility *field* is conserved, existing independent of any activity of exchange. This assumption is smuggled into the economic theory in a number of ways. The most common method is simply to posit a mathematical form of the utility function that is symmetric and path-independent. Another alternative is to rule out the phenomenon of regret in the psychology of choice (Fisher 1926, 21). A third alternative is to rule out any endogenous change of tastes. All these options really can be reduced to the same condition: there can be no divergence between the anticipation and the realization of utility. More recent innovations in probabalistic concepts of utility muddy the water somewhat, but the end result is the same.[4]

The conservation of income and/or expenditure is slightly better understood, if only because it has been the subject of more extensive controversies. It is the second half of the neoclassical litany of "given tastes and given endowments." The most frequent imposition of this conservation principle takes the form of an assumption that incomes are given and fixed outside the analysis. This assumption has become inextricably tangled up with a neoclassical version of Say's Law, which states that aggregate incomes in equilibrium are independent of the sequential path of exchanges by which they are arrived at. The explanation of the vicissitudes of these assumptions belongs in the twentieth century, with its attempt to fuse macroeconomics and neoclassical economic theory; therefore we postpone further discussion of this issue until Chapter 6.

The conservation of expenditure plus utility, the legitimate heritage of the physics metaphor, has most frequently made its appearance as a mathematical assumption in order to avoid discussion of its economic interpretation. As previously observed, it could take the form of an assumption of the constant marginal utility of money or income; but more recently, it is smuggled in under the cover of integrability conditions: most generally, the Antonelli conditions.

By this account, there have been at least two inescapable imperatives of the physics metaphor in economics. The first is that the very concept of explanation imported from the natural sciences requires conservation principles.

The second imperative of the physics metaphor is that the nineteenth-century model that comprises its basis was the pinnacle of the philosophical doctrine that identified atomistic determinism and rigid mechanical causality with explanation. The beauty of the Hamiltonian is that, once written in an appropriate and tractable format and supplemented with a set of initial conditions, it promised to predict the movement of a closed system ad infinitum. Although the neoclassicals did not directly avail themselves of the Hamiltonian formalism, they did parade about the notion that their goal was a thoroughgoing determinism, which would likewise allow them to predict the entire future course of economic events. Inauspiciously, the neoclassicals became attached to this mechanistic determinism without understanding what it entailed, and just as physical science began to retreat from it.

We have stressed the role of the generalized coordinates (equation system [3] above) in the development of the Hamiltonian formalism because they serve a critical function in the solution of a dynamic system. Hamiltonians are frequently very difficult to solve, but the process is rendered tractable if one can find a set of generalized coordinates that will in effect transform away the "potential energy"—the αs—and leave H only a function of the action variables—the βs. Systems in which such a representation is possible are called "integrable systems" in classical dynamics, and the coordinate transformation is called a "canonical transformation" (Goldstein 1950, ch. 8). In the nineteenth century, physicists spent much effort searching for the canonical transformations for the various paradigmatic problems of motion, in order to realize the dream of fully predicting all future evolution of mechanical systems. The protagonists of physical determinism were stunned, therefore, when Heinrich Bruns and Henri Poincaré proved that some of the most common problems do not lead to integrable systems (Prigogine 1980, 29–32). The core of their problem is that most mechanical systems do not possess a sufficient number of invariants to justify this procedure. The Poincaré result opened a breach in classical mechanics, which allowed the penetration of probabalistic concepts, just as they were making inroads on other fronts in physics, particularly in thermodynamics and quantum mechanics.

Henceforth, the ideal of mechanical determinism receded in physics; this, too, is an imperative of the physical model. Given that neoclassical economists never directly confronted the issues of integrability, conservation principles, and invariance, it comes as no surprise that they were thoroughly oblivious to the retreat of atomistic determinism. As long as they held fast to the simplest model of rational mechanics, they also held fast to a picture of people as inert invariant mechanical objects, while physics was becoming predisposed to see the world as subject to change and indeterminacy, as well as interaction with the observer.

Notes

1. Unfortunately, only Pareto's side of the correspondence has survived, which has been conveniently published in Chipman 1976, 45–62. Because of this fact, we have had to infer much of the content of Laurent's letters to Pareto from the ones he sent to Walras and from the content of Pareto's letters.

2. In the commentary in Chipman 1976, Laurent is made to appear as if he did not competently understand the implications of neoclassical theory, in contrast to Pareto, who had them under complete control. Moreover, the entire exchange is written off as a mere technical confusion of the following questions: (1) Was $\Sigma\phi_i dx_i$ an integrable differential equation? (2) Was $\Sigma\phi_i dx_i$ an exact differential equation? (3) Was utility a path-independent variable, that is, independent of the actual temporal order of consumption? (4) Was utility measurable? While from a purely mathematical vantage point these questions might each be given different answers—say, a differential equation *might* be integrated with the help of an integrating factor, even though it was not an exact differential—from the vantage point of the physics they are the same question: is energy-utility conserved?

3. This has a passing resemblance to Piero Sraffa's "standard commodity," however. See Sraffa (1960).

4. Although this assertion cannot be fully documented here, the key to its understanding is to see the parallels between the property of "ergodicity" in statistical mechanics and the corresponding use of that assumption in stochastic economic theory. See Davidson (1982) and Lebowitz and Penrose (1973).

3

Macroeconomic Instability and the "Natural" Processes in Early Neoclassical Economics

It may seem odd to disinter an economic theory—in this instance, William Stanley Jevons's claim that sunspots caused macroeconomic fluctuations—which no one now believes or much cares about.[1] In fact, my purpose is not to scoff at a dead theory, but to use it as a pretext to discuss the following issues: economic historians often have suggested a dichotomy between a premodern and industrial macroeconomy, with the premodern economy largely at the mercy of weather and other natural phenomena; this dichotomy is rooted in early neoclassical economic theory (here restricting ourselves to Jevons); there is little historical evidence that premodern macro fluctuations were caused by natural disturbances, such as the weather (here restricting ourselves to the case of England); and the above three theses have some interesting implications for the way economic policy is conceived, both then and now.

I

William Stanley Jevons, in his 1870 Presidential Address before the British Association for the Advancement of Science, Section F, lamented that, "There is no one who occupies a less enviable position than the political economist. Cultivating the frontier regions between certain knowledge and conjecture, his efforts and advice are scorned and rejected on all hands."[2] Although this may prompt nods of assent in the 1980s, it is important to understand the historical context of such complaints. As he said later in the same address,

> The growth of the arts and manufactures and the establishment of free trade have opened the widest means of employment and brought an accession of wealth previously unknown.... Nevertheless within the past few years we have seen pauperism almost as prevalent as ever, and the slightest relapse of trade throws whole towns and classes of people into a state of destitution little short of famine.[3]

The problem of English political economy in the 1870s was its firm association with the doctrine of free trade, which in turn was a direct corollary of

45

the fundamental theoretical principle that unfettered market structures were a superior means of organizing production and distribution. In periods of buoyancy such a stance was easy to defend; but by the 1870s doubts became more insistent in England: doubts about the stability of market organization, which resulted in sharp aggregate fluctuations, and doubts about the long-term efficacy of free trade due to the successes of Britain's foreign economic rivals.[4] Jevons personally had felt these chill winds when his father's iron firm was bankrupted in 1848, and his family bore the stigma of being the "poor relations." This experience did not sour Jevons on free trade and the efficacy of market organization, however, because he felt that by hard work from an early age he had managed, in the face of adversity, to improve his station in life, and further that such an avenue was open to all who would but avail themselves of it.[5] In practice, the early Jevons responded to the mistrust of political economy by blaming the victims. But, as he soon came to understand, that was not a winning strategy.

All of Jevons's innovations in economics—his pioneering efforts in marginalist price theory, his work on the Coal Question, and his sunspot theory—may be understood as a unified rational response to the increasing skepticism about political economy in Britain. Economists in the late twentieth century tend to view the innovations in price theory as Jevons's crowning achievement and the sunspot theory as some unfortunate lapse, or even an embarrassment. Indeed, for some the sunspot theory has attained the status of joke, whereas for others it is a cautionary parable concerning the pitfalls of inductive argument.[6] All of these interpretations are much too facile, because they ignore the unified thrust of Jevons's theoretical project. In short, his project was to portray the market as a "natural" process, so that doubts about its efficacy would be assuaged, or at the very least, countered by scientific discourse. The ultimate object was to reconstruct the foundations of the case for free trade.

In the case of neoclassical price theory the evidence for this thesis is extensive, but would be superfluous in the present context; in any event it is summarized above.[7] Briefly, Jevons's price theory laid claim to scientific status because it was identical in mathematical form and analytical content to the physics of the mid-nineteenth century, which is sometimes referred to as "energetics" by historians of science. For our present purposes, it is only necessary to survey the broadest implications of this stratagem. First, it drew a direct analogy between economic transactions and transfers of energy, which subtly endowed the transactions with the "natural" ontological status of the transfers. Second, it encouraged specialization within economics and the cultivation of an internal language (mathematics), which served to buffer the discipline from the intrusions of lay critics. Third, it demonstrated that market processes maximized utility in a regime of free competition, thus implying that no improvement was possible through conscious intervention in production and exchange. These were a much more formidable set of defenses of the doctrine of free trade than those provided by the demoralized and disheveled remnants of classical political economy.

However, effective these new foundations, they did not address the most significant objection to British political economy: If free trade was such an able method of economic coordination, why did it result in such devastating contractions punctuating economic expansion? In this respect, Jevons's sunspot theory was the necessary adjunct to his newly formulated price theory. If the market always functioned in an effective manner tended toward a configuration insuring maximum happiness, then there was only one obvious way to explain the incongruity of the misery and suffering of depressions. The natural operation of the market could only be deflected or stymied (although never fully neutralized) by another opposing "natural" force—here Jevons proposed that macroeconomic fluctuations and credit crises were caused by meteorological disturbances, ultimately caused in turn by variations in sunspot activity.[8] The advantage of this sort of explanation was that no one was to blame, or as Jevons put it,

> We must not lay to the charge of trades-unions, or free trade, or any other pretext, a fluctuation of commerce which affects countries alike which have trades-unions and no trades-unions, free trade and protection; as to intemperance and various other moral causes, no doubt they may have powerful influence on our prosperity but they afford no special explanation of a temporary wave of calamity.[9]

The issue of macroeconomic instability, then, could not be used as an argument for protection, for instance, since the cause fell on all countries indifferently as a natural state of affairs. To my knowledge, no one has adequately explored the hypothesis that the English retained their allegiance to free trade long after the Continent did because they, unlike the French or Germans, persisted in seeing economic relations grounded in a physical (and not physiological) analogy.

Throughout his life, Jevons subscribed to the principle that macroeconomic fluctuations were of natural origins, but he encountered great difficulty in fleshing out the theory. His first article on the subject in 1875 tried to establish that English grain prices from 1254 to 1400 cycled with a period of 11 years. Because astronomers at that time believed that sunspot activity also rose and fell in cycles of 11.1 years, he asserted that the coincidence of periodicities implied that observed price fluctuations were caused by exogenous shocks. Of course, this was a very flimsy argument, as Jevons was well aware: he could not cite sunspot data contemporaneous with his fourteenth-century price data. Objections that would daunt the less resolute were not sufficient to restrain him: "I am aware that speculations of this kind may seem somewhat far-fetched and finely wrought; but financial collapses have occurred with such approach to regularity in the last fifty years, that either this or some other explanation is needed."[10]

What was needed was some connection between the existing sunspot data—the Wolf Zurich relative sunspot numbers, beginning in 1749—and some contemporaneous indicator of economic activity.[11] Jevons openly admitted that he had attempted to find a regular periodicity in the prices of European grains in the eighteenth and nineteenth centuries, but the search had failed. His next tactic was to assert the existence of a very stable 11-year period between English credit crises, and to suggest that the equality of periodicity with that of the sunspots was sufficient evidence to infer causality. This argument hinged crucially upon the claim that there was a clockwork regularity in the appearance of crises in England; and it was to this thesis that Jevons committed much intellectual effort. He produced one list of the dates of credit crises in 1877–1878, but then received the unpleasant surprise that astronomers had repudiated their earlier estimate of the periodicity of the sunspot cycle, revising the estimate to read 10.45 years. Again Jevons was not to be frustrated in his quest. He simply redefined a few of the dates of his "crises" so that the average interval became equal to 10.5 years. His final list of crisis dates (with those Jevons indicated as doubtful in italics) were: *1701,* 1711, 1731–1732, *1742, 1752,* 1763, 1772–1773, 1783, 1793, *1804–1805,* 1815, 1825, 1836–1839, 1847, 1857, 1866, and 1878.[12]

At this point, Jevons became the butt of some ridicule: one example was a satirical statistical study showing that the periodicity of winning Oxbridge teams in collegiate boat races was the same as that of sunspots. Other more serious challengers pointed out that Jevons's conception of crises, as revealed in his choice of dates, was so vague as to admit of any and all interpretations.[13] He responded by maintaining that he was simply proposing the following working hypothesis:

> A wave of increased solar radiations favorably affects the meteorology of the tropical regions, so as to produce a succession of good crops in India, China, and other tropical and semi-tropical countries. After several years of prosperity the 6 or 800 millions of inhabitants buy our manufactures in unusual quantities; good trade in Lancashire and Yorkshire leads the manufacturers to push their existing means of production to the utmost and then to begin building new mills and factories. While a mania of active industry is thus set going in Western Europe, the solar radiation is slowly waning, so that just about the time when our manufacturers are prepared to turn out a greatly increased supply of goods, famines in India and China suddenly cut off the demand.[14]

In his published work, Jevons also stressed that it was the long credits given in the Eastern trade that provided a transmission mechanism for the financial credit crises.[15] The explanation was actually much more popular than we today might think, because it resonated with an ethos of the "white man's burden" prevalent in the popular English culture of the 1880s and 1890s. Jevons capped this narrative in 1879 by publishing a series of wheat prices from Delhi, 1763–1834, which he claimed displayed the sought-after periodicity and corresponded to his chronology of crisis dates.[16] From 1879 to his death in 1882 he published nothing further on the subject, but his correspondence reveals that he persisted in his defense and employment of his sunspot theory in discussions of macroeconomic fluctuations.[17]

II

Interestingly enough, Jevons's weather theory is not totally repudiated by economic theorists and economic historians: it is merely exiled to a period characterized by premodern or preindustrial economic structures. Some of the illustrious names associated with this position include Wesley Clair Mitchell, Michael Tugan-Baranowski, Joseph Schumpeter, Peter Mathias, T. S. Ashton, and W. W. Rostow.[18] This thesis has attracted little scrutiny, either in the way of empirical test or rational criticism. It is more interesting for what it implies than for its narrative value: that there either exists or did once exist a "natural economy," exhibiting market structures but lacking other structures—precisely which structures is a matter for disagreement among the cited authors. In this natural economy, breakdown, crises, and coordination failures were caused by largely exogenous shocks, such as weather fluctuations causing harvest failures, and so forth. Of course, this is precisely Jevons's theory: the substratum of market relations works well naturally and can only be undermined by external natural shocks.

One means by which to begin a reevaluation of our basic perception of macroeconomic fluctuations is to confront Jevons's thesis about the eighteenth and nineteenth centuries directly, using the historical evidence we have at our disposal. This is possible for two aspects of his theory: one, to review the possibility of a fixed decennial periodicity of fluctuations in that period; and two, to examine the likelihood that his particular exogenous shocks "caused" macroeconomic fluctuations in early modern England. Because most of the above characterizations of the "modern" English macroeconomy tend to cite 1825 as the first "modern" crisis, we shall restrict our initial quantitative inquiry to the period 1740 to 1825.

An impressionistic notion of economic fluctuations from 1740 to 1825 may be obtained from Table 3.1 below. The index of a sample of profit rates was culled from the business accounts of various eighteenth- and nineteenth-century British firms. Table 3.1 compares Jevons's crisis dates with the peaks and troughs of the profit index, the Wolf sunspot numbers, and a share price index I constructed from *The Course of the Exchange*. If one merely calculates the mean peak-to-peak durations, one finds them to 11.4 years for the sunspots, 13.6 years for the share price index, and 10.4 years for the profit index. Evidence of this nature has undoubtedly fostered the impression of a rough decennial periodicity. It would be an error, however, to infer that Jevons's characterization has been vindicated by historical research.

More than the improved and augmented historical record, another advantage we have over Jevons is a much-improved understanding of the theoretical relationship between stochastic shocks and regular cycles in time series analysis. Because of the work of Slutzky and Yule, we now know that periodicity in a time series may indeed be due to deterministic cycles in the underlying structural process (for example, a sine curve), but it also may be

Table 3.1. Peaks and Troughs of Sunspots, Share Prices, and Profit Rates compared with Jevons's "Crises"

Jevons's "Crises"	Wolf Sunspot Numbers		Share Price Index		Profit Index	
	Peak	Trough	Peak	Trough	Peak	Trough
1742			1743	1747/48		
1752	1750	1755	1753	1762	1752	1757
1763	1761	1766			1758	1762
			1768		1763/67	1772
1772/73	1769	1775				
					1775	1780/85
1783	1778	1784		1784		
					1788/91	1793
1793	1787	1798	1792	1798	1799/1801	
1804/05	1804	1810	1802	1804		
						1810
1815	1816	1823	1810	1816	1819	1823
1825	1830	1833	1825		1825	

SOURCES: Wolf sunspot numbers: Harlan Stetson, *Sunspots and their Effects* (New York, 1937), 197–99. Share price index: Philip Mirowski, "The Rise (and Retreat) of a Market," *Journal of Economic History* 41 (Sept. 1981), 559–77. Profit index: Philip Mirowski, Chap. 11 below.

due to random or autocorrelated shocks impinging upon a stable structure, producing an output exhibiting nondeterministic cycles of stable periodicity.[19] Most economic time series do not exhibit sine-wave-like deterministic cycles; the present series are no exception. The existence of stable nondeterministic periodicities is an open question, however, and there are many techniques available to provide an answer. The predominant technique is spectral analysis, but it requires inordinately large numbers of data points in order to identify periodicities with any reasonable certainty. An alternative (though less precise) technique is to fit parsimonious Box-Jenkins-style models to individual time series, and then use the estimated coefficients to calculate the theoretical spectrum peak.[20]

Using this method we find that from 1749 to 1826 the Wolf sunspot numbers have a significant frequency peak at 10.5 years (thus supporting Jevons's revised information), whereas first differences of the profit index have an insignificant frequency peak at 9.7 years, and first differences of the logarithm of the share price index have no significant discernible frequency peak. In other words, only the sunspots can be said to have a regular identifiable periodicity.

The second aspect of Jevons's theory that can be reevaluated is the assertion that exogenous natural shocks "caused" economic fluctuations in the period 1749–1826. One major problem is his characterizations of the crises. First, because of the absence of fixed periodicities, peak-to-peak durations vary from a minimum of 8 years to a maximum of 24 years for the share prices, and from 6 to 19 years for the profit index. Second, the leads and lags relative to his crisis dates are unstable. Peaks in the share price index tend to lead his crisis dates prior to the 1780s, and lag them thereafter until 1825. Profit index peaks lead his crisis dates by between 3 and 7 years, except for the years 1752, 1763, and 1825, when they coincide. Overall, his characterization of 1752–1753, 1793, and 1825 as widespread credit crisis seems fairly well grounded, whereas the identification of 1763, 1783, 1804–1805, and 1815 do not.

The question of leads and lags can be broached with somewhat more sophistication. Econometricians have recently developed a technique called "causal testing." Though incapable of solving age-old philosophical problems concerning the nature of causality, it is well suited to answer the question posed by Jevons: once we account for as much of the variance as possible of a time series variable by using as explanatory variables its own past values, how much more variance can be explained by the addition of a second explanatory variable? If the amount of additional variance accounted for is substantial according to conventionally accepted statistical criteria, the second variable is said to "cause" the first in a Granger sense. Many versions of Granger causality tests have been proposed and implemented by economists, but recent theoretical and simulation work has suggested that the variant known as the "Granger-Wald" test has the most desirable statistical properties.[21] The value of this test is asymptotically distributed as chi-square, with the degrees of freedom equal to the number of lagged values of the potentially "causal" variable.

Table 3.2 displays the values of the Granger-Wald test for pairwise comparisons between the following variables: the Wolf sunspot numbers, the

Table 3.2. Granger-Wald Chi-square Causality Tests, 1755–1826

	(1) Sunspots	*(2)* Exports to Asia	*(3)* Share Prices	*(4)* Profit Index	*(5)* Temperature
1. Sunspots	—	9.38	5.21	1.35	2.69
2. Exports to Asia	4.23	—	8.82	3.19	7.60
3. Share Prices	4.50	13.85*	—	2.68	4.43
4. Profit Index	0.84	2.07	5.24	—	2.58
5. Temperature	4.63	8.94	4.33	2.41	—

* Significant at 1 percent level.

Note: Some tests use truncated sample periods because of data availability.

Sources: Sunspots: Linearly detrended, see table 3.1. "Exports: First difference of natural logarithms," from Brian R. Mitchell and Phyllis Deane, *Abstract of British Historical Statistics* (Cambridge, 1962), 309–10. Share Prices: First difference of natural logarithms, see table 3.1. Profit Index: First differences, see table 3.1. Temperature: "No detrend, harvest-year mean temperature of Britain," from G. Manley, "Mean Temperature of England, 1698–1952," *Quarterly Journal of the Royal Meteorological Society* 42 (1953), 256–58.

value of British exports to Asia, the index of British share prices, the British profit index, and the mean temperature of England by harvest year. If the series exhibited a trend, the test required that it be removed. The columns represent the variables as potential causal agents, whereas the rows represent the variable as being the resultant of the other variables. For example, the entry of 4.23 at the top of the first column is the value of the chi-square test that sunspots "Granger cause" fluctuations in British exports to Asia. At conventional statistical levels, the null hypothesis of no causation is not rejected. All of the tests in the table are performed with four annual lags of the "causal" variable for the period from 1753 to 1822. The endpoints of this analysis are determined by data availability.

According to the Jevons hypothesis, fluctuations in sunspots should cause fluctuations in temperature, which should in turn cause fluctuations in exports to Asia, triggering fluctuations in finance (the share price index) and finally in macroeconomic expansions and contractions (the profit index). As can be observed in Table 3.2, the only link in this chain of reasoning that passes the Granger-Wald test is the relationship between exports to Asia and the share price index, which is significant at the 1 percent confidence interval in the direction of exports causing fluctuations in share prices. The result is not surprising, given that the shares of the East India Company comprise an important part of the share index. More importantly, the table shows there is no significant relationship between sunspots and any economic variable; nor, indeed, is there a significant relationship in the Granger-Wald sense between any of the "natural" shocks and any of the economic time series.

Finally, we can briefly examine the larger issue of the existence of a "macroeconomic watershed" between the premodern economy and the fully industrialized economy. Table 3.3 presents the Granger-Wald causality tests

Table 3.3. Granger-Wald Chi-square Causality Tests, 1825–1875

	(1) Sunspots	(2) Exports to Asia	(3) Share Prices	(4) GNP	(5) Temperature
1. Sunspots	—	0.93	4.28	1.57	7.74
2. Exports to Asia	1.77	—	1.91	4.57	9.05
3. Share Prices	2.31	1.50	—	12.00*	4.57
4. GNP	9.13	6.10	8.83	—	7.22
5. Temperature	9.14	3.94	4.02	2.49	—

*Significant at 5 percent level.

Note: Some tests use truncated sample periods because of data availability.

SOURCES: Sunspot, Exports, and Temperature: See table 3.2. Share Prices: Hayek's Index, in A. Gayer, W. Rostow, and A. Schwartz, *The Growth and Fluctuation of the British Economy* (Oxford, 1953), 456: first differences of natural logarithms. GNP: B. R. Mitchell, *European Historical Statistics* (New York, 1976), 797, 782: splice of Deane and Feinstein's estimates at constant prices, first differences of natural logarithms.

for the same set of variables as Table 3.2, with the single exception of the replacement of the profit index with Deane's and Feinstein's national income estimates for the period 1830–1875, as an indicator of macroeconomic fluctuations. We observe that the pattern of results is very much the same, with no significant causal relations running from the "natural" shocks to economic fluctuations. Because the share index no longer weights the East India Company so heavily, there is not a strong connection between exports to Asia and share prices in this period. Share prices, however, do seem to be influenced by changes in aggregate income.

The conception of a premodern "natural" economy that fluctuates because of shocks external to social and market processes does not hold up well under scrutiny. The problem resides in the widespread notion of a premodern economy as a baseline against which to measure industrial development. It is a form of conjectural anthropology not so very far removed from Adam Smith's "early and rude state." But after a little critical examination, we are left neither with an Eden before the advent of markets, nor a Paradise of markets "before the Fall."

We live in an era in which an increasingly influential subset of economists maintain that:

> agents' responses become predictable only when there can be some confidence that agents and observers share a common view of the nature of the shocks which must be forecast by both. . . a feature of post WWII time series has been the return to a pattern of recurrent roughly similar "cycles" in Mitchell's sense. If the magnitude of the Great Depression dealt a serious blow to the idea of a business cycle as a repeated occurrence of the "same" event, the postwar experience has to some degree restored respectability to the idea. . . . It is the similarity from cycle to cycle of co-movements among series, as documented by Mitchell, that leads to the single shock view of business cycles.[22]

The notion of a naturally stable market structure subject to random shocks has been a persistent theme of 100 years of economic history and economic theory. The major difference between Jevons and our contemporaries is that it is no longer the vogue to insist that the shocks are of natural origins; many now prefer to blame meddlesome governments for generating the disturbances. The remainder of the story is the same: macroeconomic fluctuations are generated external to market structures; macroeconomic instability is in no sense endemic nor endogenous.

Notes

1. Well, almost no one. Compare David Cass and Karl Shell (1983, 193–227) and Carlos Garcia-Mata and Felix Schaffner (1934, 1–51).
2. W. S. Jevons, "Economic Policy," in Smyth (1962, 26).
3. Ibid., 27.
4. See Karl Polanyi (1944, chs. 12, 13, 17, 18); and J. K. Ingram, "The Present Position and Prospects of Political Economy," in Smyth (1962).

5. One can observe this attitude in some rather harsh comments about the "crowning defects of the poorer classes" in his address cited in note 2. Parenthetically, this very revealing talk is omitted in Jevons's *Papers and Correspondence* and is not addressed in T. W. Hutchison (1982, 366–77).

6. For those who consider it a joke, see R. G. Sheehan and A. Grieves (1982, 775–77). As a cautionary parable, see J. M. Keynes (1963, 278–79); and Stephen M. Stigler (1982, 363–64).

7. Philip Mirowski, "Physics and the Marginalist Revolution," ch. 1, above.

8. The choice of weather rather than some other "natural" disturbance can be explained by Jevons's own background in meterology, and by his friendship at Owens College with Balfour Stewart, who was engaged in sunspot research.

9. W. S. Jevons (1977, vol. 7, 91).

10. Jevons (1884, 204).

11. Compare H. C. Willett and J. Prohaska (1960, 9).

12. Jevons (1884, 230).

13. For the boat races, see Jevons, *Papers and Correspondence,* vol. 5, 51. For crisis criticism, see ibid., vol. 4, 299–300.

14. Ibid., vol. 5, 10–11.

15. Jevons (1884, 233).

16. Ibid., 237–38. See also, in this respect, A. Siddiqi (1981).

17. Jevons, *Papers and Correspondence,* vol. 5, 103, 147.

18. W. C. Mitchell (1941, 169); M. Tugan-Baranowski (1913, 6); J. Akerman (1957, vol. 2, 249); Joseph Schumpeter (1939, vol. 2, 233, 249); Peter Mathias (1969, 228–31); Phyllis Deane (1967, 227–28); T. S. Ashton (1959, chs. 1, 2); and W. W. Rostow (1978, ch. 21).

19. John Gorman (1981, part 1).

20. Ibid., 233.

21. John Geweke (1982); and J. Geweke, R. Meese, and W. Dent (1982).

22. Robert Lucas, Jr. (1981, 125, 284, 16).

Part II
The Incompatibility of Neoclassicism and Institutionalist Economics

4

Is There a Mathematical Neoinstitutional Economics?

Daniel Fusfeld has written that "now, more than ever, economic orthodoxy has excluded from analysis the processes by which the institutional structure of the economy changes."[1] After spending some time among "orthodox" economists, it has become apparent to me that most of them would dispute the above claim, which was published in the *Journal of Economic Issues* in 1977. Yet, most economists who consider themselves institutionalists probably would subscribe to it. What is the foundation of this very substantial disagreement?

Until recently, it was the tendency of the orthodox to dismiss institutionalism as rank empiricism (or, if the writer were feeling particularly ungenerous, economic sociology), lacking in any coherent theory.[2] Of late, the attitude has been that neoclassical orthodoxy has made appreciable headway in the logical incorporation and explanation of institutions within the theory; thus, it has usurped both the problematic and the raison d'être of institutional economics. When confronted with the complication that the institutionalists do not agree with this assessment, and refuse quietly to pack up their tents and melt into the night, orthodox economists then explain this intransigence (if they are feeling generous) by the "fact" that the institutionalists are not familiar with the literature or lack the mathematical or theoretical sophistication necessary to evaluate the substance of orthodox arguments. Much as contemporary macroeconomics retreats to the high theory justification of general equilibrium analysis when under particularly heavy criticism, this recent neoclassical/ institutional literature also appeals ultimately to mathematical high theory for its justification.

It is one of the intentions of this chapter to document the forms which this new high theory literature has taken; it is contended that the components of a rigorous institutional response can be found in the pages of modern institutionalist writers. Therefore, this chapter is an attempt to assess the contention that neoclassical economics has successfully usurped the problematic of institutional economics.

The Neoclassical Challenge

Historically, there have been three methods of dealing with institutional phenomena within the research program of neoclassical economics. The first, and earliest, can be associated with the name of Léon Walras; it corresponds to the conception of institutions as outside the purview of economics and, almost as a necessity, independent of economic activities. The second method corresponds to game theoretic attempts to incorporate institutions as part of a larger economic calculus; we shall select Martin Shubik as a prime example of this group. The third category is much more heterogeneous than the first two; for lack of a better term, we shall dub it "neo-Marshallian," although the techniques more than the substance derive from Alfred Marshall.

Walrasian Institutions

At the very beginning of Léon Walras's *Elements of Pure Economics,* he feels he must distinguish among science, art, and ethics. At least in part, this arises from his desire to extricate economics from what he perceived to be the unseemly squabbling of his Ricardian predecessors. Lest my characterization be considered a caricature, I quote Walras at length:

> We may divide the facts of our universe into two categories: those which result from the play of the blind and ineluctable forces of nature and those which result from the exercise of human will, a force that is free and cognitive. Facts of the first category are found in nature, and that is why we call them *natural* phenomena. Facts of the second category are found in man, and that is why we call them *human* phenomena. . . . The operations of the forces of nature constitute the subject matter of what is called *pure natural science* or *science* properly speaking. The operations of the human will constitute, in the first place, the subject matter of what is called *pure moral science* or *history,* and in the second place, as will be seen presently, the subject matter of a study to which another name, either art or ethics, is attached.[3]

This distinction between the natural and the human becomes, a few pages later, a distinction between things and persons. Phenomena encompassing the relations between people and things are called *industry,* whereas phenomena encompassing the relations between persons and other persons are called *institutions.* "The theory of industry is called *applied science* or *art*; the theory of institutions *moral science* or *ethics.*"[4] We round out the possible combinations by noting that the theory of the natural relations among things is called pure science.

Perhaps the reader begins to see the imperative which led Walras to consider the elements of the *pure* science of economics. In his view, the road to scientific consensus was built through the creation of a solid foundation of pure science upon which art and ethics might be layered. But how could this happen in economics, which seemed to the untutored observer as the study of relations between person and person, or, with some imagination, between persons and things? Walras replies that there is one natural phenomenon in economic life, one relation between thing and thing: that is the value of a good, as Walras terms it, whereas it would be more desirable from our point of view to use the term *price*. Again in his own words: "Thus any value in exchange, once established, partakes of the character of a natural phenomenon, natural in its origins, natural in its manifestations and natural in essence. If wheat and silver have any value at all, it is because they are scarce, that is, useful and limited in quantity—both of these conditions being natural." [5] He does not mean that people have no willful influence on price; in this respect, he compares competitive prices to the law of gravity, which we can resist at will, but we cannot *alter* the essence of the law. It is in this restricted sense that his pure economic theory is "the theory of the determination of prices under a hypothetical regime of perfectly free competition." [6] These prices are natural since they cannot be manipulated by human will away from their natural state.

This attempt to elevate economics above the hurly-burly of dissension and disagreement led to a number of internal contradictions in Walras's logic, not the least of which had to do with his treatment of institutions. Under Walras's definitions, institutions are the embodiments of person-person relationships subject largely to human will, which are not natural; thus, one is predisposed not to expect much in the way of regularity in causation, and so forth, in that sphere. The market is elevated to a different epistemic plane of producing regular outcomes. But the question then arises: How does the market do this (if, in fact, it does so)? In response, Walras postulates the existence of the auctioneer, or *tâtonnement,* essentially an algorithm to alter prices, given the existence of excess demands. Far from being a harmless assumption, this analytic choice embodies the profound contradiction in Walras's position, since he has ruled out a priori the possibility that the agency conducting *tâtonnement* can be human, because that would entail person-person relations. The market would rely upon an institution, which in turn would be predicated upon human will, which would call into question the naturalness of prices. One can easily summon up related problems: How does the auctioneer circumvent his own preferences? Who enforces the trades, or even more stickily, who prevents the trades until the process converges to equilibrium prices? Why must price bear the brunt of adjustment? (Walras, through the artifice of endowments given exogenously, actually freezes pure quantity adjustment surreptitiously.) In fact, every problem in the microfoundations of macroeconomics literature that has blossomed in the last twenty years grows out of the fundamental contradiction in the Walrasian treatment of institutions. The abstract neoclassical market does not provide enough logical restrictions fully to describe the determination of price and quantity (other than in the very restricted sense of a mathematical proof of existence) in the absence of such institutions. Walras himself uneasily noted this contradiction when he wrote: "Appropriation being in essence a moral phenomenon, the theory of property must in essence be a moral science."[7] But a market without property is like a boat in a desert; it has no reason to exist; it cannot move. No matter how we try, it seems that economics cannot be made into a *pure* science.

Of course, succeeding Walrasians and neo-Walrasians did not need to preserve their master's philosophy of science along with his analytical mechanism. But oddly enough, for many, the untenable dichotomy between markets and institutions persists, even in the absence of the explicit philosophy. Standard operating procedure in this camp seems to include the *assumption* of all the (unspecified) necessary complementary institutions that buttress a functioning market. Yet, simultaneously, it also is presumed that the market produces outcomes independent of (and, for some, more "efficient" than) those very same institutions, without once examining the necessary symbiosis of these structures. This contorted position is often summarized in a sentence or two thrown out in the beginning of these texts to the effect that one will find among the givens of the analysis the governmental and institutional framework.[8] It is one thing to assert something is a given because it does not enter in any substantive way into the analysis (for example, the variation in weather does not fundamentally alter our understanding of the theory of demand, although it may conceivably influence it), and it is quite another to insist something is held fixed *simply because we do not wish to deal with it.* The first attitude states that we are fairly certain the excluded effect is of secondary or tertiary importance; the second is an uncomfortable suppression of a suspicion that we have left something out which is both important and simultaneously obscure. A great disservice is done to the economics profession by subsuming both effects under the same mathematical artifice of parameters, since no one would maintain that these two categories of excluded effects should play an identical role in economic analysis. An example from the literature may again be helpful: If Keynes genuinely believed that the marginal efficiencies of capital and liquidity preferences were *highly unstable* behavioral functions, that is, they were buffeted by a large number of causes or institutions which we do not care to examine, then what can possibly be achieved by translating this model into a Walrasian framework, which needs precisely those parameters to be exogenous and stable in order to calculate a general equilibrium?

Many general equilibrium theorists would maintain that I am thrashing a dead horse, since they long ago realized that the auctioneer and *tâtonnement* were the basic weaknesses of the Walrasian model.[9] Much recent work has set itself the task of doing away with the auctioneer and *tâtonnement,* and if critics persist in faulting Walrasian economics for its insensitivity to these issues, it is because this "skepticism concerning recent work derives from incomplete or incorrect knowledge of what is actually being done, often due to the extreme complexity of the papers."[10] I would like to suggest, rather, that the mathematical complexity of the papers is a smokescreen which prevents us from discussing the real issue, that of the appropriate role of institutions in economic theory, which is no closer to logical resolution than it was in Walras's day.

All work in Walrasian economics starts from the same fundamental question. It is stated, with minor variations, in every one of these texts: "the organizing feature [of Arrow-Debreu models and their offshoots] is the question 'how is it possible for a decentralized, individualistic system, operated on principles of self-interest, to produce coherent or coordinated outcomes?' "[11] This is a simple rephrasing of the original Walrasian problematic: How can we show that prices are natural and produce a coordinated outcome in the *absence* of other institutions? The research program of neo-Walrasian studies asks what set of qualities or attributes of individuals is sufficient to produce Walrasian-style prereconciled outcomes.

In effect, recent neo-Walrasian theory imbues individuals with increasingly prodigious psychological abilities and qualities that analytically usurp the coordination functions now performed by other social institutions. The earliest work done in this area, by Don Patinkin and Robert Clower,[12] suggested that the transactors' demand functions be augmented by including as arguments not only prices but also quantities of all of the goods in the economy. The reason for the addition was that unemployment would then be explained by the presence of excess quantities demanded, which remained unexpressed through conventional market bidding processes. This work was an early recognition that a Walrasian process without an auctioneer was incapable of determining equilibrium without some further process or interaction among transactors, but it avoided specification of the actual process by which coordination was achieved or thwarted. Later elaborations by Robert Barro and Herschel Grossman and by Edmond Malinvaud simply assumed that the transactors took some prices as rigid or given, which then resulted in less than optimal coordination.[13] Again, the reasons behind these rigidities (and therefore the underlying reasons for coordination success or failure) were left unexplored. More recently, the success or failure of coordination has been explained by the transactors' *beliefs* either about other transactors or about the future. Those economists who assert that the market system is successful in continuous coordination subscribe to the rational expectations hypothesis, which maintains that transactors are never fooled about the state of the economy. Other economists, less sanguine about the efficacy of the market system, propose instead that the conventional utility function be augmented further by a conjecture function, that is, the transactor holds some set of beliefs about the actions of other transactors in the present and in the future.[14] In all these cases, the Walrasian auctioneer is displaced by adding some psychological abilities to rational economic man, but in all these cases, the market outcome is *prereconciled* (either successfully or not) within the crania of individuals, independently of any social activities.

The institutionalist must wonder why economic coordination must always take this psychologistic form. If the original Walrasian world is incapable of a plausible determination of equilibrium, why is the model not closed with some further institutional specification, rather than through augmentation of psychological propensities of individual transactors? For example, could prices be rigid because of legal (or illegal) agreements or contractual relations, which are not themselves sole outcomes of market forces? Or perhaps conjectures are not so much innate psychological phenomena as much as suggestions planted by the communications media or the educational process. Or perhaps the setting of prices embodies an element of power struggle among various segments of society in the political arena, where the bargaining process occurs outside the market. None of these concepts is novel to an economist familiar with the work of institutionalists,[15] but it is important to recognize that these solutions to the problem of coordination indeterminacy are ruled out a priori by neo-Walrasian methodology.

What is most disturbing to an institutional economist is not so much the willful disregard of the role of social structure in the functioning of the market, but the tautology which is then derived from this research program. Having decided to abolish institutions and invent individuals who are capable of doing everything that *any* economic organization purports to do, many neoclassical economists then turn around and state that they have proven that this atomistic market is the optimal form of social organization. If other scientific disciplines behaved this way, then chemists and biologists, for example, would be proposing to solve the problem of pollution by trying to produce by genetic mutation a new breed of human beings who thrived on breathing carbon monoxide, all the while maintaining that this alteration was the direction that human evolution would take in any event.

Not only does this seem to be an unnecessarily roundabout method of "proving" the market functions in the way many have asserted, but also it leads to an indeterminacy in results which belies the insistence of neo-Walrasians that their method is "scientific" because it produces well-defined equilibria. Once one allows that the definition of the individual must change in order to model market functions, the question then becomes which alternative is the "true" model. For example, what precisely belongs in the demand function? Walras had a logical answer which followed directly from his philosophy: The only variables that belong in demand functions are current prices, because they are the only natural data; and in an economy with more than two transactors, it would probably be impossible for the actors to know all the requisite information about quantities and other variables.[16] Unfortunately, neo-Walrasians no longer feel obligated to confront this very crucial issue. As they introduce quantities of goods, expected values of variables, excess demands of other transactors, "rational conjectures," and all manner of other quanta into individual utility functions, they never once try to justify this procedure by suggesting criteria with which to judge the appropriateness of these additions. That is, what is it that fundamentally constitutes an economic transactor? (And what elements are separate from the individual transactor, that is, what is an economic institution?)

Since there is no single answer, models of individuals and, by implication, notions of equilibrium proliferate. As Allan Drazen has written, "it is often difficult in such a case to define a satisfactory concept of rationality." [17] With no well-defined notion of individual rationality, what is left of the neo-Walrasian research program?

Of the three strains of neoclassical thought we here examine, the neo-Walrasian penchant for taking institutions for granted, upon the expectations that some other discipline (psychology, or sociology) will be responsible for their study, is the least logically defensible position, and it has led to certain reactions within the neo-Walrasian camp. The first reaction is to accept the implicit challenge and try to model the institutions themselves within the neoclassical framework. This reaction has led to the work of the two groups we consider below: the game theorists and the neo-Marshallians. The second reaction is to notice the problem, give a little pep talk, and continue doing more of the same:

> Neoclassical theories rest on a set of abstractions that separate "economic" transactions from the totality of social and political interactions in the system. For a very large set of important problems, this separation "works"—since we are usually dealing with monetary exchange systems. But it assumes that the events that we make the subject of conceptual experiments with the neoclassical model of the "economic system" do not affect the "socio-political system" so as to engender repercussions on the economy of such significance as to invalidate the institutional ceteris paribus clauses of that model. [18]

The question is, how do we know that this separation purportedly "works"? This very difficult question involves issues in philosophy and the structure of scientific endeavor which we cannot discuss at great length here, but we can make one concise point: The conventional definition of the success of neoclassical explanations appeals to the supposed logical rigor of the axiomatic method, which in turn leads to determinate predictions and results. One point of this article is that neo-Walrasians will admit among themselves that their method has logical flaws and does not lead to a consensus over a determinate equilibrium. If their assessment is correct, then they have provided no logical reason for their ad hoc exclusion of institutional explanations of economic phenomena, except perhaps that this enforced separation is itself congenial to a certain ideological stance that insists upon the independent and self-sufficient efficacy of the market.

Game Theoretic Institutions

Another attack upon institutionalism is much more logically subtle than that of the neo-Walrasians and, in some ways, initially even appears quite salutary to institutional economists. This is the assertion that there are now emerging the outlines of a mathematical institutional economics, grounded in the techniques of game theory. For example, in Roy Weinstraub's popular survey of the neoclassical work aimed toward building a microfoundation for macroeconomics, he tends to suggest that the most promising work is being done in what he calls the Edgeworth framework, which is merely the game theoretic modeling of trading activity. He writes: "If the Walrasian framework is a model of how the institutions of a competitive market serve to organize and stabilize economic activity, then the Edgeworth system, which abstracts from the price mechanism, may appear as neoinstitutionalism." [19] Perhaps the most notable theorist in this tradition is Martin Shubik, who, in writing a summary of his recent endeavors in this area, called it "a survey article in mathematical institutional economics ... [even though] mathematical institutional economics is deemed by many to be a contradiction in terms." [20] Some of the more ardent advocates of this game theoretic framework claim it promises to usurp not only the institutionalist tradition in economics, but also all social science that does not explain the world by postulating individualistic rational behaviors. [21] Have these game theorists managed to capture institutional insights within a tractable mathematical framework?

Since there are many well-written introductions to game theory for the novice, [22] we shall only touch briefly upon the structure of game theoretic technique. *Games,* used in this sense, are mathematical representations of the strategic possibilities of some well-defined situations. One writer has suggested that "game theory" was coined around some poker tables at Princeton: It is those kinds of situations which are amenable to game theoretic interpretation. Game theory presumes the existence of a situation in which there are *measurable* quanta to be won or lost, rules that govern the actions of all players, and certain choice algorithms, usually dubbed "rationality." Concepts of probabilistic outcomes and probabilistic behaviors are also taken into consideration. In fact, many games only have determinate solutions because consciously randomized (or mixed) strategies are included in the definition of rationality. Games are further subdivided into cooperative and noncooperative categories. In the former, players form strategies in conjunction with other players; in the latter, cooperation is either impermissible or impossible from a rational viewpoint. It is this feature of games that is thought to capture the institutional flavor: Conflict or cooperation must be taken into account as part of the solution of the game.

To illustrate this last distinction, let us briefly examine the most famous of all noncooperative games, the Prisoner's Dilemma. Imagine a situation in which two prisoners are held isolated, and the detaining authority is attempting to extract confessions for some joint crime. If neither confesses, both can expect to receive a light sentence on some minor charge, let us say one year. If both confess, then cooperation with the authorities will be taken into account, and they will each receive a reduced sentence, perhaps eight years.

If one confesses and the other does not, the recalcitrant fellow will get the maximum sentence (ten years), while the other will go free for turning state's evidence (zero years). Each knows the same choice faces the other. These choices can be summarized in a matrix of possible prison sentences, letting N stand for "not confess" and C for "confess":

Prisoner A

		N	C
	N	(1,1)	(0,10)
Prisoner B			
	C	(10,0)	(8,8)

According to one definition of rationality, that of Von Neumann and Morgenstern, the best strategy in such a situation is to choose the option that minimizes the maximum penalty in all instances. In the Prisoner's Dilemma, this leads to the somewhat perverse result that both prisoners will choose to confess, even though the globally optimum result would be for both to remain mute. If, on the other hand, communication between the prisoners were allowed, and if there were some means at their disposal for enforcing an agreement between themselves, then they would both choose to remain silent. Thus, game theory highlights the strategic social interactions necessary to achieve some result, which is perceived to be a palpable advance over neo-Walrasian theory, with its passive zombie-like cooperation.

Given that there is a semblance of social interaction in game theory, we may ask what insights this attribute brings to models of *market* games, in which the object of maximization is conventionally some indicator of utility, although there are some games which have payoffs solely in money terms. Shubik makes several claims about the advantages of game theory vis-à-vis neo-Walrasian theory.[23] First, it allows consideration of the effects of a large or small number of market transactions; that *is,* whether there is a thick or thin market. Second, it encourages explicit specification of the amount and forms of information available to individual market transactors in the form of "the rules of the game." Third, it allows for nonzero-sum outcomes of trades, which means essentially that the level of either utility or money is not held constant in the system as a whole, but varies with the choices of the transactors. Fourth, the existence of money is logically justified within this framework, not just as an arbitrary numeraire commodity, but as a medium of exchange whose use and propagation are dictated by the reigning rule structure. Game theory also allows for a further cash flow constraint in addition to the conventional budget constraint, as well as the modeling of bankruptcy provisions. Finally, strategic interaction allows for "errors" on the part of individual transactors.

This is the sum and substance of the claim that game theoretic innovations in economic theory may be thought of as a type of neoinstitutionalism. But is this claim justified by the innovations inventoried in the previous paragraphs? A careful examination of these techniques may reveal there is much less that is new under the sun than is claimed by the champions of game theory. Our task will be not so much to dispute the claims directly as to examine their content and their use.

Let us begin with the first claim. This statement indirectly refers to the Edgeworth limit theorem, proven rigorously by Shubik and others,[24] that given certain assumptions about preferences and the rules of a market game, as the number of traders tends to infinity, the core of the game shrinks to the point of conventional Walrasian general equilibrium. If there is less than an infinity of traders, the market trading ratio is not unique. In what sense is this novel, or even an improvement upon conventional neoclassical thought? An institutionalist concerned about thick or thin markets would not seek these static convergence proofs. Rather, he would be interested in how a market is established; how it functions when it is merely a localized phenomenon imbedded in a nonmarket society; and how it spreads to the nonmonetized sectors of a society. Thus, from an institutionalist point of view, a market is not thin simply because there are few *actors;* it is thin because economic processes are organized along different lines. The way game theorists define a thin market reveals that they still conceive of a market as consisting solely of atomistic individuals floating in a void.

As for the second claim, it is certainly true that "the law, trading customs and financial institutions provide the *ad hoc* rules to completely define the economic process.... Thus a mathematical institutional economics is called for to fully specify the process."[25] However, there are two aspects of this conception which seem antithetical to an institutionalist perspective.

First, these rules are treated as if they are simply *information* for the traders, information that Walrasian traders did not need either because of assumed perfect knowledge or because *tâtonnement* obviates any need for knowledge. But conventional neoclassicists have a very easy rebuttal to this position: If institutions are nothing but embodiments of knowledge that traders require, their information can be bought and sold like any other good; therefore, what appears to be an institution is merely another market phenomenon.[26] Institutionalists would not view laws, and so forth, as information for traders, as simply instruments for their individual ends; rather, they would see them as defining many of those ends, and defining what constitutes a trade versus a gift or some other loose reciprocal relationship. From the neoclassical point of view, all failures the system in coordinating activity are imputed as failures of individual transactors; as the sheriff says cynically in *Cool Hand Luke*: "What we have here is a failure to communicate." As long as one models the economy with psychological utility as the ultimate objective, this characterization of failure as due to a flaw in individual knowledge is difficult to avoid. The problem with this position, as has been pointed out repeatedly in the institutionalist literature,[27] is that this concept of rationality can be a pot hoc rationalization for any kind of putatively purposeful activity; as such, it is empty as an explanation. Rationality itself is a function of the rules; the rules are not a simple expression of rationality.

Second, it is interesting that Shubik characterizes the rules as ad hoc. Institutionalism, which is also known as evolutionary economics, would deny this careless postulation, which has more than a trace of the neo-Walrasian tradition of the exogeneity of institutions. Ad hoc rules have no justification; one gets the impression that they were merely instituted for the traders' convenience (a position which we will consider in the section on the neo-Marshallians). Even more disturbingly, ad hoc rules are simply given and thus have no internal dynamics and no reason to change. They are something traders have to work around in order to get down to the real business of trading and maximizing utility. This is clearly antithetical to the research program of institutional economics, which is defined by Thorstein Veblen as "the economic life history of the individual [as] a cumulative process of adaptation of means to ends that cumulatively change as the process goes on, both the agent and his environment being at any point the outcome of the last process."[28] It appears that Shubik believes that merely identifying institutions as rules exhausts the theoretical implications of those institutions.

The third claim is an important improvement of the Walrasian problematic. In a sense, all past assertions that the macroeconomy was intrinsically stable presumed some sort of conservation law: For example, Say's Law argues that there can be no value lost from the system as a whole. However, the realization that zero-sum games are inappropriate models of the macroeconomy is not an institutionalist insight (although Veblen did discuss this problem many times)[29] as much as it is a prescription for *any* logically coherent macroeconomic theory. The ability of game theory to handle the nonzero-sum situation is an important technical advance, but it has no necessary relation to the institutionalist research program.

The fourth claim has some relation to the second in that Shubik has asserted that money is a necessary accessory to the market, in the sense that it is a rational choice on the part of the traders, a choice made in order to make trades easier and more efficient. Our criticism of this notion is the same criticism made in consideration of the second claim: Money is not an ad hoc choice of rule made by some traders, with no influence on their own objectives, other than as an instrumentality. (Game theory could not model this choice in any event, since the rules are given exogenously. Game theory, as a technique, is incapable of explaining rule *changes*. For further consideration of this issue, see chapter 5, below.) In institutional economics, money becomes an end in itself, to such an extent that speculation in pecuniary values can destabilize the functioning of the economy. This is, of course, the well-known antinomy between the machine process and the business enterprise in Veblen's *Theory of Business Enterprise*. Game theory is incapable of capturing this perversion of rules through use until their function comes to contradict their supposed purpose.

Another institutional economist, Wesley Clair Mitchell, described the evolutionary character of money: "When money is introduced in the dealings of men, it enlarges their freedom.... As a society learns to use money confidently, it gradually abandons restrictions upon the places people shall live, the occupations that they shall follow, the circles they shall serve, and the goods they can buy." [30] In Shubik, this insight is reduced to a much more prosaic notion of the institution of money lubricating the wheels of a preexisting trade so that transactors might achieve a higher level of utility.

Of all the claims made by Shubik, the fifth perhaps most strikingly reveals the gulf between game theorists and institutional economists. It is true that transactors are allowed to make errors in game theoretic analyses; but what kind of errors are they? Basically, it is the same sort that comes to light in the Prisoner's Dilemma: The actors, due to some flaw in the environment, are rationally led to choose a state of affairs (confession) which would not be the optimum. The optimum that eludes the players in Shubik's models is the conventional Pareto optimum of Walrasian theory, since most of the games are played for utility. As Shubik writes, "it is likely that there is a large class of somewhat different noncooperative models which differ from each other in *institutional details* to handle disequilibrium yet have the same state equilibria which turn out to be the competitive equilibria of the system modelled without attention paid to its institutional and strategic details." [31] How convenient that no matter how much institutional detail we add to the economic system, we always return unerringly to Walrasian general equilibrium! Even more outrageously, this is asserted to be true even though we have seen that the neo-Walrasian research program has lost any claim to having a unique and determinate notion of equilibrium.

This penchant for always choosing Walrasian optima as the benchmark against which we gauge all disequilibria is not the fault of game theory, which after all, is merely a mathematical technique, but of the game theorists themselves. More than three-quarters of a century ago, Veblen sharply isolated the flaw in this predisposition of neoclassical economics: "[The neoclassical perception]...may not inaptly be called the standpoint of ceremonial adequacy. The ultimate laws and principles which they formulated were laws of the normal or the natural, according to a preconception regarding the ends to which, in the nature of things, all things tend. In effect, this preconception imputes to things a tendency to work out what the instructed common sense of the time accepts as an adequate or worthy end of human effort. It is a projection of the accepted ideal of conduct." [32]

Different institutions do not necessarily mean a *different* economic order or a different notion of equilibrium for Shubik and the other game theorists; all social organization is just a veil disguising the fundamental operation of the market. The market is not one among many social organizational forms found in endless combinations in human society; it is the protean manifestation of social order itself, always returning to that desired yet vague equilibrium of general welfare. Because of this tropismatic predisposition to return to Walrasian optima, the game theoretic neoinstitutionalism falls prey to all the weaknesses of the Walrasian research program. As one example, Shubik writes in one of his papers that "noncooperative cooperation presumes the existence of an enforcement mechanism and the intelligence of all parties to understand that it does not pay to suffer the consequences of failing to repay credits granted [in the instance of bankruptcy]."[33] Shades of Walras: Appropriation being a moral phenomenon, this form of economics leaves the very existence of the enforcement mechanism out of its "institutional" orbit. But what is this unspecified enforcement mechanism but yet another reincarnation of the auctioneer? In this instance, it is not the invisible hand of the market that transmutes private vice into public benefit, but an enforcement mechanism, a power behind the scenes. Whether this power prevents false trading or exacts the penalties of bankruptcy, it remains a deus ex machina that effectively prevents the economist from examining how the market and its attendant institutions actually function; in particular, it makes it virtually impossible to model the market working "badly." Very recently, in order to circumvent these thorny problems, some game theorists have decided to alter the Von Neumann-Morgenstern definition of individual rationality rather than model the institutions which may shape economic behavior.[34] This, as the reader will recognize, is the very same choice made by the neo-Walrasian theorists. Rather than admit institutions into the theory, they opted to augment the definition of the rationality of the individual psyche. Here, we have finally come full circle, from an attempt to improve upon the neo-Walrasian treatment of institutions employing the techniques of game theory, to game theorists excluding institutional considerations by the same method as the neo-Walrasians.

Neo-Marshallian Institutions

In an important article, Lawrence Boland points out that, of all the early neoclassical theorists, Alfred Marshall was most sensitive to the importance of institutional assumptions in economic theory.[35] What is interesting for our purposes is the method by which Marshallian analysis proposes to incorporate institutions within the orbit of its problematic. For Marshall and the neo-Marshallians, an institution is parametric to the process of the individual's constrained maximization *only in the short run*. The reason for this is Marshall's Principle of Continuity: Anything that can be varied within an arbitrary length of time will be subject to change as a result of individual optimization decisions. Institutions are characterized by the fact that they change slowly relative to other "economic" variables, such as price and quantity. Therefore, in Marshall's work they are largely taken as given. In this respect, institutions and the stock of capital end up being treated in a very similar manner because of their relative "fixity" from the point of view of the optimizing individual.

The neo-Marshallians have simply extrapolated this logic by expanding neoclassical analysis through an expansion of the relevant time frame. Because the time durations of which we speak are somewhat longer than is conventional, neo-Marshallians tend to be economic historians, students of comparative systems or law, or economic theorists with substantial interests in those areas. Their concerns range from providing neoclassical explanations for the transition from feudalism to capitalism,[36] to the causes of the American Civil War,[37] to the rise of certain forms of contractual relations,[38] and to the behavior of regulated and socialist firms.[39] Although his work is not mathematical, the most avid spokesman is Douglas North, who has written that their purpose is "to analyze the parameters held constant by the [neoclassical] economist. If economics is a theory of choice subject to specified constraints, a task of economic history was to theorize about those evolving constraints."[40]

How is this research program translated into the rigorous terms of neoclassical theory? "It is necessary to define the particular utility function that reflects the decision-maker's preferences, and to determine the actual set of options (penalties-rewards) that is attainable by the decision maker... the usefulness of any such model depends on how skillfully the specification is made of the objective function and the opportunity set."[41] Unfortunately, the neo-Marshallians never return to this potentially sticky question of what constitutes a skillful specification of the appropriate objective function and opportunity set. Let us propose a single criterion: *Skill* for our purposes shall mean there are no logical contradictions in this proposed method of research. With this principle as our guide, let us examine some problems with the neo-Marshallian method.

An unobtrusive postulate of the neo-Marshallian program is that we know what quanta are parameters and what quanta are variables *prior to the analysis*. In Marshallian terms, this must mean we already know the relative speeds of change of important variables—prices, quantities, property rights, psychologies, technologies—*before* we begin our explanation; one then ranks these variables, chooses a time frame (year, decade, century, epoch), and uses it to mark off the variables from the parameters. The logical fallacy is that the analyst must assume what is supposed to be an object of proof. Somehow, the analyst must know the relative distribution of rates of change of variables/parameters as if they were independent of the analysis itself. It is instructive that the same methodology is used to parameterize both capital and institutions in Marshallian neoclassicism, because the logical fallacy of the unobtrusive postulate is also the same: The magnitude of capital cannot be logically set prior to the optimization calculation and the distribution of income, as is now fairly well understood.[42] The Marshallian *ceteris paribus* is a useful analytical device precisely because it is so vague; once one probes its meaning, it collapses under its own logical contradictions.

The second logical inconsistency in the neo-Marshallian program is the problem of what remains to be specified as exogenous to the analysis. As one expands the time frame, fewer phenomena can be considered exogenous to the analysis; when one reaches the point of working in terms of centuries, nothing exogenous is left. If, at this stage of the analysis, everything depends upon everything else, then one can make no more statements about causality; in econometric theory, this is known as the identification problem. It is solved in econometrics by placing prior restrictions upon estimation, that is, one simply asserts a priori that some things do not depend upon other things, or else that we already know exactly how some things depend upon other things. How do the neo-Marshallians deal with the identification problem? The answer varies with the particular theorist. Sometimes, population changes and new technology lead to changes in property right; sometimes, taste changes lead to legal changes; sometimes, relative price changes lead to changes in institutions; sometimes, changes in institutions lead to changes in tastes. The problem with this casual approach to the identification problem is that various theorists' rankings of the relative speed of change of phenomena differ: In each of the above examples, the first phenomenon has to be ranked slower than the second. All of these rankings cannot be true simultaneously. That means that either the work of the individual neo-Marshallian is inconsistent with the work of his peers, or the relative a priori ranking is conceded to be different across alternative times and spaces. If the latter case is so, what are the determinants of this alteration in ranking? There can be no answer to that question in the neo-Marshallian framework, since there is nothing left to specify as exogenous.

The second point to notice about this inconsistency is that these theorists always speak *as if* there always were functioning markets, even though the rest of the world (tastes, institutions, technologies, and so forth) is in flux. For example, North suggests in a recent article that the United States has opted to use political regulation of economic transactions to a greater extent and eschew pure market regulation because the relative price of these two options has changed.[43] An institutionalist would ask what structures organize this "meta-market" to allow us to buy more or less market organization. Who sets these "prices" (whatever they may look like in the real world)? Who enforces the trades? Of course, what we have is Walras's dilemma in yet a third guise. If the market is not somehow natural, etched in our very genes,[44] then the neo-Marshallian theorist is trapped in an infinite regress: Who sets the price of the market? Who sets the price of the price of the market?

I think the reason these particular confusions are papered over in the literature is that the neo-Marshallian theorist holds two inconsistent objectives: to make everything exogenous, endogenous; and to cast all problems in the form of a constrained maximization calculation. A moment's reflection will reveal that one cannot do both. This is the reason, I believe, that institutional theorists have maintained that the constrained maximization paradigm is a misspecification of the economic problem.[45]

The constrained maximization paradigm has had a powerful hold on mainstream thought for two reasons. First, it facilitates the employment of mathematical analysis, most notably the calculus, in arriving at a well-defined answer to any question. Second, it offers a thinly veiled yet salubrious interpretation that things always work out for the best. The price paid for these benefits has been a tendency for all analysis to be confined to some form of comparative statics, because the techniques demand that the constraints be fixed over the domain of the maximization procedure. This criticism is not new; Veblen made the point most felicitously with his remark about "homogeneous globules of desire of happiness... in stable equilibrium except for the buffets of impinging forces that displace him in one direction or another." If one takes away the constraints but keeps the maximization, as the neo-Marshallians propose, then what is left? Certainly not the calculus, nor the well-defined answer to the original question. (In fact there are no extrema to be found.) Although it has not yet occurred to the neo-Marshallians, there also is no implication that things work out, much less for the best. One cannot maximize if there is nothing definite to maximize over.

To attempt to portray all history as the end result of purposive constrained maximization is to make the same error as was made by early biologists who touted Darwinian evolution as proving that man was the peak of the evolutionary process. Biologists now teach that there is never a peak or a maximum in evolution, which is merely a process of incomplete adaptation to circumstances that are shifting, partly as a result of past adaptations.[46] As Victor Goldberg has written in the context of his study of contracts, "the results stemming from the establishment of new institutions or modification in existing ones are seldom known precisely and are often widely divergent from the original expectations."[47] This has been the organizing principle of institutionalist theory from the time of Veblen, John R. Commons, and Mitchell down to the present day.

Summary

We have examined three recent attempts by neoclassicists to displace institutional economics through the purported explanation of institutions within the neoclassical framework. Although the three take different mathematical forms—pure parameterization, game theoretic optimization, and a parameter/variable continuum along the time axis—all have basically the same analytical objective: to endow the individual with all the necessary "natural" powers so that the individual will embody market organization and optimization even in the most unusual or unlikely circumstances. This is generally characterized by expanding the preference set to include all sorts of hypothetical situations and by altering the perceived constraints away from a well-defined set of endowments and technologies. To summarize the gist of this research program succinctly: Since the logic of the Walrasian market as a haphazard collection of individuals is flawed in various ways that the neoclassicists will not admit, they will keep changing the definition of the *individual* until the logic works.

The institutional economist will not agree with this "neo-institutionalism," and that is why the institutionalist research program has not been displaced. As one institutionalist has written, "[for neoclassical economics]. . .it is important that the aims of individuals should be determined largely outside the system under study and should constitute the relatively stable and coherent elements in that system; otherwise it will be more interesting to regard them as determined rather than determining factors."[48] It is instructive that this concern has led institutionalists to focus their efforts upon the theoretical treatment of time (Boland, Bausor), macroeconomic instability (Veblen and Mitchell), the development of the state and the maintenance of property rights (Commons, Ellerman, Warren Samuels, Goldberg and many others), capital theory (Veblen again), and technological change; these are areas in which it is generally agreed that neoclasicism is weak. Could it be that all of these theoretical weaknesses can be traced to the neoclassical obsession for constrained maximization by atomistic individuals?

Notes

1. Daniel Fusfeld (1977, 747).
2. This passé notion can still be found in the recent edition of Mark Blaug (1978, 710–13).
3. Léon Walras (1965, 61).
4. Ibid., 63.
5. Ibid., 69.
6. Ibid., 40.
7. Ibid., 79.
8. See, for example, Paul Samuelson (1965, 8).
9. See, for example, Kenneth Arrow and Frank Hahn (1971, chs. 13 and 14).
10. Allan Drazen (1980, 2830). See also Jean Michel Grandmont (1977) and E. Roy Weintraub (1979).
11. Weintraub (1979, 74).
12. Donald Patinkin (1956) and Robert Clower (1965).
13. Robert Barro and Herschel Grossman (1976) and Edmond Malinvaud (1977).
14. F. H. Hahn (1978, 1–17); and Drazen (1980).
15. A collection of these types of suggestions is contained in Warren Samuels (1979).
16. Walras (1969, Lesson 10).

17. Drazen (1980, 298); see also Weintraub (1979, 106).

18. Axel Leijonhufvud (1977, 268).

19. Weintraub (1979, 141).

20. Martin Shubik (1975a, 545).

21. J. C. Harsanyi (1968).

22. See Michael Bachrach (1977) and Anatol Rapoport (1960 and 1970). See also ch. 5, below.

23. Shubik (1975a and 1972, 24–38).

24. Martin Shubik (1959).

25. Shubik (1975a, 558).

26. This is the position of economists such as James Buchanan and Gordon Tullock, who claim there is a market for government services. This position is considered in more detail in the section on neo-Marshallian institutionalism.

27. Alexander Field (1979, 49–72).

28. Thorstein Veblen, "Why is Economics Not an Evolutionary Science?" in Veblen (1919, 74–75).

29. Ibid., 134–69, and 1932 (ch. 5).

30. W. C. Mitchell (1953).

31. Shubik (1975a, 562n).

32. Veblen (1919, 65).

33. Shubik (1973, 37).

34. John Harsanyi (1977).

35. Lawrence Boland (1979, 957–72).

36. Douglass North and Robert Thomas (1973) and J. R. Hicks (1969).

37. Joseph Reid, Jr. (1977, 302–28).

38. Stephen Cheung (1969 and 1968) and Richard Posner (1977).

39. Eric Furubotn and Svetozar Pejovich (1970, 431–54).

40. Douglass North (1978, 963).

41. Eric Furubotn and Svetozar Pejovich (1972, 1137–38).

42. The conventional citation is Geoffrey Harcourt (1972); a condensed version is in Jan Kregal (1976).

43. North (1978, 970).

44. I think this is the only logical position to which this group can retreat. See, for example, Jack Hirshleifer (1976, 244).

45. See, for example, John Roemer (1978, 150). His later work repudiates this position, however.

46. If we finally exterminate our own species, as we periodically threaten to do through nuclear war, will some cockroach theorist then maintain that cockroaches are the pinnacle of organic evolution?

47. Victor Goldberg (1974, 482).

48. L. P. Foldes, "Comment on Harsanyi," in Imre Lakatos and Alan Musgrave (1968).

5

Institutions as a Solution Concept in a Game Theory Context

> ...he believed that human beings, when it had been clearly explained to them what were their vital needs and necessities, would not only altruistically but selfishly become honest and reasonable: they would sacrifice what might be short term advantages for long term ends. What he never saw was that in politics as in other forms of human activity, human beings are for the most part interested in struggle, in manoeuvrings for power, in risks and even unpleasantnesses; and that these are often in direct opposition to what might reasonably be seen as their long term ends. . . .
>
> This was one reason why he could so often make rings around his opponents by reasoning: he believed in it; while they, although they said they did, ultimately did not. Yet what they felt instinctively, and might have answered [him] by, was traditionally unspoken. They could not say to him in effect—Look, in your reasoning you leave out of account something about human nature: you leave out the fact that human beings with part of themselves like turmoil and something to grumble at and perhaps even failure to feel comfortable in: your economic perfect blueprint will not work simply because people will not want it to.
>
> —Nicholas Mosley (1983, 68–69)

Confounding the Critics

In the history of neoclassical economic theory, there have been two major categories of rejoinders to critics of the theory: one, that the critics did not adequately understand the structure of the theory, and thus mistook for essential what was merely convenient; or two, that the criticism was old hat, and had been rendered harmless by recent (and technically abstruse) innovations with which the critic was unacquainted.[1] The freedom of passage between these defenses has proven to be the bane of not only those opposed to neoclassicism, but also of those who have felt the need for reform and reformulation of economic theory from within. It has fostered the impression that, with enough ingenuity, any arbitrary phenomenon can be incorporated within the ambit of conventional neoclassical theory, therefore rendering any particular change in "assumptions" as innocuous as any other, and thus rendering them all equally arbitrary.

Nowhere has this impasse been more evident than in the confrontations between the various partisans of an "institutional" economics and the adherents of neoclassical economic theory. The early institutionalists, such as Thorstein Veblen, John R. Commons, and Wesley Clair Mitchell, mounted a scathing attack on neoclassical value theory in the first three decades of the century, ridiculing the "hedonistic conception of man [as] that of a lightening calculator of pleasures and pains, who oscillates like a homogeneous globule of desire of happiness under the impulse of stimuli that shift him about the area but leave him intact."[2] The unifying principles of this movement were: (a) an assertion that neoclassical economists were the advocates of a spurious scientism which insisted upon imitating physics without understanding the implications of such mimesis; (b) an expression of an alternative to the above conception of society based upon a study of the working rules that structured collective action and going concerns, such as the corporation, the trade union, the bank and the state; (c) in conjunction with the construction of theories that took as their province the explanation of the evaluation of the working rules and then attendant institutions. The institutionalists' writings on the vagaries of behavior, such as Veblen's book on "conspicious consumption," were intended to show that theories based on individual psychologies were built upon shifting sands; and that, as Commons wrote, "cooperation does not arise from a presupposed harmony of interests, as the older economists believed. It arises from the necessity of creating a new harmony of interests" (Commons 1934, 6).

The initial rebuttal to the institutionalists adopted the first tactic. To cite just one prominent example, Paul Samuelson insisted that nothing substantial would be lost if economists relinquished utility (Wong 1978), and that institutions were effectively included in the assumptions of neoclassical economic theory (Samuelson 1965, 8). When fully interpreted, this assertion meant that the study of institutions was *separable* from neoclassical economic theory, to the point of being independent of any particular institutional framework. Economics could cut itself free of the inessential institutional considerations, and preserve its core as the study of rational allocation of scarce means in a thoroughly abstract frame. Veblen and Commons were drummed out of the economists' camp, and exiled to the provinces of Sociology or Anthropology.

With the passage of time, this first rebuttal has failed into disuse, and the second option has gained favor. Among a certain subset of theorists, it has become acceptable to admit that conventional neoclassical theory is "mechanistic," in the sense that it slavishly imitates certain theoretical structures and procedures in physics, and that this might be undesirable in certain respects. In most cases, this admission is accompanied by an assertion that this flaw has been remedied by the development of new techniques in the theory of games, to such an extent that there is a "new mathematical institutional economics" which has incorporated the concerns of the earlier critics (Johansen 1983; Schotter 1981, 1983; Schotter and Schwödiauer 1980; Shubik 1975a, 1976).

It is a curious fact that the language of the critique of neoclassical theory of the game theorists is so close to that of the earlier institutionalists as to be almost indistinguishable. For example, "The neoclassical agents are bores who merely calculate optimal activities at fixed parametric prices.... No syndicates or coalitions are formed, no cheating or lying is done, no threats are made.... The economy has no money, no government, no legal system, no property rights, no banks..." (Schotter 1981, 150). "The general equilibrium model is: (a) basically noninstitutional. (2) It makes use of few differentiated actors. (3) It is essentially static. No explanation of price formation is given. (4) There is no essential role for money. (5) It is nonstrategic" (Shubik 1976, 323). However, similarities in languages can be misleading. How justified is the claim that institutionalist concerns have been absorbed by game theorists?

For the purposes of this paper, we shall choose to avoid discussion of the first variant of the neoclassical defense. We shall simply assume that the central concept of neoclassical economic theory is the application of a physical metaphor to the market.[3] This will allow us to concentrate our attention on the second variant: Are recent game theoretic models different in any substantial way from neoclassical theory? Do game theory models capture the concerns that institutionalists believed were ignored in neoclassical economics? How can one judge the various claims made for the superior efficacy of game theory?

Game Theory and Institutional Analysis: Shubik and Schotter

It is a difficult task to discern the wood from the many trees that have passed through the pulper in the cause of game theory. Game theory burst upon the scene in 1944 with von Neumann and Morgenstern's book. The solutions of games were claimed to be isomorphic to "orders of society," "standards of behavior," "economic organizations"; and yet these models also claimed to be following "the best examples of theoretical physics" (von Neumann and Morgenstern 1964, 43, ix). Forty years of development have revealed that game theory is not the philosopher's stone its progenitors had claimed: more than half of any competent textbook in game theory is occupied with developing taxonomies of the numerous variants of games—cooperative and noncooperative; constant- or nonconstant-sum; static or sequential; extensive, strategic or characteristic forms; cardinal or noncardinal payoffs; various permutations of information sets and sequences of moves, small and large numbers of players; different conceptions of uncertainty; stationary versus nonstationary payoffs and/or strategies—so that the permutations and their attendant solution concepts have far outstripped any claims for generality or unity.

Doubts about the efficacy of game theory have begun to surface— sometimes during inauspicious occasions, such as Nobel Prize lectures (see, for example, Simon 1982, 486–87). In this context, it is noteworthy that its most vocal defenders have chosen to reemphasize the potential of game theory to encompass institutional considerations. We shall therefore concentrate our initial attention on the work of the two most prolific proselytizers for a "new institutional economics": Martin Shubik and Andrew Schotter.

Shubik has built an illustrous career upon the development of game theory in economics, providing many of the basic theorems and results in that litera- ture, as well as writing the best introductory textbook (Shubik 1982). In this respect, he is particularly well qualified to judge which areas of game theory should be credited with having made substantial contributions and novel inno- vations, as well as revealing the motivations behind the prosecution of game theoretic research. In a series of journal articles, Shubik has been persistently critical of Walrasian general equilibrium because it does not explain price for- mation; it merely *assumes* it. The actors in a Walrasian world have no free- dom to make errors or even choices about process, he says; and in this, he sounds very similar to Veblen. More unexpectedly, he is also critical of cooperative game theory: "As an early proponent of the core and of the replication process for studying mass economic behavior, I am completely willing to admit that to a great extent the results on the core have helped to direct attention away from the understanding of the competitive process..." (Shubik 1975a, 560; see also Shubik 1982, 286). He believes that whole other classes of games tend to be mere repetitions of pregame-theoretic models and add little insight to the corpus; for example, constant-sum games impose conservation rules which hinder the adequate description of process (Shubik 1975a, 557; Shubik 1972).

Where, then, does the advantage of game theoretic techniques lie? Shubik claims that the future belongs to noncooperative nonconstant-sum games. "Noncooperative game theory appears to be particularly useful for the study of mass phenomena in which the communication between individuals must be relatively low and individuals interact with a more or less faceless and anonymous economy, polity or society" (Shubik 1982, 300). Since strategic considerations are linked to a perception of society as consisting of impersonal social forces, and this conception informs Shubik's notion of "institutions," he therefore proselytizes for the appearance of a "new mathematical institutional economics": "my basic approach to economics is through the construction of mathematical models in which the "rules of the game" derive not only from the economics and technology of the situation, but from the sociological, political and legal structure as well" (ibid., 10).

Shubik's research program is not so very different from the seventeenth- century dream of Hobbes, that "in the same way as man, the author of geometrical definitions can, by starting from those arbitrary definitions, con- struct the whole of geometry, so also, as the author of the laws which rule his city, he can synthetically construct the whole social order in the manner of the geometers" (Halévy 1972, 494). Just as with Hobbes, there is some equivo- cation in deciding what is *necessary* and what is *adventitious;* we are referring in this case to the notion of social structures "external" to what is identified as the "economy." Shubik has, in places, suggested that institutions are merely ad hoc rules (Shubik 1975a, 558), of which he is providing mathematical descriptions. In other places, he suggests he is actively constructing optimal rules with regard to various problems, such as the treatment of bankruptcy (Shubik 1975b, 526; Dubey and Shubik 1979). In either event, Shubik's claim to be including "sociological, political and legal structures" is in practice, reduced to the mathematical specification of rules which impinge upon the operation of a market whose basic constituents—tastes, technologies, and endowments—are essentially the same as in the conventional Walrasian models. These rules have a different analytical status than the tastes, technologies, and so forth, because they are not treated as "natural" or fundamental givens, but rather as arbitrary intrusions from outside the sphere of the economy.

The arbitrary character of the rules is only confronted once, to my knowledge, in the Shubik corpus. In (Shubik 1974, 383) he asks the two revealing questions: "Should we assume that the laws and customs are to be modelled as rules of the game which are given and never broken?... Why should individuals accept fiat money or the laws and customs of trade in the first place?" Both questions are not answered: they are instead relegated to be outside the competence of the mathematical institutional economist, and by implication, outside of the sphere of the "economic."

It is possible to attempt a summary of Shubik's cannonical institutional model. He distinguishes between "market games," which can be represented by a characteristic function, because the payoff of any subset of players is independent of the activities of the complement (that is, all other traders); and a "strategic market game," in which the activities of all traders are linked by an explicit price formation mechanism and a distinct monetary system. One valuable insight of Shubik's work has been to show how the neoclassical economists' notion of "externalities" pervades the entire price system through a demonstration that realistic descriptions of the trading process preclude the possibility of treating traders' options and objectives as independent of one another. Nonetheless, he retains the neoclassical predisposition to see prices mainly as the means of conveyance of information. He writes:

> The key aspect of many economic activities that differentiates them from the viewpoint of information processing and coding from say political or societal activities or from abstract games is that a natural metric exists on many of the strategies. In mass markets, for example, for wheat, the information that two million tons were produced last season is probably more useful to most buyers and sellers than is a detailed list of the quantities produced by each individual farmer. [Shubik 1975a, 560]

A strategic market game is modelled as a noncooperative nonconstant sum game. It consists of a list of traders[4] and their endowments, the postulation of a market structure as a set of rules governing the process by which traders may convey information about bids and offers, as well as rules for the clearing of markets, and the utility functions of and strategies available to each player. The specification of market structure may become quite complicated, including the role of a bank, the rules for bankruptcy, and so on (Shubik and Wilson 1977). Another further assertion of Shubik is that the specification of the generic types of strategies pursued by the traders captures the presence or absence of "trust" in the market. The predominance of historical strategies— i.e., where a player's move is conditional upon the past moves of a set of players—is said to represent a situation of low trust. On the other hand, the acceptance of state strategies, where a player's move depends solely upon the present state of the game, is said to represent a situation of widespread trust. There is a hint, but no more, of an evolutionary argument embedded in this distinction: as markets become more anonymous and threats, by their very nature, become less specific, state strategies slowly displace historical strategies. Shubik explicitly links this development to the spread of the use of money, which he calls "the symbol of trust" (Shubik 1974, 379).

Perhaps the most striking characteristic of Shubik's published work is the relative unpretentiousness of the claims made for its efficacy. He admits that game theory enforces a symmetry upon the personalities of the players which belies any serious intrusion of personal detail, while also abstracting away from social conditioning and role playing; he also admits that game theory requires a fixed and well-defined structure of payoffs. Even more significantly, he explains that "there is as yet no satisfactory blending of game theory with learning theory" (Shubik 1982, 358). The impression conveyed is that game theory is one of many techniques of social analysis, with its own strengths and weaknesses; the matter of choice of analytical technique is left to the individual reader without any explicit discussion. This attitude is encouraged by statements that one should choose the solution concept to fit the preconceived objective: "The [Walrasian] price system may be regarded as stressing decentralization (with efficiency); the core shows the force of countervailing power; the value offers a "fairness" criterion; the bargaining set and kernel suggest how the solution might be delineated by bargaining conditions" (ibid., 382). One cannot help, however, but receive a different impression from the collected body of his writings. There intermittent claims are made that game theoretic models are necessary prerequisites for the integration of macroeconomic and Walrasian microeconomic theory, and ironically, that Nash equilibrium points of strategic market games frequently include the conventional Walrasian general equilibrium (Dubey and Shubik 1979, 120). It would appear that all the different solution concepts really are subordinate to the one "real" solution, the Walrasian general equilibrium.

Shubik's circumspection contrasts sharply with the claims made by the other prominent mathematical economist, Andrew Schotter. Schotter (1983, 692) writes, "game theory is the only tool available today that holds out hope for creating an institutionally realistic and flexible economic theory." Schotter reveals that he is aware that other economists such as John R. Commons, also have tackled these issues, but feels that such research can be written off as ineffectual without any extended critical discussion, simply because it is not phrased in game theoretic terms.

In certain respects Schotter resembles Shubik: Schotter, also, disparages Walrasian theory for leaning on the deus ex machina of the auctioneer rather than directly confronting process (ibid., 674); and, as well, repudiates cooperative game theory and the solution concept of the core, because after limit theorems that showed the core converged to the Walrasian general equilibrium (Debreu and Scarf 1963; Aumann 1964) "what we have left is an economy that is not any richer institutionally than the neoclassical analysis, which merely assumed that this degenerate set of market institutions existed at the outset" (Schotter 1983, 682). Schotter gives voice to what many have said privately: these results stole the thunder from game theory by demonstrating that it added little or nothing to the analytical content of Walrasian general equilibrium (Schotter 1981, 152).

It is here that Schotter begins to diverge from Shubik. Whereas the latter seems to pursue a live-and-let-live policy in the house of neoclassicalism, the former is critical of the modern general equilibrium trick of handling time, uncertainty, externalities, and a host of other complications by redefinition and expansion of the commodity space. (A Hershey bar at 6 PM on Tuesday on the Boston Common in the rain is different from a Hershey bar at 7 PM etc., etc., and presumably is traded in a separate "market." See Chapter 6 in this volume.) "When market institutions fail, as in the case of economies with uncertainty and externalities, the neoclassical economist does not, as he should, try to explain what alternative sets of institutions would be created to take their place" (ibid., 151). It is the stress on the creation of institutions that Schotter believes sets him apart from Shubik and others. Shubik, as we have observed, has a tendency to define institutions as ad hoc rules which act to constrain or restrict the operation of the market; Schotter, on the other hand, insists that institutions are *solutions* to games (ibid., 155; Schotter 1983, 689). Initially, the distinction might seem to be excessively subtle: although Shubik will not commit himself on where his "rules" come from, he is not hesitant to suggest bankruptcy rules are a reaction to a perceived market failure, and then examine the spectrum of possible rules to discover which are "optimal." But Schotter insists this conception is wrong because he does not believe institutions are consciously constructed; instead, behavioral regularities "emerge endogenously" or "organically." In his book, he makes a preliminary attempt at developing a taxonomy of different kinds of institutions (Schotter 1981, 22), but quickly abandons all but one category as not being sufficiently "organic." His rationale is worth quoting in its entirety:

> If the social institutions we are investigating are created by a social planner, their design can be explained by maximizing the value of some objective function existing in the planners mind. ... On the other hand, if the form of social organization created is the outcome of a multilateral bargaining process, a bargaining theory would be required. [ibid., 28]

A number of references to the Australian school, and particularly Hayek, are provided in support of this conception of an institution.

Again, appearances suggest an affinity with the earlier institutionalists' stress on the unintended consequences of both conscious choices and evolutionary drift. For this reason, it is all the more important to be clear and precise about how Schotter conceptualizes an institution. In his scenario, institutions do not lead a separate or semiautonomous existence: "Social and economic institutions are informational devices that supplement the informational content of economic systems when competitive prices do not carry sufficient information to totally decentralize and coordinate economic activities" (ibid., 109). Institutions are stopgaps or *pis aller* which evolve naturally whenever a market is not capable of producing a Pareto optimal outcome. The failure of the market to produce these outcomes is not explored in depth, nor are there any suggestions of the ubiquity or the determinants of the presence or absence of failure; and in this it stands in stark contrast to the work of Shubik. Without any motivation, all market failures are attributed to the existence of prisoner's-dilemma structures, given presumably by "states of nature." The overall picture is of a market that organically heals itself, with health defined as the conventional Walrasian general equilibrium.

Schotter has provided us with a canonical model which can be easily summarized. His model starts by *assuming* "that the only institution existing is the auctioneer-led market institution, whose origin is left unexplained by the model" (ibid., 120). Schotter's "market" is not Shubik's "market": for all practical purposes it is not strategic; its only glitch is that it does not clear in any short sequence of "gropings" for the correct vector of Pareto-optimal prices, due to the fact that preferences are not strictly convex (ibid., 124). Traders cannot communicate directly with each other, but must communicate through the "price system" by making *quantity* offers to the auctioneer. It is asserted (ibid., 125) that this is isomorphic to a supergame played over individual component games which are both stationary and of the form of the prisoner's dilemma. The purported reason the payoff is of prisoner's -dilemma form is that it is assumed that if all parties cannot arrive at agreement upon the same aggregate quantity of the commodity both bid upon and offered, *no trades are executed.*

Before we summarize the technical details of the supergame, it will be instructive to examine the structure of one of these component "moves" or subgames. Table 5.1 is a presentation of the situation presented graphically in Schotter (1981, 125). Let us restrict our attention to two traders each with endowments of a single commodity. Because utility is not strictly convex, auctioneer-provided equilibrium prices are tangent to utility functions at more than one point: here, for simplicity's sake, let us assume there are only two possible trading points: A, where trader 1 (seller of commodity X) ends up with less of his endowment, and B, where he ends up with more. Because utility is "flat" in this region, both traders end up with the same level of util-

Table 5.1. A Trading Subgame.

		Trader 2	
		A	B
	A	(10,20)	(3,6)
Trader 1			
	B	(3,6)	(10,20)

ity whichever quantity is traded at the fixed price. However, if no trade is executed (because the traders could not agree upon relative quantities), they would be stuck with their initial endowments, and their concomitant lower utility levels. It is a curiosity of Schotter's graph that he neglects to discuss the presence or absence of symmetry in the level of utility of the two traders, because as one can readily observe, this game is not of the prisoner's-dilemma format. The problem here is not that the equilibrium point is suboptimal: it is only that there are a *multiplicity of equally desirable equilibria* and that the game does not allow any external coordination to agree upon which of these indifferently acceptable equilibria will be settled upon. If utilities are not comparable and side payments are not allowed, there are only two possibilities as one adds more traders to the market: (1) everyone is psychologically identical up to a scalar multiple, and the number of multiple equivalent equilibria proliferate; or (2) people have different utility functions, and as the number of traders increases, the solution shrinks to a single Walrasian general equilibrium, which the auctioneer effectuates. Schotter seems not to have noticed that this is not an intrinsically noncooperative game, and that only in the most idiosyncratic of special cases of utility functions is there any problem of coordination.

Far from being a niggling criticism, this observation reveals that contrary to his statement in section 4.2 (ibid.), the "market model" is not isomorphic to the supergame model in chapter 3 (ibid., 1981), because the latter model is predicated on the Nash equilibrium point solution concept applied to a sequence of generic prisoner's-dilemma games, which the former clearly is not.

Let us assume that Schotter has found a way of recasting his model of the market process so that it is in the form of a prisoner's dilemma. From whence come his claims of "evolution" and "organic developments"? First he must postulate a fixed prisoner's-dilemma situation that is repeatedly played over and over again by an identical set of players. Players are assumed to "learn" from past plays of the game, but this learning is constrained to a very small subset of experience: they are allowed neither threat strategies nor to be different from other players, and cannot "remember" past the last immediate play of the game. Technically, allowable strategies are restricted to a mixed strategy over best responses in which the probabilities attached to each response are updated with a mechanical Bayesian procedure (ibid., 72). The rule is so constructed that it will eventually converge to a pure-strategy Nash equilibrium point if that strategy is played at some juncture in the game. For Schotter, an institution is any one such Nash equilibrium of a fixed game converged upon after repeated play. He does not claim to have identified the single unique institutional outcome of the situation: there are in general multiple Nash equilibria; all he can guarantee is that the Markov chain of mixed strategies will eventually converge upon one of the equilibrium points, which is an absorbing state.

One point needs elucidation not received in Schotter's book. The necessity for the single component subgame to be of the form of a prisoner's dilemma derives from the narrow conception of learning implied in the mechanical Bayesian updating rule. The question arises, as it does in all Austrian theory, how the institutional regularity is to be "policed" if it is, in fact, "organic" or "evolutionary." If the game is not of the prisoner's-dilemma form, there is no longer any unique way for a player to "punish" the others for behavior undesirable from his point of view (ibid., 83). This can be easily observed by again looking at table 5.1. Suppose trader 1 in the last around of play has chosen A while trader 2 has chosen B. Clearly both of their situations could be improved, but how can trader 1 teach this to trader 2? No message can be sent that would not involve the recall of the pattern of all plays previous to the last, and that is prevented by the Bayesian updating rule, due to the fact that mixed strategies are allowed. In other words, no strategy is explicitly identified as punishment by the structure of the game.

Schotter, like many other latter-day Austrians, shies away from explicitly discussing *learning,* as opposed to the transmission of a discrete and seemingingly prepackaged commodity called *knowledge,* because the former suggests a social process, whereas the latter conjures up the grocer's dairy case (Field 1984). This is done largely by mathematical sleight-of-hand: assuming that everyone's psychology is identical (Schotter 1981, 88), and ruling out what Schotter calls "disguised equilibria," that is, situations where the opponent's choice of strategy cannot be divined from the actual outcome or payoff. In effect, he defines the "problem" to be so straightforward and unambiguous that only one choice can be made: it is not so much learning as it is mechanism. Any discussion of the influence of history is rendered pointless, since only state strategies (in Shubik's terms) are allowed or indeed, make any sense, given that the situation is so well defined. It should not surprise us, then, that at the end of the narrow corridor through which we are allowed to pass, we arrive at—voilà—a Walrasian general equilibrium (Schotter 1983, 185–186). It is difficult to maintain that this model transcends the passive cooperation of the zombies found in conventional neoclassical general equilibrium. The question posed at the beginning of this section remains: where has game theory gotten us?

The Rules of the Game: Game Theory
and Neoclassical Economics

What is a game? It is, as quite correctly perceived by von Neumann, a set of rules, a set of objectives or payoffs, and a ranking of those objectives by the set of players. If all of these sets are *discrete* and well-defined, they may be expressed in the format of mathematical formalism; and then further manipulation of the symbols can serve to suggest potential outcomes. However, it is also true, as Wittgenstein wrote in his *Remarks on the Foundations of Mathematics,* "A game, a language, a rule is an institution" (Wittgenstein 1978, VI 32). The copula "is" in this quote should not be confused with an equals sign, for the relationship is neither commutative nor symmetrical. To say that a game is an institution is not necessarily to say that an institution is a game.

Game theory and neoclassical market theory start from an identical premise: market trades are not adventitious, but possess a regularity and stability which permits them to be causally explained. So what is the constancy postulated by game theory? The first, and least discussed postulate,[5] is the persistence and constancy of the players (Heims 1980, 307). Within a static one-shot game the persistence of the players' identities may be ignored; but with any repetition or learning this condition becomes critical. The constancy of humans, and therefore the putative constancy of human nature is the key to the translation of any game into mathematical formalism. If humans are not to be treated with all their individual quirks and idiosyncracies (that is, are to be the subject of generalization), then their communication and behavior must be treated symmetrically. If one merely assumes that language is always adequately shared, that the content of a transmitted message is identical to the content received, and that interpretation is not problematic, then the people who are the subject of the analysis must be substantially "the same," no matter what happens.

The second postulate of game theory is the assumed constancy of the rules. As we have observed, this appeared to be the bone of contention between Shubik and Schotter. Shubik seemed content to accept the rules as arbitrarily fixed; Schotter claimed that the rules were solutions to supergames. Examination of Schotter's model revealed that the rules were no more flexible than in Shubik's models; if anything, Schotter mistakes arbitrary psychological rigidities for rule structure. As with the previous postulate, this problem is not apparent in one-shot games, but only attains importance upon repetition. The rules are what exist to be learned by the players, although this is often obscured by mathematically posting the game in strategic form.[6] We shall return to this issue shortly.

The third postulate of game theory is the relative stability of the objectives and the environment. Interestingly enough, this is not an endogenous outcome in game theory, but must be given a priori as part of the mathematical formalism. Many pages have been written about the expendability of cardinally measurable payoffs, and especially the requirement of cardinal utility, but few have realized that this is merely the tip of the iceberg. A game must have a single-valued objective function which somehow summarizes the jumbled, confused, and sometimes unconsciously contradictory desires and drives of human beings. Further, this index must generally conform to the axiom of Archimedes (Krantz et al. 1971, 25–26), which translates into the requirement that all potential outcomes be comparable before the fact; or more prosaically, every man must have his price. It is of paramount importance that these rankings be stable,[7] for without them, there is no sense in which a game can be "solved."

Now, the most important aspect of these postulates is not their tenuous connection to "reality" (game theorists have been historically thick skinned when it comes to empirical disconfirmation of solutions and/or assumptions), but rather what passes for analysis and explanation. Given the fixed actors with their fixed objectives and the fixed rules, the analyst (and *not the actors*) prereconciles the various sets, insists the prereconciled outcome is the one that will actually obtain, and calls this a "solution." The critical role of the three postulates of constancy becomes evident: without them, there is no preordained reconciliation to be discovered. The process in which the actors take part is irrelevant, because the deck has been stacked in a teleological manner. Insofar as the three postulates are "naturally" given, equilibrium is identified with harmony and natural order, while conflict and disharmony can only be expressed as disequilibrium.

This caricature is crudely drawn, and the game theorists would surely complain (at least there, if not in their published work) that the world is not that simple. I should think they would aver that the distinction between cooperative and noncooperative games was invented precisely to conjure up a more subtle and penetrating analysis of harmony and conflict. I would like to suggest that the promise of game theory to encompass conflict and strategy in a rigorous manner is more than a little illusory, and is rooted in a confusion over the role of the analyst in the solution of games.

The clearest definition of a cooperative game has been provided by Shubik (1981, 165): Pareto optimality is taken as an axiom, sidepayments of utility or other payoff units are permitted outside of the actual structure of the game, and communications and bargaining of an unspecified nature are permitted and presumed to take place (at least virtually, in that the value of each potential coalition must be well defined). Cooperation is not modelled; it is subsumed in the various payoffs to coalitions. In the presence of the three postulates, the players know what the analyst knows, and both the players and the analyst "agree" upon the feasible and desirable outcomes. It is no surprise that early partisans of cooperative games have lately been repudiating their premature enthusiasm: in this scenario, "natural order" is imposed by the analyst.

The distinctive characteristic of noncooperative games is that the players and the analyst no longer "think" the same things: in essence, the analyst would like to impose a solution that the players would not choose as a result of obeying the rules. The conflict is not located among the players as much as it resides in the tension between the rule-governed situation and the Pareto optimum. The analyst, obeying his own self-denying ordinance, resists simply imposing the naturally given optimum (or optima), and then is challenged by the need to provide a description of simple rule-governed stability in the presence of infinite degrees of freedom. The analyst is faced with the prospect of constructing some definition of the rationality that is not transparently a reflection of the natural givens.

This impasse has surfaced whenever someone tries to explain what a Nash equilibrium point means or signifies (Johansen 1982; Harsanyi 1982; Shubik 1981; Friedman 1977). Mathematically, the Nash EP is the maximum point or points on a compact convex set of the "best replies" of each player's strategy set. The Nash EP is often motivated by appealing to some lack of knowledge or ability to compare goals among players, but this is not strictly true. Each player knows all the relevant information about the other players, and has the ability to prereconcile the entire process in his own head. The only difference from a cooperative game is that the rules create the potentiality that rationality is indeterminate, in that the interpretation of strategy sets becomes an issue.

It is well know that every finite N-person game has at least one Nash EP if mixed strategies are allowed. This mathematical existence proof does us a disservice, however, once we realize that mixed strategies are only rational if deployed outside of a one-shot static game (Shubik 1981, 155). Therefore, a noncooperative game can in most cases only be seriously discussed if it is repeated; more generally, after Wittgenstein, we can say that no one is capable of following a rule only once. Games, if they are to describe behavior rather than a set of prearranged natural conditions, must be repeated. But it is precisely in repetition that the notion of a fixed strategy set slowly unravels: more and more ad hoc assumptions must be made about how each player interprets the sequences of the other players' moves over time. In general, the solutions to a sequence of noncooperative games will not be the sequence of individual solutions to each of the component games (van Damme 1981; Friedman 1977, 199). It is in this sense that rationality, as conceived in game theory, is indeterminate.

At this juncture we once again return to the postulates of constancy. Shubik is right to point out that it is a misnomer to call the Nash solution concept "rational expectations," because there is no guarantee that the outcome will meet the *analysts'* criteria of rationality (that is, Pareto optionality) (Shubik 1981, 153). He suggests it is more appropriate to think of a Nash EP as displaying "consistent expectations," in that conjectures about players' behavior match ex post outcomes. The definition of consistency, however, is a function of the time frame over which the Nash equilibrium is defined; once that is realized, it follows directly that all Nash EP require our three postulates of constancy. How else could we possibly "construct" consistency solely from the payoffs of the game, unless the players, the rules, and the objectives were identical through time?

Contrary to the claims often made in the literature on supergames, those models cannot encompass historical change. Works that claim to include change of players over time—(Schotter 1981, 127–139) for example—in fact specify the sequential agent characteristics so that they are functionally identical. In contrast, works, such as that of Friedman (1977), which vary the payoffs over time, do so in such a way that the change can be specified independent of history (that is, are stationary). If changes in strategy sets are allowed, they are restricted to stationary Bayesian revisions, by their very structure myopic and ahistorical. There is no published work that attempts to change all three postulates simultaneously. This poor showing cannot be excused as a temporary situation contingent upon further mathematical effort and virtuosity. It is a corollary of the neoclassical notion of rationality, which can only augment the psychological abilities of *homo rationalis* in order that all interactions must be virtually prereconciled in their heads, whether or not they actually occur. This conception, of course, is exactly what caused the older institutionalist school to renounce neoclassical economics.

It is easy to be lulled by all the language of "conflict," "retaliation," and "enforcement" into believing that the solvable supergames portray processes. Harsanyi (1982) and Aumann (1981) both define the Nash EP as a self-enforcing equilibrium, but we should now understand this to mean that the solution would persist if the postulates of constancy held and if the analyst imposes an arbitrary set of rules governing how players interpret each other's moves. These requirements wreak havoc with any commonsense notion of the enforcement of rules. Neoclassical economists want to portray a world where there is no active coercion, because rationality polices itself. What causes this goal to elude their grasp is that there is no such thing as a self-justifying rule (Levison 1978). Quoting Wittgenstein: "However many rules you give me—I give a rule which justifies *my* employment of your rules." (Wittgenstein 1978, I 113). "The employment of the word 'rule' is interwoven with the employment of the word 'same'" (ibid., VII 59). The exercise of rationality, as opposed to the twitches of a zombie or a machine, depends upon active interpretation of whether the rule applies in the particular instance, and on whether to regard anomalies as exceptions or failures to abide by the rule. Rationality is the deployment of judgment as a process, which cannot itself be justified by a rule at the risk of falling into an infinite regress (Field 1979).[8]

This is nowhere better illustrated than in the proliferation of solution concepts and individual solutions in game theory. As soon as someone proposes a "rational" solution to a particular game someone else generates a counterexample that questions its rationality. For example, Morgenstern and Schwödiauer (1976) criticize the core as being dominated by other imputations if the players are aware of the theory of the core. Or, Johansen (1982, 430) points out that if player X knew player Y was experimenting with his options, and had any basis for guessing the pattern of player Y's experiments, then player x would in general choose strategies outside of the Nash equilibrium. van Damme (1981, 37) shows that in certain game structures, "a player can punish the other as badly as he wishes and therefore each player can force the other player to steer the system to any state he wishes. So all kinds of behavior (even rather foolish) can appear when one plays according to a history dependent EP." Aumann (1981) reports that the solution points of supergame depend critically upon the discount rate used to calculate the present value of future payoffs; I believe no one has yet indicated how vulnerable these results are to the paradoxes arising out of the Cambridge capital controversy (Harcourt 1982, pt. V). We have already noted that the Nash EP for a one-shot noncooperative game is not identical to a Nash EP for the same game repeated over and over again.

Game theorists have opened the Pandora's Box marked "rationality," and do not know how to close it again. Walrasian general equilibrium was based upon a direct appropriation of a metaphor from physics, and this meant that the natural givens of the analysis would directly determine the optimal outcome. Planets in motion are passive and do not talk back, and neither did the passive Walrasian trader. The natural world is stable and unchanging,[9] which allowed postulations of laws that were independent of their spatial or temporal location. The Walrasian laws were also stationary and static. Then game theorists proposed to discuss bargaining which led to cooperative games, which begat noncooperative games, which begat discussions of process, which allowed the transactors the freedom to differ in their interpretations of the roles of others and the constancy of the world, all of which is now undermining the older construct of mechanistic rationality. This is not happening because game theorists have willed it so—in fact, much effort is spent demonstrating that special sorts of solutions to special sorts of games converge to Walrasian equilibria. It is happening because game theory exposes the weaknesses of the physical metaphor that all the excessive mathematical formalism served to obscure. Game theory does not, however, suggest what to put in its place. It cannot conceptualize the reduction of a language or of an institution to a game.

Rules Are Not Homogeneous

The word "institution" has been so far used loosely; the time has arrived to suggest a more precise definition. In view of the criticisms voiced in the previous sections of this paper, it may prove illuminating to conceptualize institutions as consisting of three tiers of rules. In the first tier are the rules most familiar to game theorists: these are rules grounded in stable, persistent, and independent givens of the analysis. These rules are in some sense "policed" by the stability of the environment. A good example of this type of situation is provided by prisoner's-dilemma games describing the over-grazing of a commons or the depletion of a fish species. Insofar as the "payoff" is well defined and not socially defined (i.e., fish caught or animal fed), and the players are fairly homogeneous, Nash equilibria can explain certain regularities in behavior. We could refer to these situations as "natural" rules.

The rules in the second tier are based upon the recognition that human rationality cannot be an algorithm, but must constantly be flexible and prepared for change. The rules are social, consciously constructed, and consciously policed. Into this category would fall property rights, money, religion, the family, and much else that comprises social order. The rules of this class cannot be explained as the outcome of underlying natural forces, because their enforcement mechanisms are not "natural": they possess neither persistence nor independence from the phenomena. We could refer to those situations as *bootstrap* rules.

The third tier of rules derives from the recognition that the first two classes of rules must interact over time. For example, the overgrazing game will be influenced by the institution of money, and any natural regularity of behavior may be destabilized or redefined by the penetration of market relationships: here, the "payoff" itself becomes partly socially defined. The exercise of human rationality itself transforms the environment. The recognition that there may be temporal regularities to the relative dominance or importance of natural rules versus bootstrap rules leads to the metarationality of evolutionary regularities. Unlike the first two classes of rules, evolutionary regularities by their nature cannot be teleological: they reflect interactions of natural rules and bootstrap rules beyond the imagination of any player.

It should be clear from previous comments that most neoclassical economists would insist that a scientific economics would only recognize explanations that linked any given social phoenomenon to its natural rules. Explanation in this framework is satisfied to take as given tastes, technologies, and endowments, and to identify equilibrium with the extremum of some objective function. Why can't all social processes be reduced to their natural rules? To reiterate, this program leads to a logical contradiction. All natural rules must be subject to human interpretation. Natural constraints do not inexorably compel us to do anything, because human reason intervenes. This freedom is what provides us with all the multiform variation that comprises the history of the human race. To put it in Wittgensteinian terms: A rule does not certify its own correct application. To pretend that it does so is to appeal to other rules, and can only lead in a circle. Whether a reason or an activity conforms to a rule in a particular case is a problem in reasoning and interpretation, having to do with judgments about when situations are "the same." We may feel compelled to follow a rule, but the rule itself cannot compel us.

There are also those who believe that the world is only comprised of bootstrap rules. Let us call this opinion *conventionalism.* Why cannot all social phenomena be reduced to bootstrap rules? This position also meets an insuperable logical difficulty: knowledge of this theory of social phenomena tends to undermine its efficacy. To argue that all social regularities are consciously instituted is to argue that the only prerequisite for change is will; a society based upon this premise cannot ultimately enforce or maintain the stability required to define rules. In other words, just as the natural world is intrinsically incapable of defining the totality of social life, so too is the belief that might makes right. Even if the world of language, markets, and culture were ultimately organized by bootstrap rules, these rules would themselves be asserted by some actors to be grounded in natural rules in order to provide stability and diffuse responsibility.

What then, is the function of the evolutionary regularities? These must be present because bootstrap rules influence natural rules, and vice versa. They are the locus of the understanding of change. The determination that a natural situation is producing regularities in behavior is itself a function of society's conception of science; and, as twentieth-century philosophers of science have come to argue, science consists largely of bootstrap rules. As our understanding of what is natural evolves, it cannot help but change the formal relations of bootstrap rules to natural rules in social life. These changes are not purely erratic: a good example of this is provided by Wesley Clair Mitchell in his "Role of Money in Economic History." He argues that money cannot be cogently explained by the prosaic notion that it made life naturally easier for traders. "When money is introduced into the dealing of men, it enhances their freedom. For example, personal service is commuted into money payment. . . . Adam Smith's obvious and simple system of natural liberty seems obvious and natural only to the denizens of a money economy" (Mitchell 1953, 200). More significantly, Mitchell proposes that the penetration of the money economy into social life altered the very configurations of rationality, to the extent of encouraging particular conceptions of abstraction, quantification, and thus ultimately the ontology of modern Western science. Here we have socially constructed rules, slowly transforming the understanding of natural constraints through the rational interpretative structure, finally changing the natural rules themselves.

What has all this to do with game theory and economic theory? It clearly and concisely provides a framework within which to evaluate the claim that there is a new mathematical institutional economics in the offing. Neoclassical economists will only sanction explanation in terms of natural rules. This is a reflection of their perennial search for a natural order, an invisible hand, and so forth. Since bootstrap rules and evolutionary regularities cannot be reduced to natural rules, their project is doomed to failure. One need only compare Schotter's "explanation" of the rise of money as a game theoretic solution to a naturally given problem of transactions costs to Mitchell's broad interpretation of the influence of money on economic life to see this failure.

There are other economists who believe that conscious and deliberate planning will solve all economic ills; they are partisans of the view that the world is nothing but a collection of bootstrap rules. Since neither natural rules nor evolutionary regularities can be reduced to bootstrap rules, this research project is also doomed to undermine itself.

Game theoretic explanations of human institutions fall into one of these two categories. Contrary to Schotter, all phenomenal rules cannot be reduced to their underlying natural rules. Contrary to Shubik, the postulation of rules as bootstrap or ad hoc leaves explanations without any firm foundations. A theory of institutions must operate simultaneously on all three levels. The mathematical formalism of game theory is best suited for the discussion of natural rules. It can be used to *describe* bootstrap rules. But it also reveals that notions of rationality and equilibrium are distorted beyond recognition in those models, to the point that neither the existence nor efficacy of those rules can be said to be illuminated by the analysis. Since evolutionary rules are not teleological, they are not suited to game theoretic structures.

In conclusion, game theory is not a substitute for a theory of institutions. It can only be one component of such a theory, a theory committed to the explanation of change as well as of complacency.

Notes

1. This history of the critique of the concept of the maximization provides a clear example of the peripatetic migration between one defense and the other. For recent examples of the former, the 'straw man' defense, see Boland (1981); for the latter, the insinuation of sour grapes, see Wong (1978).

2. The quote is from Veblen's "Why is Economics Not an Evolutionary Science?" reprinted in Veblen (1919). The best introduction and summary of the thought of the institutionalists is still chapters 14 and 15 of Mitchell (1950).

3. Evidence for this statement is provided in Part I above.

4. Sometimes there is postulated a continuum of traders, i.e., a nonatomic agglomeration, who therefore cannot be subject to a discrete list. This assumption is often used to "prove" that Nash equilibria converge to Walrasian competitive equilibria.

5. This absence of discussion may provide a counterexample to the common opinion that mathematical models, by their very nature, make assumptions more clear and transparent than common speech.

6. "There is a not completely innocent modelling assumption that any finite game in extensive form can be reduced to a game in strategic form, which is equivalent to the original description of the game from the viewpoint of the application of solution theory" (Shubik 1981, 157).

7. We say "stable" and not "constant," because of the tradition of probabilistic concepts of utility dating back to the original work of von Neumann and Morgenstern (1964).

8. Perhaps this explains Schotter's final chapter (1981) with its discussion of sociobiology. One way to short-circuit the infinite regress is to locate "fundamental" rules in our genes.

9. At least until the twentieth century, when physics left the economists behind.

6

The Role of Conservation Principles in Twentieth-Century Economic Theory

I

Over the last ten years there has been increasing interest in the possible conceptual connections between thermodynamics and economic theory, largely due to the masterful and provocative book by Nicholas Georgescu-Roegen, *The Entropy Law and the Economic Process.*[1] Prior to Georgescu-Roegen's clarification of some of the main issues, however, it was not uncommon to find chance off-hand references to thermodynamics sprinkled amidst the work of some of the twentieth century's most respected economic theorists. For example, Frank Knight once insisted that, "There is nothing in economics corresponding to either momentum or energy, or their conservation principles in mechanics."[2] In contrast, Paul Samuelson in his seminal *Foundations of Economic Analysis* suggested that variation of the demand for a factor with a change in its price was analytically similar to thermodynamic variation in the pressure, volume, and temperature of an ideal gas.[3] Robert Clower, on the other hand, saw the parallel between thermodynamics and *macroeconomics:* "Thus, Say's principle [that planned purchases must equal planned receipts] may indeed be regarded as a fundamental convention of economic science, akin in all relevant respects to such basic ideas of physical science as the [sic] second law of thermodynamics."[4] Clearly there is a widespread impression that there are important analogues between the structure of economic theory and the structure of thermodynamics; equally clearly, there is much confusion and imprecision in the specification of what those analogues are.

There are many potential meeting grounds between economics and thermodynamics: our purpose here is to attempt an illumination of one very small portion of that turf. Our chosen ground will be an examination of certain correspondences to the first law of thermodynamics: the "law" of the conservation of energy. This law states that all forms of energy are able to be converted, from one form to another, at fixed ratios of transformation; and that the sum total of suitably converted energy in a closed system is a constant. While many commentators, both physicists and economists, have noted the superficial similarities between the first law and an economic system of accounts,[5] we shall here restrict discussion to the question of the existence of a strict analogue between some explicit portion of twentieth-century economic *theory* and the thermodynamic principle of conservation.

The myriad relations between physics and economics is a large subject with many intriguing implications, such as: should economists emulate physicists in their methods of research and exposition? How important are the relative forces encouraging styles of intellectual discourse emanating from other disciplines? This chapter severely limits itself to the following theses:[6]

(A) Thorstein Veblen suggested at the turn of the century that existing conservation principles adopted by economic theory were leading the science into a *cul-de-sac*.

(B) Samuelson's school has unwittingly stumbled on the problems indicated by Veblen. These problems can be traced to that school's predisposition to appropriate analytical techniques from thermodynamics without fully exploring what those techniques imply about the structure of social relations.[7]

II

While Veblen catalogues[8] many of the teleological aspects of what he calls "classical" economics (which includes many theorists we would today classify as neoclassicals), one aspect of that constellation of characteristics is particularly interesting from our present vantage point. To quote Veblen:

> the resulting economic theory is formulated as an analysis of the 'natural' course of the life of the community, the ultimate theoretical postulate of which might, not unfairly be stated as in some sort of a law of the conservation of economic energy. When the course of things runs off naturally or normally, in accord with the exigencies of human welfare and the constraining laws of nature, economic income and outgo balance one another.... So it is, by implication, assumed that the product which results from any given industrial process or operation is, in some sense or in some unspecified respect, the equivalent of the expenditure of forces, or of the effort, or what not, that has gone into the process of which the product emerges.[9]

Here we recognize the implicit germ of a conservation principle in economic theory. It is presumed that some quality of the constituent inputs into production remains constant throughout the production process and is reincarnated in the final product. This can be seen, for example, in Adam Smith's "adding-up" theory of value, where the prices of inputs are conserved throughout the production process. It can also be discovered in J. B. Clark's theory of distribution, a doctrine Veblen was specifically concerned to call into question.

One theoretical implication of these conservation principles for economics is that the value of outputs and the value of inputs are necessarily identical: or more directly, the idea that exactly the sufficient quantity of incomes is created within the process of production which immediately reappears as the wherewithal to purchase those same products. This precept is generally known today as Say's Identity or Say's Law. A putative identity between the aggregate value of inputs, the quantity of money spent, and the value of the aggregate output suggested to the followers of Say that, at least *potentially*, there was no fundamental reason that any aggregate amount of production could not be sold. In its strong version, this is the imposition of an analytical conservation principle: the sum total of spending is invariant under alterations in conditions of exchange. A smoothly functioning financial sector would guarantee that everything produced would be purchased, even though various individuals might choose to save part of their incomes. The contribution of Keynesian theory was to attempt to build an economic theory which eschewed this conservation principle: aggregate production was instead to react to the distribution between *virtual* purchases (unintended inventory accumulation and liquidity preference) and the actual purchases of goods. Contrary to Professor Clower, Say's Principle in any of its variants is *not* a fundamental convention of Keynesian economics, although it is a fundamental principle of Walrasian neoclassical theory.

Veblen's critical scrutiny of neoclassical conservation principles led him to question Say's Law, and in this limited respect, anticipate Keynes by at least three decades. But in other respects he was more perceptive than Keynes, because he also recognized another conservation principle which dated back to the beginning of economic theory. To quote him again directly,

Productivity or serviceability, is, therefore, to be presumed of any occupation or enterprise that looks to a pecuniary gain; and so, by a roundabout path, we get back to the ancient conclusion of A. Smith, that the remuneration of classes or of persons engaged in industry coincides with their productive contribution to the output of services and consumable goods.[10]

Veblen understood that most economic analysis had been cast in the form of processes where an underlying value quantum remained unchanged while undergoing various social transformations, be they inputs and outputs in a production process, or exchanges of equivalents. Veblen saw nothing "natural" about this mode of analysis, and spent much of his considerable rhetorical power in trying to undermine this conception.

Although Veblen's contribution to economics has suffered neglect in the interim, there are many fruitful theoretical lessons to be learned from his work on the conservation principles implicit in the structure of neoclassical economics. One lesson is that conservation principles are *not* empirical generalizations. One does not generalize from successive observations that the value of outputs is identical to the value of inputs in a production process. Instead, conservation principles are methods of organizing both theory and observation which are imposed a priori by the theorist.[11] They are very much like filing systems, which allow us to account for important quantitative relationships. No filing system is perfect, however; and some filing systems make it nearly impossible to find what we are looking for. Veblen perceptively noticed that the Say's Law "filing system" made it very difficult to talk cogently about movements in the aggregate level of economic activity due to changes in spending behavior. He quite sensibly then suggested that the particular filing system be scrapped.

A second lesson to be gained from his work is that the choice of conservation principles in macroeconomic theory should not be arbitrary. The question which needed an explicit answer was: what precisely is the "abiding entity" in capitalist systems? Veblen rejected physical productivity, or utility, or "tastes" or incomes or endowments as being conserved throughout the operation of production and exchange (which thus meant rejection of both the Walrasian and Marshallian variants of neoclassical theory). Veblen then suggests that the abiding entity of the phenomenon known as capital is not a physical fact, but rather an institutionally defined continuity of ownership. "The continuity, in fact, is of an immaterial nature, a matter of legal rights, or contract, of purchase and sale." [12] Therefore an appeal to the "natural" foundations of economic theory, be it an assertion that human psychology varies little from individual to individual, or the assertion that the whole of the product naturally arises from and therefore belongs to the laborer, will eventually be compromised by the evolution of human society. In a very immediate sense, man makes himself; and the economist must not pretend that this changing process is determined by some supposedly innate characteristics of human nature, or by an exogenous fixed environment. [13]

The third lesson in *The Place of Science in Modern Civilization* is more implicit than explicit. Veblen believed that industrialization corrupted and finally destroyed animistic and teleological arguments in Western science, and replaced them with what he called "matter of fact preconceptions." These latter arguments never employed terms which suggested personality or desire or intention (such as that of a divine or beneficent order), but rather were cast in terms of a mechanical continuity: faceless, impartial and not a little relentless in nature. In one place, Veblen suggests that this transformation took place in physics with the widespread acceptance of the doctrine of the conservation of energy. [14] Interestingly enough, contemporary historians of science have provided partial support for Veblen's suggestion by showing that the development of the principle of the conservation of energy grew quite directly out of industrial concerns, particularly those having to do with the development of the steam engine. [15] The implication of this suggestion is that if only economics could find a non-teleological conservation principle, it, too, would finally achieve the path towards true scientific endeavor, or at least finally imitate physics as a *modern* science.

Here we stand, eighty years after Veblen's prescriptions for the upgrading of economic science. Have any of his precepts been heeded?

III

In the interim, economics as a discipline has attained many of the trappings of external recognition as a science, the most recent of which being the addition of a Nobel Prize for economics alongside the prizes for physics and chemistry. How very fitting from our point of view that the third recipient of this new prize in 1970 chose as the theme of his Nobel lecture the relationship between his life's work and parallel themes in thermodynamics! We therefore propose to examine Paul Samuelson's "Maximum Principles in Analytical Economics" [16] for indications of whether Veblen's lessons concerning conservation principles have been heeded in the course of the development of economics in the twentieth century.

Samuelson's lecture has two main theses: (a) that whenever possible, phrasing a question in economics and physics as a constrained maximization problem is both "useful" and "convenient" and leads to "grand simplicities," and (b) that many of Samuelson's own realizations of thesis (a) come from observing parallels in the theoretical framework of thermodynamics. Thesis (a) is an outgrowth of an earlier pronouncement by Samuelson that mathematics and language have the same epistemic status in economics, but that mathematics is more "convenient" for deduction. [17] Alas, in both statements, "convenience" is neither defined nor elucidated, a point we shall shortly endow with some significance.

In the Nobel lecture, Samuelson draws our attention to the fact that some of his earliest work, such as his *Foundations of Economic Analysis,* explicitly noted that his method was essentially imported wholesale from thermodynamics. [18] An example taken from his lecture may help to make this clearer.

Suppose we are plotting the pressure and the volume of an ideal gas (Figure 6.1). Boyle's Law states that the pressure times the volume of an ideal gas is equal to a constant if the gas is held at a constant temperature: thus we plot the solid curve for a single temperature in the figure. On the other hand, let us relax the constraint that the gas be held at a constant temperature, but instead impose the condition that no heat may flow from the gas to its surroundings, or vice versa. When we now plot the pressure/volume readings of the gas, we discover something like the dashed curve in the figure: there is

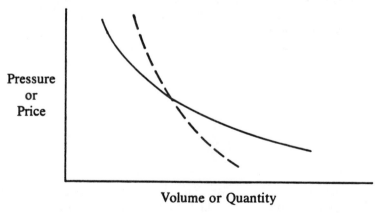

Volume or Quantity

Figure 6.1

still a negative relationship between the two variables, but the slope of the curve is more negative than in the first case. The reason for this disparity is that as a gas expands, its temperature falls. Therefore, to hold the temperature of an expanding gas constant (i.e., the dark curve), *additional energy must be added to the gas;* a corollary of this addition of energy is that the pressure of the gas is prevented from falling to the extent it would fall without the addition of energy (the dashed curve). The reason the temperature of an unheated gas falls when that gas expands is because some of the energy content of the gas is converted into work. Therefore it is important to note (both for the present argument and for later reference) that the only reason we can infer the above explanation for the two separate pressure/volume diagrams is that we have *assumed* that heat is convertible into work and vice versa, and that the sum total of these two quantities, suitably converted into a single index, is *constant* for an isolated gas: that is, we have assumed the law of conservation of energy.

Samuelson argues, quite correctly, that the pressure/volume relations can also be inferred from an *as-if* constrained extremum problem, where the constraint is in one instance constant temperature and in the other instance constant energy content. He then goes on to state this is formally the same as the constrained maximization problem faced by the neoclassical firm (or for that matter, by the neoclassical consumer) in the face of a change in the price in one of its inputs. Suppose we relabel the axes in figure 6.1 to read "price of input" on the vertical axis and "quantity" on the horizontal axis. Suppose further we wish to derive the demand curve for this input from the conventional constrained maximum relation, maximizing revenues (or utility for the consumer) subject to costs.[19] It so happens that with the appropriate assumptions about either the revenue or utility surface (and these are hardly harmless assumptions—we shall return to this issue), price and the quantity demanded will always be inversely related. However, suppose the firm (or the consumer) is unable to adjust the usage of *other* inputs for some reason. The constrained maximum problem shows that the demand curve will be less elastic than if the firm could adjust the quantities of its other inputs: that is, the input quantity-constrained demand curve corresponds to the dotted curve in figure 6.1, whereas the conventional demand curve corresponds to the solid curve.[20]

At first glance, it would appear that Veblen's concerns have been vindicated, and that some of the most respected economists of our era have managed to substitute "colorless" and "nonteleological" principles for their earlier animistic preoccupations. Notwithstanding the seeming force of the evidence, one criticism which might be made of Samuelson's Nobel lecture is that he has not sufficiently drawn out all of the parallels between his work and thermodynamics.

Historically, a rather common criticism of the neoclassical constrained maximization framework has been that firms and individuals do not continuously calculate maxima: this is the starting point of the "satisficing" literature and the evolutionary and behaviorist theories of the firm.[21] These criticisms have experienced great difficulty in hitting their mark, in part because they have passed over in silence a crucial characteristic of constrained maximization techniques: all *must* impose some sort of conservation rule. In constrained extremum problems in physics, this is always made explicit: one assumes conservation of mechanical force, or the first law of thermodynamics, or the conservation of matter and energy. In economics, the conservation rule is always hidden, buried within the assumed shape of the revenue function (for the firm) or the utility function (for consumer theory).

This can be observed by returning to Samuelson's example of the constrained maximization problem of the firm. Much of the mathematical ingenuity in his work on this problem in his *Foundations* was expended showing the necessary first and second order conditions which must be assumed for the given revenue function. By definition these must be *independent* of the firm's major activity: *selling* the resulting output. The reason for this is that without the artifice of the Walrasian auctioneer, there is no satisfactory theory of price and quantity adjustment for a competitive neoclassical market.[22] In practice, what is tacitly assumed is a form of Say's Law: at any given level of output, value is conserved through the process of exchange. Aggregate output is uncoupled from trade activities. Unhappily, all our mathematical sophistication has not advanced us any further than Adam Smith's presumptive equality of remuneration and productive contribution.

In the case of consumer theory, an exactly analogous "hidden postulate" lies buried in the utility function. As Dobb noted so many years ago, the very existence of a utility function with appropriate first and second-order properties implies the equation of "desire" with "satisfaction."[23] This, also, is an implicit conservation rule: utility is conserved throughout the exchange process. Just as in Say's Law, there is no room for the unintended deleterious consequences of good intentions. The realization of utility is made independent of the processes of consumption and exchange, just as the firm's realization of profit through sales is made independent of its production activities. If there were a theme song for this pageant of atomistic maximizing units, it would have to be, "No Regrets."[24]

One suspects that many neoclassical economists would, at this point, aver that these assumptions have been implicitly made in the past; but add that this was merely one step in a larger iteration towards more realistic and/or fruitful assumptions. If so, they would miss the major argument of this essay: without some such prior imposed conservation rules, there would be *no constrained maximization* at all in neoclassical economics. For if regret (as we have defined it) were possible, then there would be no fixed functions and no fixed extrema which could be located by the calculus. This should be the real insight of the behavioralist theorists: individuals and firms already know there is such a thing as regrets, and know that their activities are not separable into independent subsets; and therefore, quite logically and rationally, do not go about their business as if it were solely a sequence of constrained maximization decisions. The greatest irony of this situation is that neoclassical economic theorists claim to concern themselves with "general equilibrium," where "everything depends upon everything else"; but in fact their techniques persistently assume the economy is separated into isolated subsets of economic activities which *do not interact* due to the unspoken imposition of various conservation principles.

Since the technique of maximization subject to constraints is part of the "hard core" of neoclassical economics, it becomes imperative to understand what our criticism attempts to achieve and what it does not. It is *not* a claim that *empirically* people do not maximize "something." It is *not* a claim that an "as-if" methodology is flawed. It is *not* a claim that people can never attain the level or amount of knowledge required for a global maximization calculation.[25] It is instead a logical criticism that neoclassical economists, in appropriating an analytical technique from thermodynamics, have implicitly imported a physical metaphor and imposed it upon social phenomena without ever making it explicit what social conditions would be consistent with that metaphor. Those conditions are, roughly, that in the theory there never is any feedback in the economic system from market processes to the underlying value determinants (that is, the utility functions or given endowments), which are then portrayed as "natural" or "exogenous" to the analysis. This situation pertains both in Samuelson's static and dynamic models: the exogenous conditions remain the same in both. Prices are mere reflections of value and the economist need not concern himself or herself about the determinants of value, since they are grounded in noneconomic forces. Equilibrium can be described independently of the processes which purportedly bring it about, in the same way that the thermodynamic properties of the state of a system are independent of path.[26] No reasons are ever given by economists for this series of analytical choices, other than perhaps the fact that that's the way it's done in physics, and that what is good enough for physicists should be good enough for economists.

The philosopher Alexander Rosenberg has attempted to understand the fascination with the technique of constrained maximization in neoclassical economics, and has come up with three potential reasons: (a) it has been a successful research strategy in physics, which was in turn because (b) it can easily turn disconfirming empirical data into "puzzles" for the program to solve (essentially, this just restates Duhem's thesis); and (c) the only real alternative to it is the ineffectual and empty statement that actors do not maximize any objective.[27] This essay demonstrates explicit evidence for reason (a), but hesitates to lend support to reasons (b) and (c). It is not enough to show that auxiliary hypotheses can be invoked to protect the hypothesis of constrained maximization from falsification, since Duhem's thesis can be invoked to explain the relative immunization from attack of *any* hypothesis. It is not clear that the hypothesis of constrained maximization is more suited to such strategies than any alternative methodology. Further, it is a question in the history of physics as to whether there were or are any viable alternatives to the constrained extremum approach, and that is outside the scope of this essay. However, we do have one more reason to add to Rosenberg's list; but to do so, we need to return to the specific case of Samuelson's research program.

IV

Given that so many economists from Veblen onwards have been concerned to understand the role of conservation principles in economic theory, it is all the more curious that Samuelson should write in his Nobel lecture that,

> There is really nothing more pathetic than to have an economist or a retired engineer try to force analogies between the concepts of physics and the concepts of economics. How many dreary papers have I had to referee in which the author is looking for something which corresponds to entropy or one or another form of energy. Nonsensical laws, such as the law of conservation of purchasing power, represent spurious social science imitations of the important physical law of the conservation of energy.[28]

One is quite at a loss as to how to interpret this, since insofar as Samuelson's life work has involved the imposition of the constrained maximization framework upon economic phenomena, he has consistently and continuously imposed those "spurious social science imitations" of conservation laws in the course of his own work. Is it possible that Samuelson is not fully aware of the implications of his own writings?

The question brings us back to the issue of the "convenience" of mathematics for deduction and the "convenience" of recasting economic problems as if they were constrained maximization calculations. If mathematics is a language, as Samuelson has asserted many times, then we must judge its efficacy as a language: how well does it enhance the *clarity* of what is intended to be communicated, and how much of the content of what is being asserted is actually captured by the listeners and consciously intended by the speaker? In this particular instance and under these criteria, it seems mathematics receives rather low marks as a language. First, its audience is much more circumscribed than that of another language in which Samuelson is fluent, and, we might add, is frequently quite elegant in his felicitous turns of phrase. Second, many times even such a fine mathematician as Samuelson neglects the full content of what a set of mathematical relations is asserting about a social situation. The mere assertion that two quantities can be added together contains within it the implicit assumption of *some* form of conservation principle, for instance.[29] *Does the use of mathematics act to reveal or obscure which properties social phenomena must possess in order to be amenable to mathematical analysis?*

More important, to return to Veblen's characterization of a modern science, has the development of the maximization principles of neoclassical economics led that endeavor away from animism and teleology and toward more "colorless" principles of organization? Samuelson addresses this issue directly in his Nobel lecture, because he realizes that his fondness for constrained extremum problems has its precursors in physics in Fermat's "Principle of Least Time," Maupertuis' "Principles of Least Action," and Gauss' "Principle of Least Constraint." All of these physicists believed that the ability to cast problems in a constrained maximization framework was evidence that the laws of nature were the working out of a teleological (and usually Divine) purpose. Samuelson calls this the Pathetic Fallacy; all he wants to suggest is that "Often the economist is able to get a better, more economical, description of economic behavior from [the maximum principle]."[30] As is true of all of Samuelson's other dicta concerning the role of mathematics in economics, "better" and "more economical" are never defined, nor is a clear example ever proferred of the maximum principle performing this function. In fact, in this chapter we have suggested some ways in which imposing a maximum principle is "worse" or "less economical" from a certain point of view, since it entails ignoring the potentially relevant economic phenomena of realization crises and regretted purchases. Why, then, is Samuelson so very fond of maximization algorithms?

It is not clear, we would suggest, that Samuelson has completely escaped his Pathetic Fallacy. Elsewhere in this lecture, he remarks that maximization is not only a convenient procedure for the manipulation of mathematical symbols, but that it is *also* a presumed characteristic of the actors in the economic drama.[31] To restate this observation: constrained maximi.•.tion is an effective methodology because it corresponds to an actual property of social phenomena. And, in turn, if that is the case, then in the presence of a suitably constituted market, and in the absence of governmental or other constraints, there is a 'natural' order in which things can work out "for the best."

This is nothing other than the recurrence of animistic teleology which Veblen had criticized as the "standpoint of ceremonial adequacy." Quoting Veblen:

> The ultimate laws and principles which they formulated were laws of the normal or the natural, according to a preconception regarding the ends to which, in the nature of things, all things tend. In effect, this preconception imputes to things a tendency to work out what the instructed common sense of the time accepts as the adequate or worthy end of human effort. It is a projection of the accepted idea of conduct.[32]

Ultimately, the only reason for praising the maximum principles in economics is the belief on the part of the theorist that the players *should* and *do* maximize some quantum which they deem as their ultimate goal in life. This conception endows the human drama with a scope and purpose which it has not had since the intelligensia broke away from the theological institutions which earlier had performed that function.

Unfortunately, as with all other teleological conceptions of the world, it is only a case of the theorist reasoning in a circle.[33] The theorist *manufactures* a conservation principle, *imposes* a constrained maximization algorithm, *correlates* the deduced result with empirical data, and then feels assured that social life has purpose and direction (i.e., the market acts to maximize wellbeing). The rabbit, fresh from being thrust into the hat, reappears, dazed but compliant.

Notes

1. Georgescu-Roegen (1971 and 1976). Compare also Herman Daly (1980, 469–88).

2. Frank Knight (1965, xxv).

3. Samuelson (1965, 36 and 21n).

4. Clower (1970, 285).

5. See, for example, J. D. Bernal (1970, 43).

6. For the other questions, see ch. 7, below.

7. This essay refrains from explicit consideration of the work of Nicholas Georgescu-Roegen on thermodynamics and economics, mainly because he is concerned with the ramifications of the second law of thermodynamics, whereas we are restricting our attention to the first law.

8. Thorstein Veblen, *The Place of Science* (1969, 52).

9. Ibid., 281.

10. Ibid., 139.

11. Ibid., 160–61.

12. Ibid., 197.

13. The implications of this statement are developed in David Levine (1977). Even from these brief statements, it becomes apparent that Veblen's critique of neoclassical utility theory was much more rich and complex than a simple assertion that "people do not really maximize," as is suggested in Alexander Rosenberg (1979, 513).

14. Veblen (1969 repr, 103).

15. See, for example, D. S. L. Cardwell (1971) and Thomas Kuhn, "Energy Conservation as an Example of Simultaneous Discovery" in *Critical Problems in the History of Science* (Madison: University of Wisconsin Press, 1959), 330–33.

16. Paul Samuelson (1972, 249–62).

17. Samuelson (1952, 56–66).

18. See, for example, Samuelson (1965, 21): "In cases where the equilibrium values of our variables can be regarded as the solutions of the extremum problem it is often possible regardless of the number of variables involved to determine unambiguously the qualitative behavior of our solution values in respect to changes in parameters. [FN.] It may be pointed out that this is essentially the method of thermodynamics, which can be regarded as a purely deductive science based upon certain postulates (notably the First and Second Laws of Thermodynamics)."

19. For the actual procedure, see Samuelson (1965, 21–46) or any neoclassical textbook, such as that by Henderson and Quandt.

20. Samuelson (1972, 255) dubs this result the "Le Chetalier-Samuelson Principle."

21. See Herbert Simon (1979, 493–513); G. L. S. Shackle (1973); and Richard Nelson and Sidney Winter (1982).

22. This is the stated problem of the "microfoundations" literature. Compare E. R. Weintraub (1979) and F. Hahn (1980, 123–38).

23. "The subjective theory of value has continued to rest on a very slender pediment: so slender that Marshall hid it in a footnote. . . . This premise consists in the identification of 'desire' with 'satisfaction.' As Marshall said: 'We fall back on the measurement which economics supplies of the motive, or moving force to action, and we make it serve with all its faults, both for the desires which prompt activity and for the satisfactions that result from them' " (Maurice Dobb, 1937, 27–28).

24. A potential retort might be that the development of expected utility theory has effectively obviated this criticism. For the background to this theoretical development, see Paul Shoemaker (1982, 529–63). I think this objection misunderstands the present concept of "regrets"; but that is an argument best saved for a separate treatment. Likewise, the objection that modern neoclassical theory uses topology rather than functional analysis requires separate consideration.

25. This list seems to exhaust the objections disposed of in Laurence Boland (1981, 1031–36).

26. See, for example, Martin Sussman (1972, ch.2).

27. See Rosenberg (1979).

28. Samuelson (1972, 254).

29. See Emile Meyerson (1962, 178 et seq.); E. N. Hiebert (1962); and Georgescu-Roegen (1971, 318–19). See also Ken Dennis (1982, 691–712).

30. Samuelson (1972, 251).

31. Ibid., 258n.

32. Veblen (1969, 65).

33. See A. D'Abro (1951, vol. 1, 264).

7

The Philosophical Foundations of Institutionalist Economics

I

The precise nature of the relationship between the disciplines of economics and philosophy has yet to be explicated in detail. The fact that there exist certain family resemblances can be verified, and traced to a common lineage. Many of the precursors of western economic theory such as John Locke and Adam Smith were self-identified moral philosophers; many other inhabitants of the pantheon of economic theory such as Karl Marx and John Maynard Keynes are recognized as having made substantial contributions to philosophy. Nevertheless, in the modern era ontogeny does not recapitulate phylogeny, and the average economist in the late twentieth century would deny any close links between the two fields.

In economics, the facade of the repudiation of philosophical preconceptions is supported by the widespread conviction that modern economics has success-fully adopted the character and attributes of a *science*. This invocation of science is intended to settle all arguments once and for all and to expiate all sins. Of course, this has been a vain hope. Disputes over method, epistemology, and ontology have not been banished, because an invocation of science merely impounds controversy under the rubric of "the philosophy of science," without really answering any of the hard questions. Once we can get beyond the lab coats and the particle accelerators and the rest of the clanking machinery, it is not at all clear that "science" is inextricably committed to any particular program or method or ontological construction. Indeed, once we get beyond the homiletic nostrums of Physics I, some exposure to the history of science demonstrates that there is no such thing as a single "scientific method." Science may be realist or it may be idealist; it may be rationalist or it may be empiricist; it may be monistic or it may be dualistic; it may be naturalist or operationalist or it may be instrumentalist; or, most bluntly, it may be true or it may be false. Nothing is substantially illuminated by the mere invocation of science by economists, although it has in the past proved useful in cowing certain critics.

A survey of the philosophical presuppositions of modern economics is made doubly difficult by the necessity of confronting the role of "science" in both revealing and obscuring the main points of contention. Thorstein

Veblen, himself first trained as a philosopher, once began one of his articles with the deadpan sentence: "A discussion of the scientific point of view which avowedly proceeds from this point of view itself has necessarily the appearance of an argument in a circle; and such in great part is the character of what here follows" (Veblen 1969, 32). Veblen's predicament is particularly poignant for the issues at hand, because he was philosophically literate, he was the acknowledged progenitor of the Institutionalist school of economics, and he chose to raise the issue of the philosophical preconceptions of the economics of his day by attacking its credentials as a science. Ever since that time, the Institutionalist school has been distinguished from the general run of orthodoxy by a concern with the philosophical aspects of economic issues, especially in its role of a critic of neoclassical economics; however, it has not found a way to break out of Veblen's ironic circle. The problem, as we shall argue in this chapter, is a failure of comprehension of the fact that institutionalist economics was the offspring of a philosophical tradition entirely distinct from that which gave rise to neoclassical economics. These two traditions have a profound conflict over their respective images of a "science," and therefore profoundly incompatible images of "economic man" and "rationality."

II

The first urgent issue in the philosophy of economics is the question of the intelligibility of a separate discipline devoted exclusively to the explication of an abstract concept called "the economy," separate from other categories of social phenomena, and separate from the relationships we attribute to the physical or nonhuman world. This is not a new question, but one that has been broached throughout the history of economics. The debate over this issue was markedly heated around the turn of the century, with the Austrians and the German historical school disputing the possibility of the unity of the *Geisteswissenschaften* and the *Naturwissenschaften*. Those impatient with philosophical discussions have since cited the "Methodenstreit" as a prime example of the futility of methodological discourse; but such expressions of petulance do obscure the fact that most modern economists have no conception of the bounds that demarcate their discipline. There is the flippant imperialist response, that "economics is what economists do," but that response misses the whole point of raising the question. Without some notion of what makes a discipline coherent, questions concerning the efficacy of methods of inquiry flounder aimlessly without a point of reference.

In the case of economics, the issue of the relationship of the "economy" to other potential objects of inquiry already appropriated by other disciplines— say, the "mind" of an actor, or the "technology" of a society—has been a persistent sore point for economists. The threat has always existed that an external intellectual discipline will contradict or falsify some crucial tenet of the abstraction designated by "the economy"; or, conversely, that the external discipline will co-opt and absorb economics by reducing the economy to its own elemental abstractions. An example of the former was Karl Polyani's attempt to redefine the meaning of the "economy" from the vantage point of the anthropologist and economic historian (Polanyi 1968); an example of the latter would be the reduction of economic behavior to psychology, and subsequently to biochemistry. It is a fact of life that all schools of economics must be buffeted and jostled by psychology, sociology, anthropology, biochemistry, genetics, physics, and mathematics, and that they must constitute their object of inquiry as justifiably separate, despite the insistent fact of life that experience is a seamless web. The immediate implication of this thesis is that the object of inquiry cannot be simply or easily disentangled from the method of inquiry, and that both cannot be dictated by some inert and independent subject matter. One plausible role for philosophy is to analyze the forces that jointly shape the theoretical object and the method of inquiry.

The second fundamental issue in the philosophy of economics is one that does not trouble the physical scientist. It has often been observed that, when addressed, people generally talk back, but atoms are silent. The economist confronts the thorny problem that he or she is imbedded inextricably in any social process under investigation; and further, the actors involved are free to disagree with the conclusions of the economist, challenging theories as well as interpretations of the events that are imputed to them. While Nature might be portrayed as recalcitrant, it has never revolted; but people have done so. Attempts to confront this issue often surface as statements about presence or absence of controlled experiments, or mastery of the phenomenon, or the putative success of the science in question. It is no accident that modern Western thought first personified "Nature" and then claimed that science had dominated or subjected "her." Philosophy also has an important function in unpacking this presupposition of the equation of scientific success with control, and showing how it shapes inquiry.

These are the fundamental issues which any coherent discipline of economic theory must address: it must carve up reality, and have some claim to have carved artfully "at the joints"; it must have some resources to adjudicate boundary disputes with other disciplines, which requires a clear conception of its own theoretical object; it must nurture some epistemological conception of the economic actor and the economist, and presumably reconcile them one with the other; and it must build bridges to the conceptions of power and efficacy within the context of the culture in which it is to subsist. Although it is not inevitable, in the past these requirements have been satisfied to a greater or lesser degree by positing a curious symmetry between the portrait of the economic scientist and the theoretical portrait of "rational economic man" in the particular school of economic thought. This symmetry exists on many levels, both formal and informal. It is the thesis of this chapter that once the pattern of this symmetry is understood, then the philosophical distinctions that divide and demarcate institutionalist economic theory from neoclassical economic theory become transparent; and further, one can go quite a distance in explaining the evolution of institutionalist thought in the twentieth century.

The Durkheim–Mauss–Douglas Thesis

To organize the various themes in the philosophy of economics, and to explain our symmetry thesis, we shall have recourse to a very important generalization about human behavior that was generated not in economics, but in anthropology. In 1903 the anthropologists Emile Durkheim and Marcel Mauss proposed an hypothesis that has become one for the core research programs in the sociology of knowledge. They asserted that, in all primitive culture, the classification of things reproduces the classifications of men (Durkheim and Mauss 1963). Although the Durkheim–Mauss thesis was intended only to apply to primitive societies, and the original empirical ethnographic evidence which they offered in its support was widely challenged and criticized, the thesis has been taken up and revised by the Edinburgh school of the sociology of science and applied to the history of *Western* science (Bloor 1982; Barnes and Shapin 1979). Recently the anthropologist Mary Douglas has further elaborated the hypothesis by asserting its antithesis: the social classification of men is often a mirror image of a culture's classifications of the natural world. To quote her own words:

> the logical patterning in which social relations are ordered affords a bias in the classification of nature, and that in this bias is to be found the confident intuition of self-evident truth. And here, in this intuition, is the most hidden and most inaccessible implicit assumption on which all other knowledge is grounded. It is the ulti-

Figure 7.1. The "Vortex Model" of the Sociology of Science: The DMD Thesis.

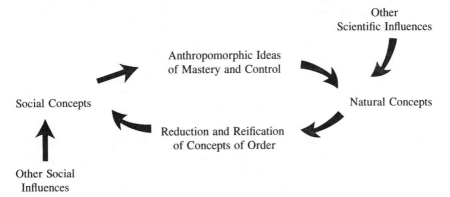

mate instrument of domination, protected from inspection by every warm emotion that commits the knower to the social system in which his knowledge is guaranteed. Only one who feels cooly towards that society can question its self-evident proposition. [Douglas 1975, 209]

For purposes of brevity, we can summarize the complete Durkheim–Mauss–Douglas (DMD) thesis in the format of the "vortex model of the sociology of science" in figure 7.1. Societies differ tremendously in their sources of inspiration and sources of validation of their social and natural concepts, but they resemble one another quite dramatically in the way in which social and natural concepts are interlinked and the manner in which belief in one reinforces belief in the other. Theories of the physical world are shaped by the social relations within the culture that generates them, and these are used in turn to express in reified format the essence of that culture's ideal of order. This ideal of order consequently molds the expression of social concepts and classifications, eventually transforming the original notions of mastery and control in the social sphere. The circuit is completed by the persistent projection of anthropomorphic concepts onto "Nature," and the intended demonstration of the efficacy and legitimacy of structures in the social sphere through its purported success in the mastery of personified nature.

While this "vortex model" is a veritable cornucopia of suggestions for the analysis of social life, the history of science, and various controversies in epistemology, its effectiveness in helping to understand the preconceptions of institutional economics is what concerns us here. Divergent assumptions about the relationship of social concepts to natural concepts, and the relationship of the possibility of mastery and control to the reified concept of order are the fundamental distinguishing hallmarks of institutional and neoclassical economic theory. The controversies around the turn of the century concerning the vexed issue of the unity or duality of the *Geisteswissenschaften* and the *Naturwissenschaften* were implicitly about the relative legitimacy of two views of science and, by implication, two views of economics. Those economists were at loggerheads over two distinct versions of the DMD "vortex," even though the various disputes were not argued out in those terms.

The discipline of economics in the Western world has always been caught in the thrall of the contemporaneous Western understanding of the physical world, particularly with respect to the concept of value.[1] It has been an even more recent phenomenon (say, since the early nineteenth century) that the idealized image of the method of natural science has played the predominant role in shaping the image of the economic actor in economic theory. At this juncture however, the cultural diversity of various Western societies has come into play: because there have been multiple variations on the theme of the correct scientific method, there have been equally numerous corresponding images of the "economy" and the economic actor. Economic praxeology may recapitulate epistemology, but it can do so only within a specific cultural setting. Schools of economic thought may subsequently interpenetrate and cross-fertilize, but their initial integrity and specificity are due to their origins in a particular construct of our knowledge of the world and hence of ourselves and other actors.

Rather than discuss the interplay suggested by the DMD thesis of the reigning scientific epistemology and the ontology of the economic actor at a terrifically rarified level, it will be more efficient to demonstrate the thesis through the display of two relevant examples: that of Cartesian analytic philosophy and neoclassical economic theory; and the American variant of the continental hermeneutic tradition in philosophy and institutionalist economics.

The Cartesian Tradition and Neoclassical Economic Theory

The Cartesian tradition in philosophy has made its appearance in the British and American contexts as a penchant for "analytical philosophy," especially in the twentieth century. Although many of the modern tenets are not intended to be faithful representations of Descartes's original concerns, the "Cartesian tradition" does serve as a shorthand for a certain sequence of canonical texts and attitudes (Rorty, Schneewind and Skinner 1984). We shall characterize (yet hopefully not caricature) this tradition by the following seven tenets (see Tiles 1984; Bernstein 1983):

1. Analytical Cartesian philosophy is not overly concerned with the thought processes of the individual scientist, nor indeed, any group of scientists. Above all, it demands that science is mechanical and impersonal, and quarantines the context of discovery from the context of justification.
2. The process of inquiry is divided into "deduction" and "induction." Philosophy analyzes the former as a discrete set of logical statements, with concepts investigated only via their functions in isolated statements. Philosophy is relatively helpless in analyzing induction, because there is no guaranteed logic of induction.
3. "Logic" is interpreted to mean mathematical axiomatization.
4. There is an unbridgeable gulf between the philosophy of science and the history of science. The best one can do is construct a post hoc "rational reconstruction" of what is, at best, a mess. Science reconstitutes itself perennially and therefore has no real need of history.
5. The role of philosophy is to prescribe and defend the right rules of scientific method. The *summum bonum* would be an automaton to which all disputes would be submitted and that would guarantee the validity of scientific work.
6. The separation of mind and body dictates that we know our own thought better than we can know the world. Hence all verification is the assuagement of personal doubt. This comes about by means of repeated personal contact with a stable external world, independent of any mediation by others as well as independent of the signs used to express such knowledge.

7. Knowledge, once attained, is passed along intact to other researchers. Knowledge is cumulative, the accretion of past individual researches.

One important corollary of the DMD thesis would be that the social theories that were prevalent in the culture dominated by the portrait of science consisting of the above seven points would project that image onto their understanding of their own social relations. If we cast our gaze upon the orthodox economics of Britain and America in the twentieth century, we indeed discover that the neoclassical portrait of the "rational economic man" conforms to the outline, very nearly point-by-point:

1. Neoclassical economics is not concerned with the actual thought processes of the individual economic actors. The actors are subject to an ideal of rationality that is mechanical and impersonal, in the dual senses that constrained optimization imitates the "behavior" of the inert mechanical world in physical theory, and that interpersonal influences and processes of interpretation are ruled out by assumption. One must separate the context of socialization from the context of choice.
2. Rational choice is divided up into rational choice rules and independently given endowments. Neoclassical economics takes as its primary subject the logic of the former and is relatively silent about the latter, because there is no logic of endowments that claims the allegience of neoclassicals in general.
3. "Logic" is interpreted to mean mathematical axiomatization.
4. There is an unbridgeable gulf between neoclassical economics and the history of any particular economy. The market is always presumed efficient, and therefore exhibits no hysteresis (see Chapter 12 below).
5. Neoclassical economics prescribes and defends the right rules of market organization. The *summum bonum* is an automatic mechanism that coordinates the economy and guarantees its legitimacy.
6. The mind–body separation dictates that we know our own thought better than we know the world. Hence economic theory must be cast in the format of self-sufficient individual mental valuations brought in contact with a stable external world of commodities, independent of any mediation or dependence upon signs.
7. Capital accumulation is treated as analogous to knowledge accumulation: an incremental aggregation of discrete units. Indeed, the former should be reduced to the latter, in the guise of an inexplicable "technological change."

Our purpose here is not to put the DMD thesis through all its paces; nor is it our intention to discuss neoclassical theory in the detail warranted seriously to illustrate the above parallels.[2] All we wish to suggest for the present purposes is that there exists a close correlation between the Cartesian epistemology and the structure of neoclassical economic theory: a familial resemblance that serves to fuse the natural world and the social world into a single coherent entity for the analytic Anglo-American mind. The social order of the economic world is reflected in the scientific order of the natural world: it hence comes as no surprise that Karl Popper has admitted that certain inspirations for his philosophy of science came from his particularly Western understanding of economics (Hands 1985).

If we accept this thesis as a given working hypothesis, the question of interest then becomes: How to account for the existence of heterodox schools of economic theory? Most germane to our present task, how can we understand the existence of the only school of economic thought indigenous to the United States, which is in many respects incommensurable with neoclassical economic theory—that is, institutionalist economics?

III

Pragmatism and Peirce

Prompted by the DMD thesis, our answer will be to search for its philosophical foundations elsewhere than in the Cartesian analytic tradition. The origins of this phenomenon must be traced back a century to the situation extant in philosophy and science in the America of the Gilded Age. In the late nineteenth-century United States, the predominant understanding of science was not that of the Cartesian tradition; indeed, as Rorty et al. (1984, 132) put it, "In the late nineteenth century American philosophical circles there were more Hegelians of various sorts than you could shake a stick at." The main influences upon the idea of science in the Gilded Age came not from Britain or France, but from the Germany of the research universities. The philosophy of science had not grown as separate and detached from the social theory as it had elsewhere, and this was manifest in the three great movements in German philosophy: the dialectical idealism of Hegel, the historicist hermeneutics of Dilthey, and a revival of neo-Kantianism. These traditions took root in the United States and by a very convoluted route, sprouted an indigenous school of philosophy in America called "Pragmatism." It is our thesis that this pragmatic conception of scientific endeavor and epistemology, which later induced a novel reinterpretation of the economy and the economic actor, were consolidated into an institutionalist school of economic theory in the first three decades of the twentieth century.

Bernstein (1966, 168) has written, "It is still a popular myth, even among philosophers, that positivism was a tough-minded variety of the more tender-minded and fuzzy pragmatism." Judging by the *Dictionary of the History of Science,* the myth is still popular, since that source defines "pragmatism" as "A variant of empiricism. . . foreshadowing both operationalism and the verifiability principle of logical positivism." These impressions are unfortunate, because they obscure the fact that it was the project of the pragmatists to provide a systematic alternative to the Cartesian analytical tradition, as well as to the naturalist doctrines characteristic of positivism. (We shall see that this confusion has subsequently spilled over into economic controversies, to the extent that, in some quarters, institutionalist economics is misperceived as a sort of naive empiricism.) The situation is further muddied by the fact that the founder of pragmatism, Charles Sanders Peirce, left no synoptic account of his philosophical system. In this respect, he resembles that other towering figure of twentieth-century philosophy, Ludwig Wittgenstein, in that he bequeathed to us only a disorganized sheaf of disconnected, epigrammatic, and oracular accounts of his mature philosophy, which had to await publication until after his death. Reading Peirce is no fun; and therefore, most who have a passing acquaintance with pragmatism base their knowledge on the more accessible but less reliable versions to be found in John Dewey or William James, or worse, simply upon their own understandings of the colloquial referents of "pragmatism."

It is frankly impossible to do justice to Peirce's writings in the space allotted in this essay; there is no reasonable substitute for reading his *Collected Papers* (henceforth referred to as CP) and the best of the commentaries upon them such as Apel (1981). Both because Peirce was the only pragmatist philosopher trained in mathematics and the physical sciences, and because it is our intention to connect Peirce (through the DMD thesis) to the institutionalist conception of the economic actor, this discussion shall focus largely on Peirce's philosophy of science.[3]

Because the Peircian corpus is so fragmented, it has been argued that certain of his texts, especially those concerned with induction, might be read as anticipatory of later neopositivist writings and some aspects of Popper (Rescher 1978, 52; Radnitzky 1973, xxv–xxvii). Contrary to these suggestions, a survey of Peirce's entire work reveals that he was openly hostile to the Cartesian analytical tradition, and is better understood as a sophisticated advocate of a hermeneutics of science and a semiotics of scientific practice. In highlighting Peirce's concern with the social aspects of science we follow the lead of numerous modern commentators (Commons 1934, 102; Dyer 1986; Apel 1981; Bernstein 1983; Rorty 1979) who have seen in Peirce a third alternative to the conventional rationalist–empiricist dichotomies.

The mainstream tradition of the philosophy of science in the twentieth century has found itself driven from pillar to post, searching for the appropriate entity in which to ground the certainty of scientific knowledge. Early analytic philosophy began by touting the single linguistic term as the primary epistemic unit, but was fairly rapidly forced to retreat to the entire sentence or proposition as the lowest common denominator of scientific intelligibility. Complaints about the incoherence of an independent object language and the consequences of scientific tests dictated a further retreat to an entire conceptual scheme as the appropriate epistemic unit, but then careful historical critiques combined with skepticism about the notion of a self-contained theory have prompted some philosophers to insist that only a research tradition in all its complex historical development can do justice to the various forms of knowledge claims of a working scientist. One amazing aspect of this progressive erosion of logical atomism in the philosophy of science is that Peirce essentially anticipated its form and consequences a century ago. His definition of "science" seems particularly relevant after the breakdown of logical atomism:

> What is Science? We cannot define the word with the precision and concision with which we define *Circle,* or *Equation,* any more than we can so define *Money, Government, Stone, Life.* The idea, like these, and more than some of them, is too vastly complex and diversified. It embodies the epitome of man's intellectual development. . . a particular branch of science, such as Physical Chemistry or Mediterranean Archeology, is no mere word, manufactured by the arbitrary definition of some academic pedant, but a real object, being the very concrete life of a social group constituted by real facts of inter-relation. [CP vii, 37–39]

Peirce's insistence that "the very origin of the conception of reality shows that this conception essentially involves the notion of a *community*" (CP v, 186) is founded on the thesis that scientific research is irreducibly hermeneutic, and therefore recourse to an independent law-abiding world or to some innate preconception of truth to account for the *process* of scientific inquiry is useless. Because the word "hermeneutics" is bandied about in a careless manner these days by literary critics, it might prove prudent to provide a brief working definition for the present audience.

Hermeneutics is the theory of the process of interpretation, be it of a text, a doctrine, or a phenomenon, by a self-identified community of inquiry. This theory concentrates on the role of shared tradition as the locus of continuity and quality control in the interpretative process; it therefore follows that the discipline of history is an indispensable accessory of hermeneutics. It freely admits that rival interpretative communities may harbor incommensurable readings of some text or phenomenon; but it also recognizes that there will be pressure to attempt comparisons as long as the communities are rivals, and that posterity may decide that traditions were eventually rendered commensurable. Hermeneutics reinstates the importance of diversity in the process of understanding, to the extent of advocating the examination of alien or pariah traditions in the course of interpretation. Hermeneutics is also concerned to acknowledge the anthropomorphic element in human knowledge, viewing it as a fruitful and necessary aspect rather than an embarrassing and regrettable anachronism (CP v, 35fn). Finally, hermeneutics is generally hostile to the Cartesian tradition of analytic philosophy, especially the presumption of the mind-body dichotomy and the program of mechanical reduction (CP vi, 15–16). Peirce was himself particularly scathing about the plausibility of the Cartesian program of radical self-doubt, which he termed a sham, merely formal, and incapable of altering any seriously held belief (Scheffler 1974, 20; Apel 1981, 62–63).

It is important to understand that Peirce's brand of hermeneutics underwent revision and transformation over the course of his life, in part as a reaction to versions promulgated by William James and John Dewey. His disaffection with their readings and embellishments provoked him in 1905 to insist that he was not at all one of these "Pragmatists," but rather a "Pragmaticist," a label so contrivedly ugly that no one would be tempted to "kidnap" it (Apel 1981, 82). Some of the fault for such a repudiation can be laid at Peirce's own door, if only because his early statements, and in particular his "pragmatic maxim," were phrased in such a way as to foster the impression of a transparent and banal common-sense philosophy of science. The pragmatic maxim of 1878 was stated: "Consider what effects, that might conceivably have practical bearings, we conceive the object of our conception to have. Then, our conception of these effects is the whole of our conception of the object" (CP v, 1).

William James read the pragmatic maxim as equating those "practical implications" with the psychological responses of the user of the concept, and therefore misrepresented pragmatism as a species of individual psychological behavioralism, thus entirely neutralizing the hermeneutic aspects of the community of inquiry. John Dewey read the maxim as dictating that there was no such thing as an end or goal of inquiry, a position that Peirce explicitly repudiated (Apel 1981, 88). Others, less sophisticated, read the maxim as a celebration of a particularly American stereotype of a hard-nosed, no-nonsense man of action, heedless of hesitation or tergiversation over fine points of reasoning. It must be admitted that some of Peirce's early writings seemed to encourage a crude know-nothingism: "pragmatism is generally practiced by successful men" (CP v, 21), or "Each of us is an insurance company" (CP v, 220). Nevertheless, in the face of attempts to portray pragmatism as a kind of crypto-capitalism in the sphere of science, Peirce went out of his way to insist that, "the meaning of [pragmatism] does not lie in individual reactions at all."

Peirce divided the process of scientific inquiry into the three categories of deduction, induction, and what he termed "abduction." He had very little of any substance to say about deduction, although he did point out that no actual novelty, and therefore no progress, could be attained by deduction *mutatis mutandis* (CP vii, 47). Induction plays a much more substantial role in his system, and here Peirce brought his extensive experience as an experimentalist into play in his discussions of empirical research. One important stabilizing influence on Peirce's community of inquiry was his postulate that *quantitative* induction was automatically self-correcting, albeit in the longest of runs (CP vi, 80; Rescher 1978).[4] Nothing in these writings, however, gave any aid or comfort to naive empiricism. Peirce commented upon the limited role that experiment occupied in the rise of modern mechanics (CP vi, 13). He observed that an hypothesis should not be abandoned immediately when contravened by empirical results, and that all good theories are always surrounded by a field of contradictory facts (CP vii, 54 and 60). In these respects he appears to share contemporary concerns with the problem of the underdetermination of theory acceptance by the "facts," and the Duhem–Quine thesis, which states that no hypothesis is definitively falsified, because it can always be immunized to adverse tests by some adjustment in the ever-present auxiliary hypotheses that accompany it (Harding 1976). Most significant, Peirce stated that induction and deduction, either jointly or severally, could not account for the progress of scientific inquiry. That effectivity was reserved for the third mode, abduction.

Peirce described abduction as "the process of forming an explanatory hypothesis. It is the only logical operation which introduces any new idea; for induction does nothing but determine a value, and deduction merely evolves the necessary consequences of a pure hypothesis" (CP v, 106). Of the three modalities of method, abduction explicitly assumes a hermeneutic demeanor, because it is responsible for creativity and innovation, which is an historical process made manifest in language and social behavior, subject to the self-discipline of a normative logic. This is why "the question of pragmatism . . . is nothing else than the question of the logic of abduction" (CP v, 121).

To discuss abduction Peirce often employed the language of "instincts" or evolutionary talents, and these metaphors were often carried over into the works of Dewey, Veblen, and others influenced by pragmatism; however, one must note that the more racialist connotations, not Peirce's more subtle concept, tended to predominate in later works. Peirce's equation of abduction with instinct and meaning with habit (Apel 1981, 71) probably strikes the modern reader as odd, but Peirce's unrelenting hostility to mechanical reductionism should signal that these passages are not to be read as anticipations of sociobiology. Instead, they seem to posit the existence of a naive common-sense metaphysics that provided physics with its early fundamental hypotheses about natural law. Given Peirce's further thesis that natural laws themselves evolve (CP vi, 84), it follows that he would likewise expect the sources of inspiration for scientific hypotheses also to evolve. Peirce expressly asserted that *physical* laws evolve over time because laws of homogeneity could be discerned only against the backdrop of stochastic phenomena, from which they would be emergent. One can only marvel at his prescience in this respect, since it was not until well after his lines were written that physicists began to plumb their significance in quantum mechanics, cosmology, and else-where.[5]

No summary of Peirce's philosophy could be complete without some acknowledgment of his role as the founder of semiotics, the theory of the interpretations of signs and their interrelations. Peirce saw the sign relation as fundamentally triadic, a relation between the denotation of a word, the designated object, and the interpreter. The importance of this triad for Peirce lay in his conviction that previous philosophers had attempted to understand language by concentrating attention on only one or two aspects in isolation, a practice he claimed served to quarantine the hermeneutic aspects of human inquiry. An important corollary of the triad was that it is impossible to discern the rules of sign-mediated behavior by simple external observation; in other words, there is no such thing as the passive observation of rule structures. Not only did this anticipate the mature Wittgenstein's critique of rules and language games, but it also has profound relevance for the positivist attempt to explain rule structures by mechanistic models.

Finally, in a philosopher so concerned to explore the links between social processes and scientific inquiry, it should come as no surprize to discover that he also had a reasonable familiarity with the social theories of his day. It has not often been noted, however, that Peirce was hostile to orthodox economic doctrines, and became downright livid when it came to hedonism and utilitarian doctrines (CP vii, 43; CP v, 59–60). He wrote,

> Bentham may be a shallow logician; but such truths as he saw, he saw most nobly. As for the vulgar utilitarian, his fault does not lie in pressing too much the question of what should be the good of this or that. On the contrary, his fault is that he never presses the question half far enough, or rather he never really raises the question at all. He simply rests in his present desires as if desire were beyond all dialectic. [CP v, 98]

In a few essays, Peirce trained his sights on American political economy, accusing it of an "exaggeration of the beneficial effects of greed" (CP vi, 193), and complaining of a tendency to want their "mammon flavored with a soupçon of god" (CP vi, 194). These indictments were directed not only at the more vulgar apologists of political economy, but also at some of its more illustrious writers. (Peirce's sophistication in this respect might be illustrated by his correspondence with Simon Newcomb, which includes, among other interesting tidbits, an early discussion of the role of mathematics in the theory of supply and demand [Eisele 1957, 414].) The presuppositions of utilitarianism offended his hermeneutic view of science in a number of ways: it denied the role of tradition in human understanding; it blithely ignored the incommensurability of valuations; it gave short shrift to the dependence of behavior on community interaction and semantic processes; it was incompatible with the idea of evolutionary change, and with abduction; and it smacked of Cartesian mechanical reduction. Although Peirce was not concerned to sketch out an alternative political economy, in retrospect it would seem obvious that anyone deeply influenced by his thought would certainly be skeptical of the encroaching tradition of neoclassical economics.

The modernity of Peirce's package of concerns, or as he put it, his "architectonic," is striking. With some generosity of exegesis, one could credit him with the anticipation of the DMD thesis in certain respects, because he saw that one of the most fruitful sources of abduction in science was the transfer of metaphor from one sphere of inquiry to another.[6] Nevertheless, Peirce was definitely out of tune with his era of American culture. It is tragic that the theorist of the infinite community of science was himself expelled from that community in 1884, never to hold another academic position. He repaired to Milford, Pennsylvania, in 1887 to reside in almost total isolation, scribbling away at manuscripts that remained unread and unpublished during his lifetime. In part because of this exile, many learned about pragmatism either through William James or John Dewey.

John Dewey

Dewey was the conduit through which many of the precepts of pragmatism migrated over to American social theory in the early twentieth century. From a certain point of view this was unfortunate, because the quality of his thought was not often up to the standard of Peirce. Yet, he managed to achieve much greater renown than Peirce. Peirce himself once rebuked Dewey for a lack of logical subtlety, despite the fact that Dewey (along with Veblen) was one of the few illustrious students during his stint at Johns Hopkins (Apel 1981, 5). Richard Hofstadter was shrewdly on the mark when he wrote of Dewey: "His style is suggestive of the commanding of distant armies; one concludes that something portentious is going on at a remote and inaccessible distance, but one cannot determine just what it is" (Cahn 1977, 9). Even an enthusiastic supporter such as Richard Bernstein was forced to admit: "Imagination and insight must be explicated and modified in detailed analyses, and this is what Dewey failed to do for us. Insofar as philosophy requires the funding of fertile imagination with systematic elaboration, his philosophy fails" (Bernstein 1966, 171–72).

We shall not attempt a summary of Dewey's philosophical writings. Instead, we shall restrict our scope to the indication of a few ways Dewey altered the Peircian legacy as he popularized it. In effect, Dewey extended some of the hermeneutic themes found in Peirce to explicit application in social theory, especially generalizing the concept of habit into the broader concept of social custom. Many have observed that Dewey equated pragmatism with social psychology (Apel 1981, 87); indeed, he seemed to approach philosophy as if it were a branch of a more encompassing instrumentalist social science.

Unfortunately, Dewey was quite innocent of any familiarity with any actual science, or the history of science, or mathematical logic; therefore, in retrospect, his numerous appeals to the scientific method appear awkward, strained, and pedantic. His favored sources of inspiration were Hegel and Greek philosophy. The path of his intellectual evolution can be traced from the psychologistic idealism of his early career to a vague and politicized pragmatism toward the end of his life.

Dewey's crusade was to argue against the idea of truth as accuracy of representation, which took the form in his later life of an insistence that reality could not exist prior to and independent of the process of inquiry (Dewey

1939, 308). The idea of "warranted assertability" was as close as he ever got to Peirce's richer notion of the complex interaction of the interpretative community and the object of inquiry; in Dewey, this assumed the rather more prosaic cast of a comparison of scientific inquiry with a jury trial (ibid., 898–900). Dewey followed Peirce in his skepticism concerning the Cartesian analytic tradition, but as was his inclination, he tended to reinterpret philosophical problems as amenable to reduction to problems in psychology: "the older dualism of body and soul finds a distinct echo in the current dualism of stimulus and response" (Dewey 1931, 233). Dewey also imitated Peirce in viewing human inquiry as an evolutionary process, but diluted his legacy by reducing the sweeping portrayal of the evolution of natural law itself to the diminished banality that "tool and material are adapted to each other in the process of reaching a valid conclusion" (Dewey 1939, 929).

Whatever one's opinion about the poverty of Dewey's conception of science, it is demonstrably true that his work in social theory found a sympathetic audience in an America that had previously associated evolutionary theory either with atheism or with social Darwinism. Although it had remained a familiar idea in the Continental tradition of philosophy, it was a jolt to find an American arguing that

> History is the record of the development of freedom through the development of institutions.... Here we have instead an anticipatory criticism and challenge of the classical liberal notion of freedom, a deliberate reflective and reactionary one. Freedom is a growth, an attainment, not an original possession, and it is attained by the idealization of institutions and law. [Dewey 1931, 285)

As a consequence, Dewey also maintained Peirce's hostility to utilitarianism, although his objections appeared to spring primarily from an aversion to the idea of given and immutable tastes:

> Not even the most devoted adherents of the notion that enjoyment and value are equivalent facts would venture to assent that because we once liked a thing we should go on liking it.... Desire and purpose, and hence action are left without guidance, although the question of the regulation of their formation is the supreme problem of practical life. Values (to sum up) may be connected inherently with liking, and not yet with *every* liking but only with those that judgment has approved. [Dewey 1939,786]

As a champion of the importance of the process of change over static notions of optimality, Dewey became associated with groups opposed to economic laissez-faire notions; he was a vocal advocate of the position that classical liberalism had avoided all the hard questions of coordination and the definition of order by surreptitiously postulating that each citizen came naturally equipped with an innate complement of rights, desires and powers that were sufficient to do the job (Dewey 1931, 281). It is relevant to later developments in economics that he saw this flawed predisposition as part and parcel of the larger Western predisposition to yearn for natural laws (Dewey 1939, 745). As he put it, "the existing limitations of 'social science' are due mainly to unreasoning devotion to the physical sciences as a model, and to a misconception of physical science at that" (ibid., 949). Unfortunately, here Dewey became tangled in his own lack of system, for not only was he incapable of describing the actual activities of the physical sciences, but he was also bereft of any coherent vision of social order. This led him in later life to compound these weaknesses by proposing the non sequitur that the natural sciences would themselves provide the progressive ideals of social order (ibid., 791). Democracy was said to be a pronounced improvement over previous modes of political organization because it deployed the same techniques as science to mediate freedom and authority (ibid., 358–60). All social problems would be thus purportedly solved (or dissolved?) by the scientific method, because democracy was the analog of the scientific method in the political arena.

The Pragmatic Tradition and Institutionalist Economic Theory

We now return to the DMD thesis to ask whether the alternative philosophical program of pragmatism did provide an alternative template for rational economic man. As we did for the Cartesian tradition, we can generate a brief bill of particulars that characterize the Pragmatic philosophy of science:

1. Science is primarily a process of inquiry by a self-identified community, and not a mechanical legitimation procedure of some preexistent goal or end-state. Science has conformed to no set of a-historical decision rules, and for this reason history and science are inseparable.
2. Possible methods of inquiry consist of deduction, induction, and abduction. No one method is self-sufficient without the other two as complements. Abduction is the explicit source of novelty, whereas induction and deduction provide the checks and balances.
3. There is no single logic, but rather a logic of abduction, a logic of deduction, and a logic of induction.
4. Because there are no foolproof impersonal rules of scientific method, decisions concerning the validity of scientific statements reside with the community of inquiry. The community of inquiry is the basic epistemological unit.
5. Without a strict mind-body duality, science has an irreducible anthropomorphic character. Natural laws themselves evolve, as do the members of the community of inquiry. Social and natural concepts interpenetrate; therefore hermeneutic techniques are a necessary component of scientific inquiry, on the same epistemic level as mathematical techniques.
6. The study of semiotics and the interrelation of signs constitutes an integral part of the philosophy of science.
7. Because pragmatism must ultimately depend upon the community of inquiry, it often wavers between a defense of the status quo and an advocacy of a technocratic utopia.

Just as with our previous experience with the connection between the Cartesian tradition and neoclassical economic theory, here too the conception of the rational economic actor in institutionalist economics can be read off the pragmatic program. In our drawing of parallels, we shall concentrate upon the first generation of institutionalist economics, from roughly Thorstein Veblen to John R. Commons. Proceeding point-by-point:

1. The economy is primarily a process of learning, negotiation and coordination, and not a ratification of some preexistent goals or end-state. Economic rationality is socially and culturally determined, and therefore history, anthropology, and economics are different perspectives upon the same inquiry.

2. Economic actors are defined by their habits, customs, and "instincts," the physical or material relations that impinge upon them, and the expedients developed in order to adapt one to the other. This portrayal seeks to find a middle way between "nature" and "nurture."

3. There is no unique logic of choice. "Passion and enjoyment of goods passes insensibly and inevitably into appraisal.... Enjoyment ceases to be a datum and becomes a problem. As a problem, it implies intelligent inquiry into the conditions and consequences of the value-object; that is, criticism" (Dewey 1939, 260–61).

4. Because there exist no innate rules of rational economic behavior, the only gauge of the validity of such behavior resides in the particular economic community. Laws are made by people, not nature. The appropriate epistemological unit is the institution. Institutions are transpersonal rules that endow individual economic actors with the ability to cope with interpretation of action and with change.

5. Acceptance of the thesis that science embodies anthropomorphic concepts prompts the social theorist to incorporate hermeneutics or a sociology of knowledge approach when comparing certain incommensurable interpretations of the behavior of economic actors. Diversity of interpretations is as important for the viability of social structures as are simpler economic indicies such as profit or growth.

6. Because rule structures cannot be comprehended by external detached observation, economists must self-consciously engage in participant observation. Economics is based upon a theory of the semiotics of trade, production and consumption, which serves to explain how actors interpret the significance of transactions. (Examples are Veblen's "conspicuous consumption" and Commons's typology of transactions.)

7. Institutional economics has displayed a certain vulnerability to a technocratic conception of the economist.

These seven points do not capture the whole of institutionalist theory, but they do give some indication of the divergence of the conception of economic rationality from that characteristic of neoclassical theory. As previously noted, the first generation of institutionalists generally derived their pragmatism from William James and John Dewey and other sources more accessible than Peirce. This path of influence made a mark on their writings; among other more subtle effects, it induced an image of science that was excessively vague. This weakness, especially in Veblen, resulted in a vulnerability to neoclassical complaints that their appeals to science were less legitimate than those of the neoclassicals. Somewhat later John Commons made more explicit reference to Peirce's philosophy of science, and consequently built upon a more robust philosophical foundation. Nevertheless, Commons's *Institutional Economics* signals the end of the first phase of the development of institutionalist economic theory. This watershed was due not so much to the merits or demerits of Commons's work as it was to the rapid decline of the pragmatist philosophy of science in the United States and its supercession by a Cartesian logical positivism.

Thorstein Veblen

It has been observed that Veblen owed a number of debts to the pragmatist tradition (Dyer 1986). What has not been noticed is that Veblen's conception of science and economic rationality owes more to Dewey and James than to Peirce, with its stress that science is a process which has no goal or end. In his famous essay *The Place of Science in Modern Civilization,* Veblen wrote:

> Modern science is becoming substantially a theory of the process of cumulative change, which is taken as a sequence of cumulative change, realized to be self-continuing or self-propagating and to have no final term.... Modern science is ceasing to occupy itself with natural laws—the codified rules of the game of causation—and is concerning itself wholly with what has taken place and what is taking place.... A scientific point of view is a consensus of habits of thought current in the community. [Veblen 1969, 37–38]

Unfortunately, Veblen confused pragmatism with "maxims of expedient conduct" (ibid., 19) and a "Metaphysical postulate of efficiency" (Veblen 1914, 331fn), and consequently idealized the scientist as being in possession of a "matter-of-fact" approach to "the facts" and their evaluation. Ultimately, this led to an extremely naive sociology of science, where a class of industrial workers and engineers nurtured a set of colorless and nonteleological habits of thought as a result of their proximity to the "machine process" (Veblen 1969, 30; 1921; 1923, 254–55).

The fatal flaw in Veblen's portrayal of science was his desire to apotheosize it as the opposite pole to his otherwise withering skepticism; it was to be the one ideal not besmirched by the common self-delusion of social categories. In many ways, because he thoroughly misunderstood Peirce's hermeneutics, he instead opted for a unilineal historical materialism not unlike that of Marx:

The technology of physics and chemistry is not derived from established law and custom, and it goes on its way with as nearly a complete disregard of the spiritual truths of law and custom as the circumstances will permit. The reality with which technicians are occupied are [sic] of another order of actuality, lying altogether within the three dimensions of the material universe, and running altogether on the logic of material fact. [Veblen 1923, 263]

Veblen believed he could break out of the "logical circle" cited above in section I by resort to this lofty and otherworldly conception of science, and then using it to claim that he himself was merely applying the "mater-of-fact" attitudes to the economic sphere. Instead of Peirce's community of inquirers, scientists were for Veblen almost automatons, mere individual reflections of materialist theories. In another similarity to Marx, Veblen also wished to argue that there was a certain inevitability to the whole process: the matter-of-fact efficiency characteristic of the technician would necessarily clash with the anachronistic appeal to inefficiency propped up by the legitimation of natural law by the "captains of industry"; and Veblen intimated that the technicians would defeat the business interests in the long haul.

Although Veblen's writings are a fertile source of insights into economic theory, the Achilles heel of his system was his naive conception of science and the exalted place of the engineer. This epistemological weakness led to two further flaws: first, Veblen misunderstood that the neoclassical theory that he so adamantly opposed had a more legitimate claim to his brand of scientific legitimacy than he realized, his ignorance of physics leaving him blind to this possibility; and second, certain particular evolutionary or Peircian aspects of Veblen's thought stood in direct conflict with his overarching theme that science developed independently of cultural and social phenomena.

The first flaw can go some distance to explain the neglect of Veblen's profound critiques of neoclassical theory, particularly the theory of capital and the theory of production. Veblen clearly believed that natural law explanations were on the wane in physics, and that economics would follow suit. His neglect of the hermeneutical aspects of science prevented him from understanding how deeply rooted natural law explanations are in the Western cultural matrix, and how significant they were in the nineteenth-century science which he admired: in mechanics, in chemistry, and in energetics. In other words, Veblen had no inkling of the DMD thesis. Because of this, he could not comprehend the primal attraction of neoclassical theory, which was that it was a model appropriated lock, stock, and barrel from nineteenth-century physics. Veblen's assertions that he was a partisan of modern scientific methods appeared weak and unavailing in comparison with the practices of neoclassical economic theory. The engineers, with whom Veblen was so enamored, flooded into economics after his death and opted to work for the theoretical tradition they recognized as closest to their previous training: neoclassicism.

The second flaw in Veblen's epistemology was that he did not realize that some of the more intriguing aspects of his economic theory were in open conflict with his conception of science. In his early essay on Kant, he claimed that "the play of the faculties of the intellect is free, or but little hampered by the empirical elements in its knowledge" (1934, 181), and this predisposition was later used to satirize the foibles of his day and age. He was also very scathing when it came to others' adherence to a naive sense-data empiricism, as in his critique of the German historical school (Veblen 1969, 58). In his profound series of essays on the preconceptions of economic science, he observed:

> Since a strict uniformity is nowhere to be observed in the phenomena with which the investigator is occupied, it has to be found by a laborious interpretation of the phenomena and a diligent abstraction and allowance for disturbing circumstances, whatever may be the meaning of a disturbing circumstance where causal continuity is denied. In this work of interpretation and expurgation the investigator proceeds on a conviction of the orderliness of natural sequence. . . . The endeavor to avoid all metaphysical premises fails here as elsewhere. [ibid., 162]

This heightened awareness of the presumption of natural sequence was put to good use in Veblen's critique of the "obvious" proposition that the value of outputs must necessarily be equal to the value of inputs, for example.

Yet, acknowledging all this, Veblen still thought he could simultaneously indict neoclassical theory as unscientific because it had metaphysical presuppositions. Because he was reluctant to expose his own metaphysical presuppositions to scrutiny, he never evolved beyond the role of a wickedly entertaining but ultimately destructive critic.

A more consistent Peircian position would have been to admit that any economic theory would find itself forced to impose some metaphysics of uniformity and continuity upon the phenomena, but then to compare and contrast the structures imposed by neoclassical theory with those envisioned by an institutional economics. Had he hewn to such a program, many of his more perceptive comments might have fallen into place in a formidable system. For instance, neoclassicism is fundamentally based upon a putative equality between income and outgo, between costs and returns, between anticipation and realization, and between effort and reward. Veblen brought two perceptive criticisms to this imposition of uniformity: that the balancing terms were not strictly commensurable (Veblen 1969, 134), and that this vision of uniformity was merely "what the instructed common sense of the time accepts as the adequate or worthy end of human effort. It is a projection of the accepted ideal of conduct" (ibid., 65). This metaphysical uniformity was reified in the actor as passive entity, the famous "homogeneous globule of desire" (ibid., 73). Now institutionalist theory may reject the portrait of human nature as uniform state, but it must replace that vision with some other uniformity or regularity. Veblen himself hints at the alternative in a number of places: "The continuum which is the 'abiding entity' of capital resides in a continuity of ownership, not a physical fact. The continuity, in fact is of an immaterial nature, a matter of legal rights, of contract, of purchase and sale" (ibid., 197).

Unfortunately, Veblen then turned around in his *Theory of Business Enterprise* to assert that this institutionally defined continuity of legal rights and accounting entities that was somehow illegitimate, or at least less "real" than the more fundamental "machine process" that underlay it, since the inevitable conflict between the two resulted in business cycles, anachronistic industrial buccaneers, monopolies, and other deleterious effects.

There are other Peircian themes in Veblen that languish in an underdeveloped state because of his epistemological position on science. His earliest work on the theory of the leisure class could be read as a prologomena to a semiotics of economic transactions. The phenomenon of conspicuous consumption indicates that desires and wants cannot simply be read off of economic behavior (as has often been claimed under the rubric of "revealed preverence"), but that the interpretative and intentional problems of the actors must also enter into the picture, undermining any unique reference for the concept of self-interest. In essays such as "The Economics of Women's Dress" (in Veblen 1934), he shows how the hermeneutic practice of approaching familiar behavior as if we were producing an ethnographical report of the behavior of an alien tribe reminds us the extent to which our explanations are shaped by our interpretative community. His conception of capital as an evolving linchpin of our economic system has interesting parallels with Peirce's idea that natural laws themselves evolve, and thus our interpretations are forced to evolve as well.

These possibilities did not receive the attention they may have deserved; instead, Veblen became associated with the politics of the technocratic movement and a "soviet of engineers," as the extrapolation of his faith in a self-assured materialist science.

John R. Commons

The Peircian legacy in the work of Commons was more self-conscious and more direct. In his magnum opus *Institutional Economics* (1934), he surveyed the philosophical traditions he saw as nurturing the primary schools of economic thought, and argued it was time for recent advances in philosophy to prompt a new economic theory.

> In the stage of Pragmatism, a return is made to the world of uncertain change, without fore-ordination or metaphysics, whether benevolent or non-benevolent, where we ourselves and the world around us are continually in a changing conflict of interests. . . . Not till we reach John Dewey do we find Peirce expanded to ethics, and not until we reach institutionalist economics do we find it expanded to transactions, going concerns, and Reasonable Value. [Commons 1934, 107, 155]

Commons followed Peirce in many respects. He, too, was hostile to the Cartesian duality of mind and body (ibid., 16 and 105), and suspected that said doctrine had served to obscure the problem of conflicts of interest in earlier economic thought. For Commons, both truth and value were defined as the consensus of the relevant investigative community. Mind was not assumed to be a passive receptacle of sense impressions, contra neoclassical biases, but rather as an active inventor of meanings, which displayed "an inseparable aspect of valuing, choosing and acting" (ibid., 18). Commons brought these philosophical convictions to bear in his economics, by isolating value as the central epistemological term in economics, and postulating that the definition of value is tentative and evolutionary, constructed by courts in the course of their adjudication of conflicts of interest.

The hermeneutical character of science is an important presupposition of Commons's economics. He insisted that "False analogies have arisen in the history of economic thought by transferring to economics the meanings derived from the physical sciences" (ibid., 96). If economists had not been so spellbound with the slavish imitation of the outward trappings of physics, they might have admitted that the structures and meanings they had constructed frequently conflicted with the interpretations of the actors so described, and that there had to be some rational means for reconciliation of such divergent constructions. All economic life is interpretative, and there is no more certain recourse than the interpretative practices of the community. This explains why Commons dubbed his theory "Institutional Economics": "we may define an institution as Collective Action in Control of Individual Action" (ibid., 69).

Commons's theory of transactions follows directly from his embrace of Peircian hermeneutics, as it attempts to supply a theory of semiotics to explain the actors' interpretations of the meanings of legitimate transactions. To portray a transaction as simple physical transport between two spheres of relative need assumes away all problems of rational cognition.

> It is significant that the formula of a transaction may be stated in terms of psychology.... All that is needed to shift it to institutional economics is to introduce rights of property; legal units of measurement; the creation, negotiability and release of debt; the enforcement of the two duties of delivery and payment by the collective action of the state. [ibid., 438–39]

In effect, Commons was invoking Peirce's dictum that every semiotic act must be analyzed in terms of the sign itself, the signifier and the interpreter. In his taxonomy of transactions, the signifiers were the actual traders, the interpreters were to be the virtual buyers and sellers and the state apparatus, and the signs were to be the contracts, the debt instruments, and all the rest.

Once one sees the transaction for the complex social phenomena it is, it should become apparent that conflicts of interest and interpretation would be endemic. Hence, problems of coordination within a market system will be rife, and there will be an imperative for some notion of "reasonable value" to be negotiated. This concept of value can only be historical, and contingent upon the evolution of the interpretative community.

Commons's legacy as an economist was surprisingly consonant with his stated philosophical premises. As is well known, both he and his students were active in legal and governmental circles, attempting to get courts and legislatures to recognize their role as experimenters as well as mediators. Commons's stance was that he was openly advocating the gradual improvement of capitalism through governmental intervention. Many of the economic functions of American government, which we today take for granted, were the handiwork of Commons and his students in the first half of the twentieth century.

Nonetheless, his greatest triumphs in the arena of practice were viewed as liabilities in the arena of economic theory in the next generation. His refrain that there were no "natural" grounds for economic institutions was read as implying that Commons left no systematic economic theory. The conjuncture of the decline of pragmatism in the United States in the 1930s with the rise of a particularly narrow form of positivism sealed the fate of the pragmatist institutionalist program.

IV

Post–1930s Institutionalism

The pragmatist view of science had fewer and fewer partisans in the United States from the 1920s to the 1960s. The causes of this decline are too baroque to discuss here, but it is obvious that a Cartesian-style positivism rose to predominance and became the premier cultural image of natural knowledge. The Institutionalist school of economics found itself very frail and vulnerable in this harsh new climate. The rival tradition of neoclassical economics was patently more attuned to the trends in philosophy and science and even went on the offensive, branding its rivals as "unscientific." In reaction to this threat, the "second generation" of institutionalists tended to distance themselves from their heritage of Peircian pragmatism. Two prominent representatives of this reaction were Wesley Clair Mitchell and Clarence Ayres.

Mitchell was a student of Veblen and received from him an extreme skepticism about the analytic claims of neoclassicism, a skepticism he maintained throughout his career. His early works on monetary history and business cycles were extrapolations of some major Veblenian themes, such as the divergence of financial from material expansion as a cause of macroeconomic instability. As Mitchell rose in professional standing, however, he chose to emphasize some of the more technocratic biases of Veblen's world view, in the sense that Mitchell became an advocate of the economic scientist as a neutral and impartial gatherer of facts. One of his crowning achievements was to be the prime mover behind the founding of the National Bureau of Economic Research, an organization originally dedicated to the nonpartisan support of the collection and analysis of quantitative economic data such as the fledgling national income accounts.[7]

From some of his comments (such as those in Mitchell 1937, 35), it seems he thought that statistical analyses were somehow separate from and immune to the mechanical analogies imported by neoclassical theory. Nonetheless, it is also clear that his formidable success in capturing funding and support for his bureau hinged crucially upon his willingness to use prevalent impressions of the trappings of scientific rigor. As a result, it was largely due to Mitchell that by mid-century the Institutionalist school was perceived as promoting a species of naive empiricism without any theory (Koopmans 1947). Protests to the contrary were met with the challenge, Where is your scientific theory? which really meant, Why aren't you using the conventional techniques of physics, such as constrained maximization, as we do? Mitchell had no coherent response, since he had already acquiesced to so much of the positivist program.

Clarence Ayres was another well-known institutionalist who stressed the more technocratic side of Veblen's legacy. Ayres posited a dichotomy between "ceremonial" social processes and science similar to Veblen's dichotomy between business practices and the imperatives of the "machine process"; but in his hands, the dichotomy became a kind of Manichaean contest between darkness and light. Ayres was prone to such *obiter dicta* as "nothing but science is true or meaningful" or "Any proposition which is incapable of statement in scientific terms, any phenomenon which is incapable of investigation by scientific methods, is meaningless and worthless as meaning and value are conceived in that universe of discourse" (in Lepley 1949, 59). Ayres did temper the harshness of this pronouncement by his reference to the relevant universe of discourse, but he had obviously come a long distance from Peirce's hermeneutics. This increasing stridency in the evocation of science became painfully incongruous to a positivist audience, and pushed institutional economics further and further out on a limb: how could they praise scientific discourse as the only relevant truth criteria, and simultaneously eschew scientific practice as it was understood in mid-twentieth century America? Where was the mathematical formalism and axiomatization, the systematic hypothesis testing according to the canons of classical statistical inference, the mathematical models, and the style of studied anonymity of the physics report?

Revolutions in Science and Philosophy

A funny thing happened on the way to the Temple of Science. Just as neoclassicism and institutionalism were vying to be the sole legitimate claimant of the mantle of science, science itself changed dramatically. First in the theory of relativity, and then more dramatically in quantum mechanics and cosmology, physics was severely warping the complacent vision of natural law. The particularly Laplacean notion of rigid determinism came unstuck, and the prosaic conception of percepts of sense data got lost in a whole sequence of counterintuitive and perverse accounts of space, time, discontinuity, and the interaction of the observer with the natural phenomenon. Eternal verities, such as the conservation of energy and the suprahistorical character of physical law, were progressively undermined. Things got so bad that physicists started going around telling people that there could be such a thing as a free lunch.[8] The amazing thing is that much of this drift had been anticipated by Peirce as part of his hypothesis that natural law was itself the product of an evolutionary process.

Philosophers of science felt the tremors under their feet in the 1960s. Not only had analytical philosophy of science been subject to devastating internal criticism, but historians of science such as Thomas Kuhn, Paul Forman, Richard Westfall, and others were demonstrating that respected scientists of the past did not conform to the strict positivist code of correct scientific behavior. Perhaps because they were historians, they grew more curious about the hermeneutic aspects of scientific behavior. As Kuhn wrote about scientists:

> When reading the works of an important thinker, look first for the apparent absurdities in the test and ask yourself how a sensible person could have written them. When you find an answer, I continue, when those passages make sense, then you may find that more central passages, ones you previously thought you understood, have changed their meaning. [1977, xii]

Now, if we have difficulties in understanding the paradigm scientists sanctioned by our culture, it is but a short step to assert that the contemporaries of pivotal scientists also had problems in interpreting and understanding their peers. Explicit rules of deduction and induction could not be expected to resolve this problem in all situations, and as a result the entire Cartesian portrayal of science came unraveled for philosophers (Suppe 1977; Laudan 1984; Rorty 1979, 1986).

By the 1980s it was common to find historians, philosophers, and sociologists of science employing hermeneutic techniques (Latour and Woolgar 1979; Knorr-Cetina and Mulkay 1983; Laudan 1984; Radnitzky 1973). This development in turn encouraged philosophers to rediscover Peirce and resuscitate the pragmatist tradition in America. Writers such as Richard Rorty, Richard Bernstein, and Karl Apel have put pragmatism back on the philosophical map, proposing to reunite a theory of language and social interaction with a theory of scientific inquiry. As Rorty has written of the new pragmatism:

> It is the same as the method of utopian politics or revolutionary science (as opposed to parliamentary politics or normal science). The method is to redescribe lots and lots of things in new ways, until you have created a pattern of linguistic behavior which will tempt the rising generation to adopt it, thereby causing them to look for appropriate new forms of non-linguistic behavior—e.g., the adoption of new scientific equipment or new social institutions. Philosophy, on this model, does not work piece by piece, analyzing concept after concept, or testing thesis after thesis. Rather, it works holistically and pragmatically.... It does not pretend to have a

better candidate for doing the same old things which we did when we spoke the old way. Rather, it suggests that we might want to stop doing those things and do something else. [1986, 4]

The irony of this revival was that the legitimate heirs of the tradition of Peirce in economics were basically unaware of their legacy, and remained wedded to the Cartesian conception of science, which bartered away their legitimacy to neoclassical economics. Although many institutionalist economists maintained a lively interest in philosophical issues, they tended to get sidetracked into such controversies as the meaning of Milton Friedman's essay on the "methodology of positive economics" (an article so incoherent that it could support any reading), or else into behavioralism of a mechanistic cast, which neutralized all hermeneutic problems of interpretation.

Worst of all, the technocratic bias that had been a hallmark of institutionalism from the 1930s to the 1960s grew more and more an embarrassment, both because of the overt scientism of neoclassical theory, and because of the increasing skepticism about the competence and benevolence of the technocrat in a society where the very institution of science seemed an instrument of subjugation and a juggernaut careening out of control. The tragedy was that institutionalism had lost sight of its bearings, making the mistake of pretending to be a better candidate for doing the same old things that were done when speaking the same old language. In consequence, the research agenda had been set by the neoclassical economists. It was a no-win situation.

The Modern Revival of a Pragmatist Institutionalist Economics

There is one more nod to be made in the direction of the DMD thesis, and that is to discuss certain nascent hopeful trends in institutional economics. As the vortex model suggests, one might expect that profound transmutations of our "natural" concepts would be felt (perhaps with a lag) in the construction of social theory. I will argue that this is indeed the case in some recent institutionalist economic research, and that one might extrapolate from present trends to anticipate a full-scale repudiation of Cartesian philosophy of science and an increased reliance on pragmatic and hermeneutic conceptions of the economic actor as well as the role of the economic researcher.

Twentieth-century innovations in physical science have come quite a distance in denying a mechanically determinate world, reinterpreting our ideas of limitation and scarcity, and filling us with disquiet at the boundlessness of chance, chaos, and emergent novelty. Science is making us rudely aware of our role in constructing the world or, as Rorty puts it, "making truth." If the DMD thesis is any guide, then we should expect that this progressive awakening should eventually show up in economics. Because neoclassical economics is irreparably committed to the imitation of nineteenth-century physics, the DMD thesis predicts that it will find itself progressively isolated from cultural conceptions, defending an increasingly reactionary conception of Natural

Order as mechanically deterministic and static. Institutional economics, on the other hand, with its Peircian pedigree, should be well positioned to participate in the reconstruction of economic theory from a hermeneutic perspective. This reconstruction is not merely wishful thinking; there are signs that it is already well under way.

The revitalized institutionalist tradition cannot consist of a return to Peirce; too much has happened in the interim, in science, philosophy, and economics for that to be a practical course of action. Nonetheless, Peirce and his work might serve as a symbol of the central concept of institutional economics, the idea of Collective Rationality. The primary lesson of Peirce's philosophy of science is that the validity of science is not encapsulated in a "method" for all time, and that our criteria of knowledge will always be bound up with the constitution of the community of inquiry. Further, this will not just be true for "science" writ small, but for all human endeavor. Consequently, the philosophical definition of an institution (with a bow toward Commons) should be "Collective Rationality in pursuit of Individual Rationality." This does not imply a reversion to a Hegelian *Geist* or Bergsonian élan vital; it is not an idealism. Institutions can be understood as socially constructed invariants that provide the actors who participate in them with the means and resources to cope with change and diversity; this is the nonmechanistic definition of individual rationality.

A prodigious body of institutionalist economic theory can be systematized around this philosophical conception of an institution. We have already mentioned Commons's discussions of transactions as a semiotics of economic trades, as well as his portrayal of value as the outcome of a long history of negotiation in the legal system. There is also Mitchell's gem of an essay on money in economic history, which suggests that money itself is a socially constructed invariant that is intended to stabilize the concept of price, but which inadvertently transforms the very idea of freedom.

Yet it is in more modern writings that one can observe the impact of a hermeneutic philosophy upon economic theory. Wilbur and Harrison (1978) have proposed the vocabulary of "pattern models" to highlight the evolutionary and holistic themes in recent applied work in institutional economics. Samuels (1978) has surveyed the alternative portrayal of information and preferences in many articles in the *Journal of Economic Issues*. The role of mathematics in obscuring the hermeneutic problem of interpretation has been explored with great insight by Dennis (1982).

But more important, hermeneutic considerations are beginning to show up in the actual theoretical portrayal of the social actors and their problems. The idea of rule creation as the outcome of a constrained maximization problem has been critiqued with great subtlety by Field (1979, 1984). The proliferation of solution concepts in game theory has been interpreted in Chapter 5, above, as the breakdown of the mechanistic notion of individual rationality, which had been already anticipated in the philosophy of Peirce and Wittgenstein. Bausor (1986) has demonstrated how complicated it is to model the passage of time from the transactor's point of view. Levine (1986) has suggested that the problem of firms' interpretations of each other's activities has a direct bearing upon the rate of growth of the macroeconomy. I have argued (Chapter 4, above) that institutions cannot be explained within the ambit of neoclassical models, because the only legitimate explanation in that sphere is one that reduces the institution to antecedent natural givens, which renders their function incoherent and superfluous. Elsewhere (Mirowski 1986) I have attempted to outline the mathematical foundations of institutionalist economics, arguing that the quantitative character of prices and commodities is socially constructed, and suggesting that the institution of money imposes an algebraic group structure that permits the mathematical manipulation of economic categories, and hence reifies the notion of value.

Notes

1. Evidence for this assertion is presented in detail in Part I above.

2. See, however, Mini (1974).

3. We shall ignore in this essay questions of the wellsprings of Peirce's influences, or the tangled question of his metaphysics. We should caution, however, that some works in the institutionalist literature, such as Liebhafsky (1986, 13) have tried to absolve Peirce of any Hegelian or continental influence. On this issue, see CP (viii, 283) and Apel (1981, 201n).

4. This assertion of the self-correcting nature of specifically quantitative induction is perhaps one of the weakest parts of the Peircian corpus, because it does not give any cogent reasons for the priviledged character of quantitative evidence. On this issue, see Kuhn (1977). Further, it is easy to devise numerous situations where repeated measurement does not converge upon any particular value. This would especially be true of nonergodic situations, such as those envisioned in Peirce's own "evolutionary" laws.

5. Peirce made a number of observations on the role of conservation principles in the construction of the static mechanical world picture, such as CP vi, 15, 20 and 100. It is interesting to compare these statements with the definition given above in chapter 5 of an institution as a socially constructed invariant.

6. "But the higher places in science in the coming years are for those who succeed in adapting the methods of one science to the investigation of another. That is where the greatest progress of the passing generation has consisted in. Darwin adapted biology to the methods of Malthus and the economists. Maxwell adapted to the theory of gasses the methods of the doctrine of chancs, and to electricity the methods of thermodynamics. . . . Cournot adapted to political economy the calculus of variations" (CP vii, 46). On this issue, see also chapter 8 below.

7. Conventional histories of economic thought have not given sufficient attention to the importance of the institutionalist school for the rise of twentieth-century macroeconomics (see Mirowski 1985). The position of NBER as a nonpartisan purveyor of data and research was repudiated in the 1970s when Martin Feldstein was installed as director, at which point institutionalist themes disappeared from its agenda.

8. "I have heard it said that there is no such thing as a free lunch. It now appears possible that the universe is a free lunch" (Guth 1983, 215).

Part III
Co-opting the Unorthodox

8

Rhetoric, Mathematics, and the Nature of Neoclassical Economic Theory

They have indeavor'd, to separate the knowledge of Nature, from the colours of Rhetorick. . .   —Thomas Sprat, *History of the Royal Society*

The greatest thing by far is to have a command of metaphor.
                                                    —Aristotle, *The Poetics*

Wild in the Streets

Don McCloskey likes to make out that he runs with a fast crowd, or as he put it: "riding into town on their Harley- (or Donald-) Davidsons, spurning warrants for belief and good reasons, reading pornographic comic books (the new literary canon), and snarling at the townsfolk huddled behind the local syllogism" (McCloskey 1985b, 134). Life among the Econ *does* get dull now and then, and a little stir might liven things up. The town elders, smelling trouble in the air, predictably lock up their daughters and climb onto soap boxes to thunder ponderously about the folly of Rhetoric and the doom consequent upon straying from the One True Path of Science. The youngsters, curious at all the fuss, whisper naive questions to one another when the parents aren't looking. The barbarians are at the gates, but the Econ have deputized a street-smart sheriff to meet the gang at the edge of town. They stand massed in an anarchic (or is it just libertarian?) huddle, formidable in their black leather jackets with some obscure French phrase stitched above the gang's name, "The New Fuzzies." The sheriff, who can read them like a book, knows that they are merely under the influence of fads imported from the Big City, but that they are basically good kids: all they want is to be heard. In his younger days, the sheriff himself had sported a fashionable Viennese hair shirt; he had traded it in when he got his badge. He says to the gang: "I know your parents are out of it. They're uncool, they've got no style. But they've got their problems too. . . . If only you could *communicate* with them. . . . Maybe sit down, have a conference." Of course, it's impossible for the gang to agree upon who should be the representatives of an anarchists' convention, and a few of the kids have a brush with real trouble. They are captured at the edge of town and sent away to be incarcerated someplace in Iowa. Nevertheless, the sheriff knows best, and the shock brings the rest of the kids to their senses. Everyone who has seen *Rebel Without a Cause* comes away convinced that eventually James Dean will clean up his act and take over dad's Chevy dealership.

People who watch too many movies like this one are predisposed to believe that the medium is the message. I suppose that this is the reaction of most economists to Don McCloskey's crusade to describe economics as a Rhetoric. For them the move to demote economic methodology to the status of literary theory is only so much strutting and posturing, perhaps what you would expect from someone who spent too much time reading novels and philosophy.

Is Rhetoric just a new and trendy way to *épater les bourgeois*? Unfortunately, I sometimes think that McCloskey gives that impression. After economists have worked so hard for the past five decades to learn their sums and their differential calculus and their real analysis and their topology, it is a fair bet that one could easily hector them about their woeful ignorance of the conjugation of Latin verbs or Aristotle's Six Elements of Tragedy.[1] Moreover, it has certainly become an academic cliché that economists write as gracefully and felicitously as a hundred monkeys chained to broken typewriters. The fact that economists still trot out Keynes's prose in their defense is itself an index of the inarticulate desperation of an inarticulate profession.

There is nothing new in all of this: the average economist knows it in his bones. Hence the exasperation that must greet a passage such as that found in McCloskey (1985a, 28): "the overlapping conversations provide the standards. It is a market argument. There is no need for philosophical lawmaking or methodological regulation to keep the economy of the intellect running just fine." Isn't this just what the average neoclassical economist believed anyway? So what else is new? Dr. Howard Littlefield turns from the passage in disgust, and returns to thinking about estimating the demand elasticities in a general equilibrium system for a local real estate consortium (cf. Sinclair Lewis, *Babbitt*).

I maintain that there is more to Rhetoric than that. There is something in McCloskey's original 1983 *Journal of Economic Literature* article that touched a nerve but is in danger of becoming lost amid all the (small-r) rhetoric. McCloskey's "Rhetoric" can be fully understood only in its dual historical contexts: the older context of the decline of classical Rhetoric, and the more modern context of the ongoing methodological defense of neoclassical economic theory. Examination of these trends will lead us directly to a prosaic discussion of mathematical expression as a species of metaphor, and its dominant influence upon the rise of neoclassical theory. Meditation upon this sequence of events will redouble our curiosity concerning the philosophical implications of rhetorical analysis in the fourth section below. Finally, in pursuit of that virtuous emotion which Aristotle calls *catharsis*, we shall conclude this essay with the words of others.

War of the Worlds

Don McCloskey has asserted that the canons of Rhetoric provide a suitable set of concepts for understanding how arguments among economists fail or succeed. On a superficial reading, he appears to be concerned soley with "style". To be sure, this is one connotation of the term "Rhetoric": it is *l'art de bien dire,* defined as the correct and agreeable demeanor of address in conformity with the rules of communication in a civilized society. But there is another connotation of Rhetoric, one that is also relevant: this is the art of persuasion. In a civilized society, it should be possible to change another person's mind without force or coercion. Hence Rhetoric is also a form of a theory of social order, a prototype of morality, statecraft, and of Philosophy itself. As the great Philosopher himself said, "The perfection of style is to be clear without being mean" (Aristotle 1961, 101).

Classical Rhetoric was one of the pillars of education in the fifteenth through the seventeenth centuries, the others being Grammar and Logic. Rhetoricians sought to instruct the student in the techniques of the arts of persuasion, beginning with drills in Greek and Latin and continuing on to translations of the ancient Greek and Latin and continuing on to translations of the ancient masters, such as Aristotle, Cicero, and Quintilian. Advanced exercises included practice in declamation and disputation, and instruction in the tropes and figures of speech appropriate to the three duties of the orator, which were to instruct, to please, and to move.

This situation began to change in the seventeenth century, when Rhetoric came under severe attack by the partisans of the new sciences. In France, for instance, the primary antagonists of the rhetoricians were recruits from the Cartesian camp, who insisted that the conviction of certainty arose from introspective knowledge, mathematical expression, and the reduction of all the epiphenomena of the world to a few simple rules of matter in motion. Malebranche, for one, feared that audiences were too frequently swayed by what he termed nonrational considerations, and he denounced the appeal by rhetors to the senses, the imagination, and the passions (France 1965, 19 et seq.). The archtypical complaint of the new scientists was that the rhetor engaged in an irrelevant display of verbal or literary pyrotechnics; he aimed more to provoke applause and admiration than to get on with the real business of analysis and information. Some critics went so far as to insist that all embellishment got in the way of communication, whereas others suspected that rhetorical refinements served to convince people against their wills. The Cartesian antidote to all of this puffery was immersion in the bracing environment of austere mathematics and rational mechanics. A goodly dose of that purgative would reveal a truth that was self-evident and independent of the authority and eloquence of others.

We are all aware that the Cartesian idea of a natural science has had its instrumental and tactical successes, and as a consequence it has pushed Rhetoric from the standard curriculum of Western education into exile at the very margins of the curriculum. The rise of the modern university further encouraged a tendency toward professionalization more attuned to the Cartesian ideal. One salient aspect of the process was the cultivation of an arcane jargon in each little department, both for purposes of differentiation and to prevent the intrusion of outsiders. The *lingua franca* of the natural sciences became mathematics, and its influence became apparent in every discipline that pined for the status and legitimacy of the Cartesian natural scientistic style became conflated with the ideal of legitimate suasion, a format McCloskey calls "modernism," but given its geneology, is more aptly called "the Cartesian vice."

There now exist quite a few competent descriptions of the Cartesian vice (Tiles 1984; Rorty 1979). In simple terms, for the Cartesian, the only reasoning is formal reasoning and the only thought is conscious thought. Reasoning is formal when knowledge of the subject matter is deemed irrelevant to the principles of formal demonstration, and therefore irrelevant in any acknowledgment of the validity of an argument. Indeed, it is claimed that formal principles of reason are embodied in mathematics alone, a computational scheme that could ideally be programmed into an automaton, which could then settle all disputes "objectively." Moreover, for the Cartesian the most perfect thought is reflective thought, because the "mind" knows itself better than it knows any external condition or circumstance. Self-reflective thought is transparent to the thinker, beyond all doubt, unclouded by brooding unconscious forces or irrational emotions. Thus all knowledge must be grounded in the original assent of the self-reflexive individual. It should be clear that the Cartesian tradition is hostile to the idea that the process of argumentation and persuasion should have any bearing upon rational knowledge; hostile to the idea that there is an inextricable social component to the growth of knowledge; suspicious of historical claims to authority; suspicious of the slippery connotations of words in the vernacular. In short, it is hostile to Rhetoric. Assent of an audience of rational individuals is only to be expected upon the demonstration of the impersonal and self-evident truth of the mathematical syllogism.

The irony of McCloskey's article on the Rhetoric of economics was that he opted to champion the vanquished foe of Cartesianism as the best methodological defense of the social science most addicted to the Cartesian vice, neoclassical economic theory. The neoclassical school of economics had only recently adopted all the trappings of the Cartesian world view—mathematical formalism, axiomatization, derogation of literary narrative, and mimesis of natural science terminology and attitudes—but had earlier endowed their model of rational economic man with exclusively Cartesian powers and abilities: transparent individual self-knowledge, mechanical algorithms of decision-making, independence from all historical determination, and all social action ultimately explained by rational individual assent. Suddenly, along came McCloskey, insisting that neoclassical economists had been too long caught in the thrall of the Cartesian vice. Irony was piled upon irony when he further asserted that addiction to the Cartesian vice was nonlethal. If only economists would acknowledge that the persuasiveness of their arguments hinged upon rhetorical considerations, they would discover that orthodox theories now ascendant would be preserved, if not actually strengthened.

McCloskey's crusade could not help but sound dissonant and appear self-contradictory. One common reaction was to view it as just another installment in the continuing Decline of the West, the dissolution and squandering of our rational heritage. Another common reaction was the American admonition "If it ain't broke, don't fix it." Both reactions were really beside the point, although they did stoke the swirling fires of controversy. What was missing in both the Rhetoric manifesto and in the ensuing controversy was any *historical* understanding of why McCloskey's article appeared in the *Journal of Economic Literature* when it did, and why an advocacy of rhetorical analysis could lay claim to some legitimacy in 1983 rather than in 1963 or 1933.

Since the 1930s neoclassical economic theory has increasingly allied itself with the natural sciences—or more exactly, the image of physics (a claim documented in Part I above)—in the process of inquiry, imitating both style and substance. Examination of neoclassical manifestos, from Robbins's 1952 *Essay* to Koopmans's 1957 *Three Essays*, from Friedman's 1953 essay to Blaug's 1980 *Methodology*, reveals an escalation in the appeal to scientific legitimacy through citation of the practices that purportedly constituted the core of the scientific method, be they prediction, falsificationism, axiomatization, or the use of mathematical formalism. In deference to the Cartesian vice, these practices were portrayed as self-sufficient abstract methods independent of any examination of what physicists actually did, or how they did it.

It was precisely this oblivion when it came to the actual practices of scientists that set neoclassical economics up for a fall in the 1970s. Physics itself had been going through a period of turmoil, trying to assimilate the disturbing implications of quantum mechanics and the attendant proliferation of subatomic particles. The increasing politicization of science had fostered the growth of political movements skeptical of the claims of scientists (Krimsky 1982). These first two trends led to a third, the revolution in the philosophy of science and the explosion of science studies in areas such as the history and sociology of science. Everyone who was not intellectually moribund in the 1970s had at least heard of Thomas Kuhn's *Structure of Scientific Revolutions*, and many who were not professional philosophers took to reading the works of Paul Feyerabend, Steven Toulmin, Imre Lakatos, David Bloor, and others. It was the combined project of these and other authors to explode the myth of a single scientific method by means of detailed historical investigations into the origins and development of specific scientific theories.

In this context the neoclassical appeals to *the* scientific method appeared anachronistic and almost naively quaint (McCloskey 1985a, 12). Testimonials of faith in falsificationism ran smack into the Duhem-Quine thesis, which states that every test is so inextricably imbedded in auxiliary hypotheses that rational adjustment of some subset can reverse the verdict of any adverse test (Harding 1976). Proponents of austere axiomatic formalism were chastened by Gödel's Theorem and Wittgensteinian puzzles of interpretation (compare Mirowski 1986). Prophets of prediction were humbled by the appearance of ARIMA models as statistics with little or no a priori theory. And to add insult to injury, physicists began to undermine some of the neoclassical economists' most cherished tenets of faith, such as the supposed impossibility of a free lunch. By the 1980s, some cosmologists were claiming that the entire universe was itself a free lunch, nothing more than a vacuum fluctuation.[2]

Eternal verities were crumbling; the barbarians were at the gates. One should not infer that many or most economists were au courant with the latest scientific trends. Indeed, most neoclassical economists were innocent of any awareness of developments in science of the reexamination of scientific practices, their notions of scientific inquiry having been formed by earlier experience of introductory physics or engineering courses, or else by idealized vignettes found in general cultural sources such as science fiction or the hagiographies of famous scientists. Nevertheless, the rumblings on the frontier were beginning to be audible, however indistinct and jumbled, and neoclassical economists felt them as part of the continuous lay litany that economists are charlatans and economics is not a science. Earlier defenses of neoclassical economics based on the progressively discredited conceptions of science were rendered ineffectual.

The genius of McCloskey's 1983 manifesto was that it promised an escape from this impasse. McCloskey's advocacy of a rhetorical defense was an exhortation to abjure all reliance upon "science" or the "scientific method." In criticizing scientism—what he called "modernism"—he made use of many of the philosophical theses of Kuhn, Feyerabend, and others on the radical underdetermination of scientific theories by data, the absence of a neutral observation language, and the importance of 'external' considerations for the acceptance or rejection of scientific theories. Many historians of science— most notably, those associated with the Edinburgh school—had interpreted those external conditions as mediated by sociological forces, but McCloskey introduced his own innovation here, substituting classical Rhetoric for sociological or anthropological theories. As he later admitted in the book-length version of his work, "The project here is to overturn the monopolistic authority of science in economics by questioning the usefulness of the demarcation of science from art" (McCloskey 1985a, 56). The bottom line was that, while neoclassical economists were not the most artful of souls (or artful of dodgers?), they did manage to improve the tenor of their conversations over time: hence, basically, I'm OK and you're OK.

This solution to the problem of the methodological justification of neoclassical economics was not destined to please everyone. Of course, some will cling to their outdated scientism, blind to both Rhetoric and science. Others will pronounce a plague on all methodological houses as long as their own career meets the market test: that is, they get paid for doing economics. The remainder who do detect some valuable insights in McCloskey's work, however, will eventually find their curiosity frustrated and stymied by some deep contradictions inherent in his overall program. The first, already alluded to, is the painful incongruity of the assertion that a Cartesian model of economic man can be justified with an anti-Cartesian paradigm. This argument displays an antisymmetry that could easily be used against it: If people in general are optimizers, and if economists are people, then shouldn't economists also maximize over a set of personal objectives that might be contrary to their pursuit of open and honest conversations?[3] In other words, Classical Rhetoric embodies a specific theory of social order. Shouldn't that theory be consistent and congruent with the theory of social order in the theory it was intended to defend?

Second, there is an extreme incompatibility between the ideal of Rhetoric as the study of all the various techniques of persuasion and McCloskey's own study of the rhetoric of particular arguments in economics. In one place, he insists that economics itself is "a historical rather than a predictive science" (1985a, xix); yet elsewhere in the same volume he insists that the rhetorical analysis of economists' arguments, as well as the content of the arguments themselves, are necessarily ahistorical (ibid, 64–65, 93). The problem with this position is that Rhetoric, by most accounts, is intrinsically and essentially an hermeneutic and historical form of inquiry; whereas it is neoclassical economics that is generally conceded to be an ahistorical explanation of social activity. Some of the very best examples of rhetorical analysis of economic arguments, such as Klamer (1983), are by their very nature historical inquiries: investigations into the "external" determinants of theory rejection or acceptance beyond the acknowledged arguments to be found in the economic literature.

I believe that McCloskey understood that the implicit theory of social order in Classical Rhetoric is diametrically opposed to the atemporal existence of the neoclassical *homo economicus,* and therefore a full rhetorical analysis would be congenitally critical of neoclassical economic theory. Of course, this would never do for his purposes, so to restrain and repress this tendency, McCloskey tried to restrict his definition of Rhetoric to an atemporal consideration of the style of argumentation of economists independent of all historical context. Thus, in his chapter on the impact of Robert Fogel upon the discipline of economic history, he arbitrarily quarantines any discussion of the historical fact that Fogel and his Cliometrics movement were the vanguard of the penetration of neoclassical economics into a stronghold of institutionalists, historicists, and others united by their distate for the atemporal character of neoclassical economics. In his chapter on John Muth and rational expectations theory, he neglects entirely the running controversy over whether Keynesian economics was (or could be) consistent with the premises of neoclassical theory, as well as the relevant psychological literature that had suggested that the process of learning could not be adequately captured by neoclassical theory. It is not at all inconceivable that what starts out as a rhetorical defense of neoclassical theory could rapidly become a poison pill, if all the directions on the label were followed. Perhaps this explains some of the disdain that greeted the appearance of McCloskey's original article.

I should like to take very seriously McCloskey's primary thesis—that "the scientific method" is inadequate to explain how economists choose to advocate the theories that they do—but to maintain that his subsidiary hypotheses are false. I would like to suggest some amendments to his manifesto:

1. Rhetorical analysis can provide valuable insights, but only when it is diachronic as well as synchronic;

2. The style of economic arguments cannot be adequately understood independent of their content;

3. Rhetorical analysis is invariably critical and will never constitute a satisfactory defense of neoclassical economic theory.

I am aware that the spirit of these assertions runs counter to contemporary deconstructionist credos in literary theory, but then, what would you expect, coming from an economist? If economists with their "pig philosophy," as Carlyle called it, don't insist on the existence of a world outside of the text, then who will?

Rather than shuffle a deck of methodological fiats and slap them down on the table one by one, it may be more edifying and instructive to focus attention on just one of McCloskey's rhetorical claims: that "mathematical theorizing in economics is metaphorical, and literary" (1985a, 79). This assertion is almost certainly correct, but extended rhetorical analysis reveals that it has implications undreamed of in McCloskey's market argument.

The Absent-Minded Professor

The most subversive doctrine (from the vantage point of neoclassical economics) in the armory of McCloskey's Rhetoric is the idea that mathematical expressions are "merely" metaphorical. In a discipline that has arranged its pecking order largely on the basis of the appearance of mathematical sophistication, this must surely sound like the tic-tic-tic of the barbarians pecking at the gates. To drive home the inversion of conventional values, McCloskey has written that "What is successful in economic metaphor is what is successful in poetry, and the success is analyzable in similar terms" (McCloskey 1985a, 78). The average neoclassical economist might be willing to agree with Bentham that pushpin is as good as poetry, but would resist to the death the idea that poetry is a good as a polynomial.

It is important to realize that McCloskey himself does not think this is a disruptive doctrine, and indeed, thinks it a defense of the behavior of neoclassical economists in some of their most recent *contretemps*, most notably in the erstwhile Cambridge Capital Controversies.[4] These sometimes acrimonious controversies forced certain neoclassical theorists to admit that their Cambridge (UK) cousins' criticisms did possess some merit; however, it remains somewhat of an embarrassment that this has not curbed the ubiquitous employment of neoclassical production functions in mathematical models. Whatever happened to the bracing discipline of the austere logic of mathematics? McCloskey would respond that, if one regards the production function (and, indeed, capital itself) as a mere metaphor, then there is little harm done. No metaphor is premised upon the precise identity between the object and the thing compared, or, as he put it, "The reason there was no decision reached was that the important questions were literary, not mathematical or statistical. The debate was equivalent to showing mathematically or statistically that a woman cannot be a summer's day. Yet no one noticed" (1985a, 80).

Such a cavalier summary of what was an extremely labrynthine and subtle dispute cuts two ways. Superficially, it seems to say that the differences that divided the two Cambridges were *merely* metaphorical, and therefore inconsequential. Surely this cannot be McCloskey's message, because such an interpretation implies an invidious comparison between questions literary and questions mathematical contrary to the spirit of his rhetoric. On the other hand, neither can this be interpreted to suggest that the disputants be absolved of their respective pig-headedness merely because they neglected to subject the metaphorical content of their respective mathematical models to sustained analysis. Simply because Paul Samuelson insisted that J. B. Clark-style capital was a "parable" did not get him off the hook: he had made mathematical errors that were doubly grievous because so much of his authority derives from mathematical expertise. Surely the rhetor is not satisfied to mumble that "everyone has his or her own opinion, and there is nothing you can do to change it"? On the contrary, one would reasonably expect the proponent of Rhetoric to plumb the depths of the metaphorical sources of apparently technical disagreements, with the eventual goal of clarifying the points of the dispute. There is no getting around it: some parties are going to be criticized. Yet this is precisely the sort of analysis that McCloskey is not inclined to do.

The metaphorical character of mathematical analysis is not a novel idea. The great mathematician Henri Poincaré defined mathematics as the art of giving the same name to different things, a phrase more than adequate to do double duty as a definition of metaphor (Kline 1980). Wittgenstein, with his characteristic acuity, got to the crux of the matter: "Mathematical conviction might be put in the form, 'I recognise this as analogous to that'. But here 'recognise' is not used as in 'I recognise him as Lewy' but as in 'I recognise him as superior to myself' " (1976, 63).

The problem of what enforces the acknowledgment that one set of mathematical relationships are "the same" as another set is a major theme of Wittgenstein's later philosophy. One profoundly disturbing implication of this inquiry is that mathematics cannot be considered an independent mechanical decision procedure (as portrayed in the Cartesian tradition) because there are no self-enforcing rules concerning the sufficiency of mathematical analogy. Why is a geometric circle "the same" as the equation $(x - a)^2 + (y - b)^2 = r^2$? Does one still consider it the same if the y-coordinates are complex numbers? Or if we are concerned with a non-Euclidean geometry? In what sense is matrix multiplication "the same" as the multiplication of integers or rational numbers? These types of questions led in the later nineteenth century to the concepts of "isomorphism" and "homeomorphism" as an attempt to codify some of the principles of "sameness" and to reveal the analogies between various branches of mathematics (Kline 1972, 767). While this in turn led to very profound results in the theory of groups and semigroups, one should not conclude from it that the principles of metaphor and analogy in mathematics are formalized and settled for all time. The fact that Hesse (1966, 64–77) tried to formalize the process of analogic reasoning in science using abstract algebra and failed should warn us that the latter has not sufficiently subsumed the former. There can be no more poignant illustration of this fact for economists than the case of the writings of William Stanley Jevons.

Although it is not common knowledge, Jevons was at least as famous as an expositor of the philosophy of science (such as it was in his day) as he was renowned as an economist. The second edition of his textbook *The Principles of Science* devotes an entire chapter to the role of analogy in science, and he specifically discusses the function of analogy in the development of mathematics. He admitted that "generalization passes insensibly into reasoning by analogy," but as a good Cartesian, he could not bring himself to express unrestrained enthusiasm over the method of reasoning by analogy. The stumbling block was the same as that indicated by Wittgenstein: When could one say metaphorical relationships were really "the same"? How does one decide that a resemblance or lack thereof is fundamental, and when incidental? Jevons chose to illustrate the problem of analogical reasoning with an example from mathematics:

> analogical reasoning leads us to the conception of many things which, so far as we can ascertain, do not exist. In this way great perplexities have arisen in the use of language and mathematical symbols—mathematicians have needlessly puzzled themselves about the square root of a negative quantity, which in many applications of algebraic calculation, is simply a sign without any analogous meaning, there being a failure of analogy." [1905a, 643]

This passage was anachronistic when it was written; its error is glaringly apparent today. In the nineteenth century there were reasons to think that the square root of a negative number should not be accorded the same treatment as the square root of a positive number, but these reasons were not written in stone, and in some cases the pure aesthetic appeal of the metaphor induced some mathematicians to persist in its development and elaboration. Quite unexpectedly, these "imaginary numbers" were then found to have applications in periodic functions, in probability theory and in quantum mechanics. Jevons had suspected that analogy is pernicious, luring the unwary into false paths. Instead, the analogy had become a sort of self-ratifying reality, with curious analytical constructs being developed for their own sake, and later further analogies being forged with physical phenomena.

The profound ramifications of the thesis that "mathematics is analogical reasoning" are being debated in the philosophical literature; a summary of those debates would carry us too far afield from our present concern, which is to analyze the rhetoric of mathematics in neoclassical economics. Nevertheless, we cannot pass by one fascinating thesis, which may prove useful. Mary Tiles has recently argued that it is the metaphorical character of mathematics that can explain the uncanny feeling that the mathematician "discovers" Platonic essences and grasps preexisting mathematical relationships independent of the process of inquiry—the widespread conviction that the mathematician is a discoverer, not an inventor (Wittgenstein 1978, 99).

While the fact that two separate mathematicians arrive at the same solution for the problem $x = \sqrt{(56)(32)}$ may be traced either to a mechanical calculation procedure or to the heavy hand of authority, the discovery of new mathematical structures cannot be explained by the same means. Bachelard and Tiles claim that the new structures are a byproduct of the drive of the mathematician to unify his or her discipline (Tiles 1984, 87). The scheme for creating this unity is to apply the theory of one existing mathematical structure to the domain of another—that is, to reason by analogy. Because the two domains are never identical, there will be some ways in which the initial analogy appears to be a bad fit: the heterogeneity of domains produces "analogical interference." Tiles uses the example of a ratio of integers and the idea of a ratio between the diameter and the circumference of a circle, an analogy that induced cognitive dissonance and resulted in the discovery of π and other "irrational numbers" (ibid., 93). She could have used the noncommutativity of the multiplication of quaternions, or any of a plethora of similar instances in the history of mathematics. The fact that the analogies are not perfect, and never can attain perfection, leads mathematicians to ask novel questions. The answers to these questions are curious, in that they do not seem to be predetermined by the previous corpus of mathematics, and yet they produce answers that have the aura of objectivity. Hence, the mathematics appears to "resist" the original drive to unify the subject matter, fostering the impression that it exists independent of the objectives and choices of the researcher. In a rhetorical twist worthy of O. Henry, it is the metaphorical practices of mathematicians that conjure the impression of the cold objectivity of mathematics.

The practice of analogical reasoning is of course not restricted to the activities of mathematicians. This should appear self-evident to the neoclassical economist whose time and energy is spent constructing "models" of increasing levels of complexity and abstraction. What the neoclassical economist may not realize is that a substantial proportion of the activities of the physicist also consists of the transport of analogy from one domain of science to another. This has been recognized by numerous historians and philosophers of science from Duhem to Hesse, including W. S. Jevons. Duhem wrote, "The history of physics shows us that the searching for analogies between two distinct categories of phenomena has perhaps been the surest and most fruitful method of all the procedures put into play in the construction of physical theories" (1977, 95–96).

Those forced to suffer through courses of electrical engineering will recall the light that dawns when one realizes that any mechanical or acoustical system can be reduced to an electrical network and the problem solved by circuit theory, or vice versa (Olson 1958). The very success of the theory of energy in the nineteenth century was due to the newfound capacity to see analogies between phenomena that had previously appeared distinct and unrelated. Now one could state that mass was "like" inductance and that velocity was "like" current, and hence use the mathematical formalisms developed in the sphere of rational mechanics to describe other phenomena in novel spheres, such as electricity and light. Other analogies that were critical for the development of physics in the nineteenth century were comparisons between heat and electrostatics, and comparisons between light and the vibrations of an elastic medium. The physicist James Clerk Maxwell was so impressed with the fecundity of these analogies that he elevated the postulation of analogy to a principle of research method, a method he conceived as a middle way between the sterility of a strictly mathematical analysis and the excesses of pure speculation. His method paid off handsomely with the postulation of the famous Maxwell equations and the subsequent discovery of the electromagnetic nature of light (Nersessian 1984). Examples of the role of analogy and metaphor in physics could be multiplied indefinitely.

The prevalence of metaphor and analogy in the history of the physical sciences is no accident. It is a corollary of another trend, the increasing use of mathematics as the preferred mode of communication within the disciplinary matrix. Mathematics, as we have observed, is the method par excellence for the transfer of metaphor. Once mathematical expertise has come to be the badge of the theorist in any science, theory becomes isolated from that subset of the discipline responsible for empirical implementation and experiment. The mathematical theorist is given carte blanche by his or her prestige and separation from the nitty-gritty of everyday observation to prosecute any mathematical analogy or metaphor that captures her fancy. The negative component of any of these metaphors (for instance, the fact that light waves are not "really" like water waves because we can't identify the substance light waves move through) can be effortlessly set aside for the time being, or dismissed as irrelevant, impounded in *ceteris paribus* conditions or otherwise neutralized, because for the theorist, it is only the mathematics that matters (Colvin 1977).

Many appeals to "beauty," "simplicity," "clarity," and suchlike by the mathematical community can be rendered comprehensible as comments upon the aesthetic qualities of analogies. It is ironic that the existence of the closed community of those fluent in mathematics permits the mathematical theorist to indulge in wilder flights of fanciful metaphor than might be condoned were they expressed in the vernacular. As it stands, the closed community of mathematical theorists can independently invest a metaphor with legitimacy, and leave it to the "applied scientists" to clean up the negative components of the analogy and make the messy bits fit with recalcitrant reality. It should go without saying that this constitutes an excellent sociological structure for the protection of a theory from its critics.

Don't Look Back

Fortified with these observations, we now return to explicit consideration of neoclassical economics and McCloskey's thesis that mathematical models are metaphors. The preceding considerations suggest that there is substantial truth to this claim, simply because most extensions of mathematical formalism proceed by metaphor and analogy. Nevertheless, this simple observation has little cash value, because a potentially limitless number of possible metaphors might have been proposed, and a myriad of mathematical metaphors might have been deemed to warrant sustained elaboration. The questions that should concern the rhetor are: Which metaphor(s) were chosen? Why were they thought plausible when they were adopted? What happened to the negative components of the analogy? Are they still thought to be plausible? Why? Are the metaphors "dead" or "alive"? The very process of persuasion dangles without rational support in the absence of such an inquiry.

A metaphorical analysis of this format already exists that can stand as an alternative to McCloskey's "Rhetoric" of neoclassical economic theory. This analysis claims that there is a coherence to neoclassical theory because it all has grown out of a single metaphor, a mathematical metaphor. It asserts an empirical hypothesis, that the progenitors of neoclassicism did what all mathematical theorists do: they appropriated a mathematical model lock, stock, and barrel from somewhere else, in the guise of a metaphor. In particular, the early neoclassicals took the model of "energy" from physics, changed the names of all the variables, postulated that "utility" acted like energy, and then flogged the package wholesale as economics. In lieu of a sustained attempt to convince the skeptical reader, we shall merely sketch in the main outlines of the metaphor, restricting ourselves to what is needed to evaluate our later rhetorical theses.

At one point in his *Three Essays*, Tjalling Koopmans notes in passing, "A utility function of a consumer looks quite similar to a potential function in the theory of gravitation" (1957, 176). Although he opted not to elaborate the analogy, let us explore it further. Suppose we are to describe a mass point moving in a three-dimensional Euclidean space from point A to point B.

The conventional physical description, developed in the middle of the nineteenth century, postulates a "force" decomposed into its orthogonal components, each multiplied by the spatial displacement, also suitably decomposed. To incorporate cases of nonlinear displacement and acceleration, the "work" done in the course of motion from A to B was defined as the summation of the infinitesimal forces multiplied by their displacements:

$$T = \int_A^B (F_x\, dx + F_y\, dy + F_z\, dz) = (1/2)mv^2 \big|_A^B$$

The writings of Lagrange and Hamilton insisted that the total energy of this system depended in a critical way upon the position of the mass point in a gravitational field. This was subsequently clarified in the following manner: suppose that the expression $(F_x\, dx + F_y\, dy + F_z\, dz)$ was an exact differential equation. This would imply that there exists a function $U(x,y,z)$ such that:

$$F_x = \partial U/\partial x; \quad F_y = \partial U/\partial y; \quad \text{and } F_z = \partial U/\partial z.$$

The function $U(x,y,z)$ so defined was asserted to represent a gravitational field, which by the 1860s was also identified as the field of potential energy. The sum of the kinetic energy $(1/2mv^2) = T$ and the potential energy U was understood as being conserved in the confines of a closed system. The law of the conservation of energy, in turn, clarified and encouraged the use of constrained maximization techniques (such as the Principle of Least Action, Lagrangean mutipliers, and the Hamiltonian calculus of variations) in the description of the equilibrium motion of a mass point under the influence of impressed forces.

As Koopmans indicated, the similarity between this model and the conventional canonical neoclassical model is quite striking. Let the forces 'F' be the prices of individual goods x, y, z, and the displacements be infinitesimal changes in the quantities of the goods dx, dy, dz. The rest of the metaphor falls into place: "kinetic energy" is the sum of prices times quantities, and hence is the total expenditure or budget constraint; the potential field defined over the commodity space is clearly "utility."[5] Constrained maximization (or minimization) of an imponderable quantity over a conservative field leads directly to the equilibrium configurations of forces–prices.

Is this remarkable similarity merely an accident? Koopmans is prudently silent on this issue, but examination of the origins of neoclassical theory reveals that its progenitors consciously and willfully appropriated the physical metaphor in order to render economics a "mathematical science". Jevons (1905b, 50), Walras (1960), Edgeworth (1881) and nearly every other early neoclassical economist admitted this fact. Here the rhetor pricks up his ears; his blood starts to race; could this be a "rhetorical ploy"? And they all admitted it? Then why is it news a century later? Could this be a "dead" metaphor—has it become so fully detatched from its sources of inspiration that it is now effectively independent of the conditions of its genesis? Curiously enough, this was the position of that most pugnacious defender of economic mechanics (or mechanical economics?), Pareto:

> Let us go back to the equations which determine equilibrium. In seeing them somebody—and it might be the writer—made an observation of the kind above and said: "These equations do not seem new to me, I know them well, they are old friends. They are the equations of rational mechanics." This is why economics is a sort of mechanics or akin to mechanics.... mechanics can be studied leaving aside the concept of forces. In reality all this does not matter much. If there is anyone who does not care to hear mechanics mentioned, very well, let us disregard the similarity and let us talk directly about our equations. We shall only have to face the drawback that in certain cases we shall have to labour greatly in order to deduce from those equations certain consequences that we would have perceived at once had we kept in mind the fact that mechanics has already deduced them from its own equations, which are similar to ours. All told this does not alter the consequences. [1953a, 185]

The rhetorical analyst, forewarned and forearmed by our previous discussion, smells the Cartesian vice in the neighborhood. Here is the insistence that sources of inspiration are irrelevant; the actual process of inquiry is irrelevant; the composition of the audience is irrelevant. All that purportedly matters is the formal mathematical expression, which alone renders truth more transparent. The fact that the mathematics was appropriated wholesale from physics merely speeds up the research and does not influence the content of the theory. However much Pareto wishes to appear a pragmatical and no-nonsense type of guy, the fact is that his *prosopopoeia* is eminently rhetorical, in that it is meant to persuade and *not* to be a literal account of his activities, or the activities of other neoclassical economists.

I maintain that the physics metaphor in economics is not a dead metaphor, and that the attendant mathematics have not served as the simple heuristic device, *pace* Pareto. In the first place, neither Pareto nor any of his comrades in the marginalist revolution made explicit use of the mathematical analogy for the purposes of speeding up the process of inference, or even to provide an independent check upon their analytical prognostications. This was not because the metaphor was dead on arrival; rather, it was because none of the neoclassicals understood the physics well enough to follow up on the implications of the metaphor. This fact is illustrated by the numerous occasions when physicists, upon recognizing the physical equations, wrote letters to the neoclassicals to query them upon various points. The early neoclassicals—Walras, Fisher, Pareto—to a man replied with bombast, farrago, and finally a frustrated and sullen silence, simply because they did not understand what was being asked of them (see Chapter 2, above).

In the second place, no neoclassical economist has *ever* treated the physics metaphor as a scientific metaphor rather than a poetic metaphor. Evoking a distinction made below, this means that no neoclassical economist has ever seen fit to plumb the energetics metaphor for its "positive" versus "negative" components, weighing those parts of the metaphor that seemed relevant against those that appeared odd, strained, or even downright perverse. This could not be attributed to the possibility that the metaphor of utility as energy was so elegant, so felicitous, and so very right that it would be futile to look for its negative aspects. Indeed, with only minor effort we can generate six profound disanalogies:

1. There is nothing obvious about the definition of human rationality as the maximization of an objective function over a conserved entity. This elevation of the significance of extrema did not arise first in social theory, but rather in physics, as the principle of least action. The physics of constrained extrema was interpreted as evidence for the existence of a God who had constructed the world in the most efficacious and coherent manner. That maximization or minimization was global in the most comprehensive sense, and encouraged an attitude that "efficiency" could be defined in some absolute framework. In its evolution from Maupertuis to Euler to Hamilton, the principle of least (or varying) action shed its theological skin, but the notion of absolute efficiency persisted, and it was this connotation that was recruited to tame the multiform and unruly concept of rationality.

The predisposition of the modern neoclassical economist to "optimize" over someone's "objective function" is neither an empty tautology nor a harmless metaphor: it surreptitiously presumes an inordinately large amount of structure about the nature of desires and objectives, the role of time, the understanding of causality, the unimportance of process, the conservation of the domain of the objectives, the relative construction of the world of the actor vis-á-vis its reconstruction by the social analyst, the strict separation of the thing desired and the act of choice, and much, much more (Bausor 1986).

2. The metaphor of energy–utility that was appropriated by neoclassical economics was derived from the physics of a specific historical moment, namely, the middle of the nineteenth century just prior to the elaboration of the second law of thermodynamics. The mathematics of pre-entropic physics is not thought to have been the pinnacle of the development of static mechanism (Prigogine 1980). In this vintage of physics, all physical phenomena are portrayed as being perfectly reversible in time; there was no room in theory for hysteresis. In other words, nineteenth-century physical law could have no history. This stubbornly antihistorical bias of neoclassical economics has frequently been excoriated by critics such as Joan Robinson, and bemoaned by such partisans as Hicks (1979) and Shackle (1967). What the latter have not realized is that it is futile to attempt to superimpose history onto neoclassical stories without thoroughly wreaking havoc with the very physical metaphor that was its inspiration and the mathematical techniques that were responsible for its success.

3. In pre-entropic physics, all physical phenomena are variegated manifestations of a protean energy that can be fully and reversibly transformed from

one state to another. When this metaphor was smuggled into the context of economic theory, it dictated that all economic goods be fully and reversibly convertible into utility, and thence into all other goods in the act of trade. Now, most economists would admit that the introduction of money into neoclassical economic theory has been an awkward marriage at best and a shotgun marriage at worst (Clower 1967). The problem has been, curiously enough, metaphorical. In the mathematics, the analogue to money has not been some lubricant that greases the wheels of trade, but rather a superfluous intermediate crypto-energy which all other energies must become in transit to their final state. The mathematics says one thing; the accompanying commentary something else.

4. As a prerequisite for the application of techniques of constrained extrema, it has long been recognized that energy must be conserved as a mathematical rather than an empirical imperative (Theobald 1966). Neoclassicals have not yet understood the significance of this imperative in their own models. If one takes the metaphor literally, it would dictate that the sum of realized utility plus the money value of the budget constraint be equal to a constant. Much of the hoopla concerning the constancy of the marginal utility of money around the turn of the century can be understood as the making of a worse muddle of this problem than it already was.

5. A flurry of activity in the 1940s and 1950s portended the liberation of neoclassical value theory from dependence upon the utility concept. The motivations behind this self-denying ordinance were never openly discussed, although a rationally reconstructed history (Wong 1978) can be organized by asking how our understanding of the folk psychology of utility makes it dissimilar to energy. It can also explain why economists cannot bear to take psychology seriously. The failure of this abortive research program can be gauged by the extent to which the axioms of revealed preference are isomorphic to those of a gravitational field.

6. Problems with the energetics metaphor can also assume less lofty and philosophical proportions. For example, the components of physical forces can assume negative values without disrupting the physical intuition, but negative prices really do seem beyond the pale (Mirowski 1986).

The more one is willing to become embroiled in the history of physics and mathematics, the more one could expand this list. For our present purposes, I hope we have examined sufficient evidence to counter the claim that it makes no difference where the mathematical analogies come from, because once appropriated, they are freely amended to express only what was consciously intended. Mathematics is not a colorless and secure cloak into which the analyst can slip in order to shield himself from the vagaries of human discourse.

A vast rhetorical process is going on here, and it cries out for analysis. It is not simply a matter of writing style, or conversational tactics, or an incident in which a single individual flashes into fleeting fame. It is not the saga of a

John Muth or a Robert Fogel. It is the narrative of the displacement of all other schools of economics (with the obvious exception of Marxism) by means of a single mathematical metaphor appropriated from nineteenth-century physics. It is the story of the persuasion of the majority of Western economists to pledge allegiance to a particular ideal construction of economic life by means of a single rhetorical technique.

This is where the idea of mathematics as metaphor takes us. It takes us to the historical origins of neoclassical theory, into its content. Inexorably, it also draws us into *critique*, into looking at the present with something far short of warm admiration. This is where rhetorical analysis takes us, but it is a place where Don McCloskey does not want to go.

Blow-up

Don McCloskey rode into town on his Donald-Davidson, a mean machine, and it did turn some heads. But as always, mundane reality intrudes, and it is time to find a gas station for the dual overhead cam, four-cylinder, high-compression monster machine so that the biker can once again put the pedal to the metal. Unfortunately, the Donald-Davidson only runs on the most austere high-test fuel, the supersyllogism that "metaphors mean what the words, in their most literal interpretation, mean, and nothing more" (Davidson in Johnson 1981, 201). Neoclassical economists have been trying to siphon this stuff out of the tanks of the BMWs and Caddeys since the year one. Witness Pareto:

> [Social scientists] can therefore derive no advantage from words. They can, however, incur great harm, whether because of the sentiments that words arouse, or because the existence of a word may lead one stray as to the reality of the thing it is supposed to represent, and so introduce into the experimental field imaginary entities such as the fictions of metaphysics or theology. . . . Literary economists . . . are to this day still dilly-dallying with the speculations such as "What is *value*?" "What is *capital*?" They cannot get it into their heads that things are everything and words are nothing. [1935, 61–62]

This search for the perfect fuel, the real stuff, has been frustrated for more than a hundred years. Induction, that most imperfect of methods, suggests that the Rhetoric Express will not leave town under its own power.

Neoclassical economic theory is founded upon a single mathematical metaphor that equates "utility" with the potential energy of mid-nineteenth century physics. From Walras to Pareto to McCloskey the tendency has been to admit the metaphor in a coy and indirect manner, hedged about with the qualification that it is merely a matter of words and therefore of no conse-quence to evaluations of the content and significance of the theory. If a "good metaphor depends, too, on the ability of its audience to suppress incongrui-ties," and "What is successful in economic metaphor is what is successful in poetry, and the success is analyzable in similar terms" (McCloskey 1985a, 77fn and 78), then the prognosis is clear. All that modern neoclassicals must do is suppress all the uncomfortable or silly bits of the founding fathers' metaphor—and this they have done by their blinkered concentration upon the technical aspects of the mathematics, come hell or high water—and evaluate the "artfulness" of the resulting product using their own internally generated criteria. This, of course, is nothing other than the "market test" in sheep's clothing. Just as the Realpolitik version of Great Art is the art that still sells, the Realpolitik version of Great Economics is the stuff that neoclassicists still flog in the classroom. If the metaphorical genesis of neoclassical theory is no longer mentioned in the classroom, well, then, it must have been expendable.

One of the virtues of the rather more broad conception of Rhetoric herein advocated is its mandate to describe the *process* of persuasion in all its multi-form splendor, from the literal reference of "mere words" to the social construction of the object of discourse. In the more narrow case that concerns us here, the importance of metaphor (vernacular or mathematical) is that its role, contrary to Donald Davidson, is *never* limited to a literal representation of the concept of reference. The use of metaphor sets up a field of secondary and tertiary resonances, constrasts, and comparisons that not only describe, but also reconstruct and transform the original metaphorical material. It is a commonplace among philosophers that there are no rules for definitively identifying metaphors, because the original thing compared and the object of comparison frequently undergo figure–ground reversal, and the forcefulness of a metaphor often derives from the unstated synergistic impliations. This is not to say that the analysis of the efficacy of metaphoric reasoning is a hopeless project, trapped at the ineffectual level of aesthetic appreciation.

The foundational metaphor of mathematical neoclassical economic theory is palpably different from poetic metaphor and therefore must be analyzed in a distinct manner. Mary Hesse, who has considered the role of metaphor in physics at great length, has described the fundamental distinctions between metaphors in science and metaphors in poetry (1966; 1974; 1980, 118–123). It is a distinguishing characteristic of successful poetic metaphor that the images chosen be initially striking, unexpected, shocking, or even perverse. (Here we may recall Baudelaire's comparison of his lover's body to a piece of carrion.)[6] A poetic metaphor is meant to be savored, to be entertained in the way one sips a wine, not to be analyzed further in pedantic detail. (This most certainly explains the pariah status of literary critics in certain quarters.) The poetic metaphor sports a penumbra of further metaphors and implications that may themselves be contrary to conventional usage and the tacit knowledge of the reader, be flagrantly contradictory with one another, and fly in the face of previous comparisons in the same text. Far from being considered an error, this is part of the calculated impact of poetic language. Finally, only the confused pedant takes a poetic metaphor to be a research program. A poem is intended to be self-contained; it is a rare occurrence for a poem to recruit missionaries who go out to remake the world in its image.

Scientific metaphors clearly have different criteria of efficacy and success. Although a scientific metaphor initially may appear incongruous, this is not generally conceded to be a point in its favor, and much of scientific activity can be interpreted as an atempt to render unseemly metaphors intelligible and pedestrian. A distinguishing characteristic of scientific metaphors is the fact that they are considered failures if they can muster only temporary impact and do not become the object of pedantic explication and elaboration. (Here one might cite examples of mathematicians rooting out the most obscure and arcane implications of the idea of a continuous function, or of the metaphor of "infinity.") Scientific metaphors should set in motion research programs that strive to make explicit all of the attendant submetaphors of the original. They should provoke inquiry as to whether the implications are consistent, one with another, as well as consistent with the background tacit knowledge.

There is no such thing as a perfect scientific metaphor with no negative aspects. It is the job of the scientist to reconcile these inconsistencies with the tacit knowledge of the profession as well as with the "facts." Scientific metaphors can fail; but this is not generally due to some mythical *experimentum crucis*, but rather to an increasing realization on the part of the scientific participants that the metaphor is cumbersome, awkward, and throws up intractable inconsistencies with its penumbra of meanings. However tentative and non-teleological this process seems, metaphors are an indispensable component of the scientific vocabulary, because they are a means to permit the expansion and adaption of theory to a changing world.

Thus a rhetorical analysis of scientific and mathematical meaphor will diverge from the rhetorical analysis of a poem in distinct and critical respects. The former must ask, Is the metaphor consistent with itself? Is it consistent with the rest of the science? What properties of the metaphor are essential, and which expendable? Which aspects are those of similarity, and which of causality (Hesse 1966, 86–87)? In these areas, McCloskey's version of Rhetoric gets low marks, because it abdicates all responsibility for the tough questions. The probable cause of McCloskey's watered-down Rhetoric is that neoclassical economic theory does not fare well under more intense cross-examination.

As already indicated, the progenitors of neoclassical theory did admit that they were asserting that something in economics was "like" energy in physics, but not a one of them ventured beyond coy references to the examination of the consistency of the metaphor in any detail. When various physicists and mathematicians challenged the consistency and adequacy of the metaphor, particularly with respect to what they considered to be the fundamental property of energy (that is, its conservation), the neoclassicals responded with nonsense and incomprehension. This situation did not improve over time. Later neoclassicals wavered between affirming and denying that the metaphorical "utility" was required by the very structure of their economic theory, or quibbled about whether it only needed to be ordinal rather than cardinal, as if the denial of the metaphor as the very rock upon which the theory was founded would somehow exorcize all the negative components of the analogy with energy (Wong 1978; Shoemaker 1982). Hence twentieth-century neoclassicals tried to suppress the negative components of the energetics metaphor by trying to suppress the metaphor itself, to the extent that neoclassicals are still surprised and a little shocked when confronted with the fact that their economic theory was appropriated from nineteenth-century physics. This was not science, and it was not even passable poetry.

Because of this fact, critics of neoclassicism over the last century have been put in the unenviable position of having to unwittingly reinvent the wheel. When Veblen complained that man was not a lightning calculator of pleasures and pains who oscillates like a homogeneous globule of desire or happiness under the impuse of stimuli that leave the man intact; or when Schumpeter complained that the firm would not exist as a static maximizer; or when Sraffa complained that there are no increasing or decreasing returns; or even when the exceptional undergraduate frowns skeptically at the idea of a utility function—all are unwittingly questioning the scientific propriety of the metaphor of utility as energy. The fact that the modern proponents of utility were innocent of the genealogy of the theory and its implications resulted in a palpable degeneration in the quality of discourse. The critics were testing the limits of the physics metaphor, whereas the defenders felt free to tender any response that was convenient, since they had no clear conception of what was necessary and what was superfluous in their adopted model. If attention had been paid to the physics metaphor, it would have become apparent that some attributes of the energy concept are indispensable: that it be conserved in a closed system; that it is a variable of state, and therefore cannot be time-dependent; that it posited a fundamental symmetry between the past and the future; that it was not a substance but a relation; that it was an integral, and therefore determinate only up to a constant of integration. Many acrimonious debates in the history of economics, including the Cambridge capital controversies, would have been clarified tremendously if these tenets had been kept in clear view.

The Discreet Charm of the Bourgeoisie

Unhappily, neoclassical economists have not used their metaphor the way scientists generally use metaphors. But if this has been the case, then why has neoclassical economic theory been so persuasive over the course of the last century, to the extent of "marginalizing" all other schools of economic thought? The answer takes us outside the realm of McCloskey's rhetoric, but remains well within the bounds of our broader notion of Rhetoric as the social construction of knowledge. This expanded Rhetoric draws its theoretical inspiration from fields disparaged by the neoclassical economist because they have remained relatively impervious to the siren song of the Cartesian vice: anthropology and the sociology of knowledge.

Tracing their influences from Durkheim and Mauss on primitive classification, Mary Douglas and David Bloor have recently argued that the act of persuasion in any human culture is intrinsically metaphorical and social:

> I feel we should try to insert between the psychology of the individual and the pub-lic use of language a dimension of social behavior. . . . Persons are included in or excluded from a given class, classes are ranked, parts are related to wholes. It is argued here that the intuition of the logic of these social experiences is the basis for finding the *a priori* in nature. The pattern of social relations is fraught with emo-tional power; great stakes are invested in their permanence by some, in their overthrow by others. This is the level of experience at which the gut reaction of bewilderment at an unintelligible sentence is strengthened by potential fury, shock and loathing. Apprehending a general pattern of what is right and necessary in social relations is the basis of society: this apprehension generates whatever *a priori* or set of necessary causes is going to be found in nature. [Douglas 1975, 280–81]

In other words, *all* societies must appeal to their understanding of natural order for the purpose of legitimizing their social order. The works of Douglas (1973; 1975; 1982) describe how this process operates in non-Western societies; the fascinating work of Bloor (1982) and Barnes & Shapin (1979) applies the same sort of analysis to the history of Western physics, mathemat-ics, and medicine. The relevance of this work to a revitalized theory of rhe-toric is that it unites social theory with the original quest to understand how audiences are won over by certain general techniques of communication. The appeal to Nature and to a Natural Order pervades our discourse in ways nei-ther literal nor transparent; this submerged content accounts for many of those subversive and troublesome emotions that color any rational argument. The Cartesian plot to banish emotional discourse and to denigrate the process of argumentation was yet another instance of this general pattern of appeal to Natural Order.

Thus the appropriation of a mathematical metaphor from physics and its reification as neoclassical economic theory is rendered comprehensible as part of a much larger pattern, one that we share with such precapitalist societies as the Tiv and the Lele, as well as with our predecessors in earlier Western social formations. The success of neoclassical economic theory cannot be traced to the scientific criticism and elaboration of the positive and negative aspects of the original physics metaphor. Rather, it can be traced to the fact that the appropriation of a physics metaphor expresses a basic principle of human understanding, that social order must be understood as being rooted in and a reflection of natural order. Because this principle has been expressed in economics indirectly as a metaphor, it has proven profoundly more effective than if it had been stated baldly and prosaically, perhaps as a philosophical dogma or a tenet of faith. The Cartesian predispositions and the scientific pretensions of economists would in that case have clashed with an explicit authoritarian fiat. It has proved more consistent to allow the individual scientist through reflective contemplation to discover for himself or herself the implied metaphors of natural order inherent in the mathematical model appropriated from physics.

So what precisely is this metaphorical content of neoclassical economic theory that has proved so successful in displacing all other schools of economic thought? Our expanded rhetorical analysis can be adequately carried out only in the detailed analysis of texts and conversations, but the architectonics can be summarized briefly. The physics metaphor implies that economics is a *science* and deserves all the legitimacy that is granted to physics itself, because no great difference exists between the two modes of inquiry. The economy is portrayed as a self-contained and separable subset of social life, and as such has the character of a stable natural process. "Capitalism" as a natural entity is implied to be timeless: it has always existed and will always continue to exist. Human beings within this sphere of social life behave as if they were automatons, in that their rationality is conflated with the existence of mechanical decision rules, most notably constrained maximization over a conserved vector field. Humans may behave differently in other spheres of social life, but since that behavior is "irrational" by definition, there is nothing left to be explained. Finally, the physics metaphor endows differential ontological validity upon sets of social phenomena: the "individual" is taken to be more real than any other social formation, be it the family, the firm, the nation state, and so on.

The Words of Others

Let me tell you why I hate critics. Not for all the normal reasons: that they are failed creators (they usually aren't; they may be failed critics, but that's another matter); or that they're by nature carping, jealous and vain (they usually aren't; if anything, they might be accused of over-generosity, of upgrading the second-rate so that their own fine discriminations might thereby appear the rarer). No, the reason I hate critics—well, some of the time—is that they write sentences like this:

"Flaubert did not build up his characters, as did Balzac, by objective, external description; in fact, so careless is he of their outward appearance that on one occasion he gives Emma [Bovary] brown eyes (14); on another deep black eyes (15); and on another blue eyes (16)."   —Julian Barnes, *Flaubert's Parrot*, 74

Surely here is an opportunity to get rid of that great stick of a character *Homo economicus* and to replace him with somebody real, like Madame Bovary.
          —Donald McCloskey, *The Rhetoric of Economics*, 66

Notes

1. For the curious, they are Plot, Character, Diction, Thought, Spectacle, and Song (compare Aristotle 1961, 62).

2. I mean this literally, not figuratively. See Guth (1983, 215): "I have often heard it said that there is no such thing as a free lunch. It now appears possible that the universe is a free lunch."

3. McCloskey (1985a, 124) admits this possibility, but does not seem to realize the extent to which it could cripple his entire thesis: "the Announcement, the more bold, unargued and authoritarian the better, is the favored form of scholarly communication. . . . One wonders why unargued cases are accepted more readily than argued ones, even among professional arguers."

Others have already noticed the possible symmetry between the neoclassical theory of social behavior and a neoclassical theory of the behavior of scientists. See, for instance, Garner (1979).

4. The best blow-by-blow commentary is still Harcourt (1972), supplemented by Harcourt (1982). Does it say something about the tenor of American rhetoric that the most cogent defense of the Cambridge, Mass., position also comes from the other side of the Atlantic, viz. Blaug (1974)?

5. Fisher (1926, 85–86) presents a table that lists the correspondences between the physics and economics labels for the variables in the same mathematical formalism.

6. "Une Charogne" in Baudelaire's *Les Fleurs du Mal*. In the Pléiade *Oeuvres Complètes* it can be found on pages 29–31.

9
Nelson and Winter's *Evolutionary Theory of Economic Change*

Economic theorists have flirted with the metaphor of "natural selection" for a hundred years, but they have been mere dalliances until now.[1] If it is true that neoclassical economics is nothing more than bowdlerized physics, then the work of Richard Nelson and Sidney Winter, *An Evolutionary Theory of Economic Change*, is an epoch-making departure from orthodox theory.[2] It is one of the most significant books of the decade, as much for what it leaves unsaid as for what it contains.

This book, in a much more explicit manner than the authors' previous journal articles, is a full frontal attack on the hard core of neoclassical *method*, and a suggestion of an alternative. Nelson and Winter expressly dispense with "all the components of the maximization model—the global objective function, the well-defined choice set, and the maximizing choice rationalization of firms' actions" (14). It is noteworthy that the target of their attack is very circumscribed: they disagree with casting *firm* behavior as the outcome of a global constrained maximization; they do not comment on the appropriateness of the characterization of the consumer. Partly due to this selective and limited vantage point, their reasons for dispensing with constrained maximization are the weakest part of this book, especially in view of the fact that they later claim that their framework subsumes the neoclassical orthodoxy (73). Nelson and Winter's indictments of maximization are in no way novel, particularly coming after the writings of G. L. S. Shackle and Herbert Simon; they are: (a) processing information is itself costly; (b) perfect knowledge of the underlying structure of the economy is unrealistic; (c) all behavior that is fully preplanned is not consistent with free choice; (d) maximization ignores firm decision-making structures; and (e) global probability statements cannot analytically encompass novelty and surprise (66–67). Neoclassical economists already have well-developed responses to these sorts of criticisms, along the lines that inductive proofs are not necessary for true knowledge, and true knowledge is not necessary for successful or determinate decision-making.[3] Neoclassical theory has always abstracted away the actual reports of individuals' motivations and the actual mechanisms of market interactions, and since its inception has proved incapable of incorporating these considerations in any logical manner.[4] Therefore, simply to indict neoclassicism for lacking realism

161

is rather like whining that one was not born rich and beautiful: the sympathy of the audience wanes rapidly. One can picture most neoclassical economists reading a hundred pages into Nelson and Winter, then giving up with the conviction that the authors plainly did not understand the true generality of the neoclassical paradigm.

To do so would be a great mistake, nonetheless. One theme of Winter's work, dating back to his thesis, is that the defenses of firm maximization can take two forms: one, a tautology, outlined above, invulnerable to any empirical attack; and two, an assertion that there is some form of selection mechanism that weeds out firms that do not behave as if they maximize something, generally profits.[5] Various defenders of neoclassical theory, such as Milton Friedman or Fritz Machlup, have shifted indiscriminately between the two positions, and this is their logical error. Winter's thesis and his book with Nelson show that the latter position cannot be defended on purely logical grounds, because they can conceive of many plasible situations in which the mean survivor need not be a maximizer, or even particularly efficient from some global viewpoint. This aspect of Nelson and Winter is valuable and important, because it reveals the *post hoc ergo propter hoc* character of neoclassical rationalizations of economic events, and the tautological nature of neoclassical "equilibrium."[6]

The other major contribution of *An Evolutionary Theory* is to provide a paradigm of evolutionary economic research that is not some minor variant of neoclassical methodology. Even though this is the most thoughtful and sustained attempt to do so since the writings of Thorstein Veblen and J. R. Commons, I harbor serious doubts that Nelson and Winter are successful in this quest. The remainder of this view is devoted to an explication of Nelson and Winter's models and then expression of these reservations on the technical level, on the level of the biological metaphor, and on the level of appropriate tactics in attempts to provide alternative research strategies to neoclassical economic theory.

There are three generic evolutionary "models" in *An Evolutionary Theory*. The first, which appears in chapter six, portrays firms probabalistically receiving physical units of "machines" in the event that they are profitable. The model purportedly describes a situation where a market environment selects firms that differ from each other according to different capacity utilization rules; these firms grow by adding machines. Once one understands the assumptions, the chapter six model becomes vacuous as an analytical device: machines have no price so firms don't really buy them. In conjunction with the assumption that firms sell everything they produce in the same period that they produce it, one can see that their conception of capacity utilization has no sensible interpretation, in contrast to the conventional conception of behavior that tries to adjust costs to fluctuating sales.

The second generic model, found in chapter seven, is a needlessly intricate search algorithm for a single firm for alternative techniques using two variable "inputs," given factor prices and holding the capital/output ratio constant. Since this model holds all of the same things constant as the conventional neoclassical theory of the firm, and derives essentially the same results as that theory, it seems redundant in light of Nelson and Winter's earlier criticism of orthodoxy theory. The authors themselves seem somewhat embarrassed by this, as they conclude this chapter with a section entitled "What Difference Does It Make?" (184).

The third generic class of models is the only substantial alternative to neoclassical theory offered by Nelson and Winter. In chapters nine and twelve the authors present models of firm behavior that leave a number of options open to each individual firm, such as the ability to search for a new production technique conditional upon past experience. Since the wider range of options leaves more degrees of analytical freedom than are conventional in orthodox analyses, Nelson and Winter find they can discuss the outcome of selection processes only through the use of the technique of computer simulation of an aggregation of synthetic firm histories. The broad outlines of this third class of models can be summarized in five equations (302–3):

$$q_{it} = A_{it} K_{it} \tag{1}$$

$$Q_t = \sum_i q_{it} \tag{2}$$

$$P_t = D(Q_t) \tag{3}$$

$$\pi_{it} = (P_t A_{it} - c - r_{im} - r_{in}) \tag{4}$$

$$K_{i,t+1} = I[(P_t A_{it})/c, (q_{it}/Q_t), \pi_{it}] + (1 - \delta)K_{it} \tag{5}$$

where: q_{it} = quantity output of firm i at time t
Q_t = aggregate output
A_{it} = "capital" requirement per unit output
P_t = price per unit output
K_{it} = capital stock of firm i at time t
π_{it} = firm profit rate
c = cost of capital per unit
δ = depreciation rate per unit capital
r_{im} = cost of imitative search per unit capital
r_{in} = cost of R&D per unit capital

Equation 1 displays the Leontief-style technology; each firm uses the same identical homogeneous input ("capital") to produce a single homogeneous output. Equation 3 is a conventional downward-sloping neoclassical market demand curve, which is fixed over the duration of all simulation runs, and sets the price of the output. Equation 4 describes the firm's profit rate as its return per unit capital minus the "cost of capital" and expenses of imitative and exploratory search; all costs are constant and identical for all firms. Equation 5 describes the growth path of the firm's capital, combining an investment function (with the explanatory variables: the firm price/cost ratio, market share, and profit rate) with a depreciation function; the functional forms are the same for all firms. Search itself is triggered by a shortfall relative to a profit-rate satisfying criterion. Success in imitation of other firms, technologies and/or technological innovation is stochastic, with moments of distributions conditional upon the size of the firm's capital.

Equations 1 through 5 describe a stochastic difference equation in "capital" for each firm; runs for a number of firms comprise a population history. The authors then choose two different settings for each of the parameters, and create synthetic population histories based on those settings. The reader may easily get lost in this section of the book, since independent population histories are identified only by binary digit codes; so little information is provided about each individual run that the reader has no independent ability to draw his or her own conclusions about pairwise comparisons of histories.[7] The runs are then employed to make statements about the effects of parameter settings upon industry concentration, innovations, price dynamics, the adoption of best-practice technology, and other matters of concern. The only unambiguous result of the runs seems to be an unwavering tendency for unconcentrated situations to assume relatively stable concentrated forms over time. Other results seem to hinge crucially upon the specific parameter settings, and since we are presented with only two discrete settings for each parameter, the reader may be hesitant to agree with Nelson and Winter's confident assertions that more of "X" leads to more or less of "Y." Indeed, I expect much dissatisfaction with Nelson and Winter will arise from the essentially arbitrary nature of their simulations. But since they themselves make no claim to striving for historical accuracy (220), and see their models as tentative suggestions of an alternative research strategy, then any substantial critique must be conducted upon the same plane.

Initially one's attention is drawn to the technical inadequacies of their model. It is a glaring asymmetry of their generic model that the price of the output is determined by a neoclassical demand curve, but all other prices are given, mainly by setting them as constants. One anticipates that this is where neoclassical economists will press their counteroffensive: it has always been their contention that the absence of markets in certain areas will give rise to the indeterminacies and nonneoclassical results that engage Nelson and Winter. For example, they might claim that if a functioning neoclassical market (that is, a stable demand curve with appropriate arguments and market clearing conditions) for "capital" were incorporated into their model, the distribution of firms would rapidly collapse to a conventional no-profit equilibrium. Were Nelson and Winter to retort that they do not believe such a market exists, then we should be equally justified in asking why a neoclassical market for output exists as well. The theoretical lesson here is that one cannot remain aloof and agnostic, as Nelson and Winter do on price theory, and simultaneously claim to be offering an alternative to orthodox theory. (One would have thought the recent history of the Keynesians would be sufficient warning in this respect.) It would be a minimum requirement of consistency that Nelson and Winter should provide an explicit answer to the following question: What is the theoretical basis of their demand curve, our equation 3? If it is derived from the constrained maximization of utility of individuals, subject to a market clearing condition, then they have undermined their entire manifesto against orthodox method.

Second, Nelson and Winter also adopt elements of neoclassical capital theory that seriously compromise the logic of their models. The reader can observe from equations 1 and 5 that capital is treated as if it were some sort of protean jello, immediately assuming the characteristics of any adopted technological change; and further, its magnitude and depreciation are treated as though they were independent of prices. It would seem that Nelson and Winter have missed the significance of the last thirty years' controversy over capital theory. Suppose a change in the price of output (equation 3) were allowed to affect the price of capital, thus altering its magnitude in a non-monotonic direction. In that case, equation 5 could no longer be a simple difference equation, and the authors would lose their recourse to the theory of Markov processes. This objection is far from a quibble over the realism of assumptions, since the only actual identity a firm has in these models is the *magnitude* of its capital (a point to which we shall return). Nelson and Winter also fail to see that the reason they find results supporting Robert Solow's work on the aggregate neoclassical production function in chapter nine is that they have assumed the same "unobtrusive postulate" as Solow: a capital-substance having a magnitude independent of its price(s).

Other technical criticisms follow from these first two, and are merely indicated here. Nelson and Winter indiscriminately mix the physical and financial aspects of capital (157–58), to the point of maintaining that it is possible to identify a firm's capital stock without analytical attention to its balance sheet (408). It is beyond me how one could discuss the survival and growth of capitalist corporations without considering their financial structure, unless, of course, one nurtured the neoclassical predisposition to believe that monetary phenomena do not substantially alter Walrasian equilibrium configurations. Moreover, it is also beyond me how anyone could make any cogent statements about economic growth employing a model that allows no linkage between the growth of output and the growth of demand in the aggregate (part 4): the "demand curve" for output is exogenous and stable for all runs. Of course, this is nothing other than the Marshallian *ceteris paribus*, popping up in more and more contexts where it never belongs. Finally, one might express a little irritation with Nelson and Winter's studied neglect in reporting anomalous results. In their original unpublished draft of chapter nine, they admit that some initial parameter settings resulted in "crises," in which gross investment was negative, both for individual firms and in the aggregate.[8]

Their a priori and unreported juggling of parameter settings might itself have had some bearing upon whether readers will think the simulations "plausible".

Perhaps of more interest to the general economist than technical modeling considerations are the viability and plausibility of the biological metaphor itself. The adoption of a biological metaphor does not rigidly imply a single style or method of economic research, as historians of economics are well aware. Nelson and Winter do not provide an explicit discussion of the role of the metaphor in their work, a fact all the more incongruous given Winter's earlier careful consideration in his thesis of the misuse of the metaphor by Friedman and others. The closest thing we get to such a statement is the claim that "our theory is unabashedly Lamarkian: it contemplates both the 'inheritance' of acquired characteristics and the timely appearance of variation under the stimulation of adversity. We explicitly disavow any intention to pursue biological analogies for their own sake" (11). In one sense, this attitude is laudable, since so much of modern economics has slavishly copied the natural sciences, without deliberation as to the appropriateness of those methods and metaphors in the social sphere.[9] But in the case of Nelson and Winter's book, they adhere neither to a Lamarkian nor a Darwinian framework with any consistency; and this lapse causes the reader to wonder what their notion of "evolution" signifies. In other words, they do not treat their metaphors in a "scientific" manner, as explained above in chapter 8.

In their early chapters, Nelson and Winter insist that "routines" are the analogue of genes in their theory, and that searches for new routines, either by imitation or active R&D, serve as the analogue of mutations. This scheme might be meaningful, except for the fact that Nelson and Winter then say they will not consider firms as altering their Chandlerian strategies or structures; nor, indeed, will they pay any attention at all to the internal structure of the firm (37–38). This is a grave lacuna, because the question then arises as to what precisely is identical over time: that is, what is the object of the selection mechanism? In their explicit models, the only "routine" is a technology involving a capital-jello that expands over time. Nevertheless, the capital-jello in these models is continuously undergoing transformations that allow it to assume a new technology. For all practical purposes, the firm is a black box with no stable characteristics that could be subject to selection over time: it is only a bowl of capital-jello with a name (although it lacks even that grace in the world of high-tech simulation runs). There is nothing for the environment to "select," because there are no stable "species" in Nelson and Winter-style "evolution."

Haven't Nelson and Winter evaded this criticism in advance by opting for "Lamarkian" evolution? Even Jean-Baptiste Lamark understood the necessity of the existence of *relatively* stable species if there were to be a selection process: otherwise, it would be a world where most organisms so rapidly adapted themselves to any and all novel circumstances that there would be very little differentiation at any point in time. Nelson and Winter claim that their assumption that firms "satisfice" provides the needed species inertia; but they do not realize that it is not sufficient for an argument concerning *selection*. The first rule of any selection model is that the selected entity must have a high degree of permanence (meaning that one can truly identify it as the *same* entity) and a low rate of endogenous change, relative to the degree of bias for or against its favor in the environment.[10] In Nelson and Winter's models, there is no high degree of permanence because the rate of endogenous change—that is, the rate of the search—is roughly equal to the rate of bias in the environment—that is, profitability less than a relatively high trigger value. Nelson and Winter don't seem to understand that the reason that Darwinian evolution superceded the Lamarkian version was logical: pure natural selection reduces the frequency of mutation to a level approaching zero, or as George Williams puts it, "evolution takes place, not so much because of natural selection, but to a large degree in spite of it." [11] A portrait of a world where organisms are always undergoing self-initiated transformations in reaction to environmental alterations is already available: neoclassical economic theory.

Nelson and Winter misuse the metaphor of evolution because in their world nothing is ever the same, and nothing really dies, either. One of the more fascinating aspects of the evolutionary metaphor is the analogue between the death of the organism and firm bankruptcy, a phenomenon that attracts very little research interest in neoclassical theory. Because Nelson and Winter have exercised their analytical choice to neglect firm structure, they admit they have nothing to say about "the degree of owner versus management control, merger opportunities, tax and bankruptcy law consideration, [and] the liquidity or illiquidity of firm assets" (122). The capital-jello of a few firms dissolves in Nelson and Winter's simulations, although we have seen that they have admitted elsewhere that they have set their parameters so that it happens very infrequently. If death is only a remote possibility, then the selection metaphor has been stripped of what little analytical substance it still retained in their models. A serious evolutionary theory would begin with the premise that bankruptcy–death is what gives selection mechanisms their bite. The genetic entity that was to be selected could not be firm technology *per se*, both because firms regularly change their technologies, and because under present bankruptcy statutes, the firm's physical technologies are often kept in operation, even though the balance sheet may be restructured or absorbed by other firms. Patently, bankruptcy is a financial and monetary phenomenon, whereas Nelson and Winter don't seem to rank those phenomena high in theoretical importance.

Evolutionary metaphors have often been imported into social theory, from Herbert Spencer and Social Darwinism to E. O. Wilson and Gary Becker and Sociobiology. All these attempts have fallen prey to what Marshall Sahlins calls "the fallacy of the a priori fitness course." [12] In these theories, the traditional roles of the organism and the environment in natural selection have been reversed. The environment is presumed stable, and the organism is seen as rapidly changing. Nelson and Winter can be interpreted as also having run afoul of this pervasive fallacy. Much of what firms react to in Nelson and Winter's models are exogenous conditions, such as the state of technologies yet to be discovered and a fixed demand schedule and fixed factor costs. Upon making this list, one realizes these are not "natural" conditions that present barriers to firm expansion, but are rather the conditions that the evolutionary process itself changes; an adequate evolutionary theory must explain those changes. One observes this clearly in actual firm histories (which do not much interest Nelson and Winter), such as recent work by David St. Clair on the U.S. auto industry, which shows that General Motors would rather transform the very structure of American cities than rest content with the state of the market dictated by the technological and demand configurations of the 1930s and 1940s.[13]

Contrary to the impression that my nagging succession of criticisms may have created, I still believe that this book portends a new departure in economic theory, not because it is successful on its own terms but because it is the first book to reveal the great complexity and potential riches of the application of the metaphor of natural selection in economic theory. It indicates that the extension of the metaphor will require a new theoretical language, new research methods, and a substantial reconceptualization of the question of how a market does or does not "work." Unfortunately, I think Nelson and Winter's choice of computer simulation as a research method is an error, because it will not convince those who become acquainted with the arbitrary nature of their runs. A more effective tactic might be to adopt the research methods employed by evolutionary biologists: population genetics, demography, and paleontology (firm histories). Researchers could then admit that they were dealing with phenotypes (firm accounts, Chandlerian strategies and structures, work organization, and so forth), rather than pursuing some quest to identify genes with ephemeral and ill-defined "routines." Researchers might then be able to build simple models of firm formation and bankruptcy, which might lead to insights concerning business cycles and prices.[14] More important, such a research program would be fundamentally linked to a concerted program of empiricism, something which Nelson and Winter's book leaves stranded in a cul-de-sac. Information on firm size distribution, age structure, survival rates, formation and bankruptcy rates all become grist for testing and formulating hypotheses that have no place in the neoclassical program. Some of this empirical work already exists, and needs only to be put in the theoretical context of an evolutionary framework.[15]

If an evolutionary program is to succeed, however, it will probably have to avoid Nelson and Winter's *strategy* in dealing with orthodox economic theory. *An Evolutionary Theory* wants to have its cake and eat it, too. On the one hand, it purports to speak for every group of economists who have every expressed the mildest disaffection with neoclassical theory: the behavioralists

(34), Schumpeterians (39), neo-Austrians (41), classical and Marxian economists (43), historians of technical change (203) and, finally, institutionalists (404): "On questions of evolution in the larger system, we converge substantially with the older tradition of evolutionary thinking in economics that has had institutional evolution as its principal concern-a tradition maintained today by the AFEE and its journal, the *Journal of Economic Issues.*" But on the other hand, it doesn't want to ruffle any neoclassical feathers, providing results that are only marginally differentiated from those of the orthodoxy to the point of claiming that their book "*subsumes the orthodox*" view (73). Why are they loath to believe that different traditions generally produce incommensurable results? If this book fails to generate sustained research interest, it will be due mainly to this milk-and-water strategy, rather than to any dearth of provocative intellectual content. The results they proffer are so close to neoclassical results that I can't think why any neoclassical theorist would grace it with any more than a cursory reading. Conversely, the disaffected groups are so roundly misrepresented (and in the case of the institutionalists, not even consulted), that they too would probably choose to ignore it rather than argue with it. A careful reading of Veblen's essay "Why Is Economics Not an Evolutionary Science?," for example, should serve to disabuse Nelson and Winter of any notion that neoclassical price theory could be effortlessly linked to an evolutionary research program. Perhaps Nelson and Winter's error has been to apply their own model of the firm to the history of economic thought: they must think that bounded rationality will sustain localized search only in the near neighborhood of orthodoxy.

Notes

1. Among the neoclassical economists who have dallied in the groves of Darwin are Alfred Marshall (1925); H.S. Houthakker, "Economics and Biology," Office of Naval Research Technical Report no. 30, January 1956; R.S. Goodwin, "A Growth Cycle," in *Capitalism and Economic Growth*, ed. C.H. Feinstein (Cambridge: Cambridge University Press, 1970); Armen Alchian (1950, 211–21); and Gary Becker (1976, 817–26).

2. Richard Nelson and Sidney Winter (1982). All page numbers in parentheses refer to this work.

3. Lawrence Boland (1981, 1031–36).

4. See Chapter 4, above.

5. Sidney Winter (1964).

6. The fundamental misreading of maximization as the outcome of a process rather than an imposed tautology is present even on the dust jacket of Nelson and Winter's book. A. Michael Spence there suggests erroneously that Nelson and Winter show how markets "substitute" for maximizing behavior.

7. These reports are so confusing that in the few cases where comparisons across runs are possible, there appear to be errors in the reports. For example, if Table 9.1 (218–19) is to conform to Table 9.2 (221), then 9.1 should describe run 00000 and not

00001, as reported in the text. One might suggest that the simulation method makes sense only if all of the raw results are reported, if only in a microform appendix.

8. R. Nelson, S. Winter, and H. Schutte, "Technical Change in an Evolutionary Model," University of Michigan Institute for Public Policy Studies discussion paper no. 45, July 1973, 31–32.

9. See Part I, above.

10. George C. Williams (1966, 23).

11. Ibid., 139.

12. Marshall Sahlins (1976, 83–128).

13. David St. Clair (1980, 62–78) and (1981, 579–600).

14. Perhaps something along the lines of Ronald Lee (1974).

15. William Crum (1953) and Richard Edwards (1975, 428–56).

10

Morishima on Marx

It is almost tragic, however, that Walras, who was usually so acute and clear-headed, imagined he had found the rigorous proof, which he had missed in contemporary defenders of free-trade dogma, merely because he clothed in a mathematical formula the very arguments which he considered insufficient when they were expressed in ordinary language. —Knut Wicksell, *Lectures on Political Economy*

This predilection, to which Wicksell himself was not entirely immune, has continued to bedevil the economics profession down to the present day. It is one thing for neoclassical economists to hawk proto-physics models as "proofs" of the natural order of the market. It is quite another level of hubris to wish also to teach some long-dead economists the error of their ways by nattering at them about lacunae in their educations concerning sums and topology.

The fervent desire to emulate physics has left neoclassical economists with a deep ambivalence concerning their discipline's past. Most, under the mistaken impression that physics has sloughed off its history, would wish economics to do likewise. Others, perhaps more worried about how posterity will treat them, feel impelled to go back to the hallowed texts and reinterpret them, with an eye toward demonstrating that all that is valuable in economics has led up to the current orthodoxy. Combined with a fervid faith that the adoption of mathematical argument has accounted for most of said progress in economic theory, these reinterpretations have been constrained to assume a particularly curious format. Usually they consist of a marshaling of quotes, which are dragooned to justify the casting of some economic relationships in a specific functional form, which are then used to arrive at one of the two alternative conclusions: (a) the esteemed late economist in question merely had anticipated a special case of existing neoclassical theory; or (b) the esteemed late economist in question had tripped himself up in self-contradiction, due to his unfortunate weaknesses in the area of mathematical expertise. (See, for example, Hicks 1972; Barkai 1959; Eagly 1974; Brems 1986). Ricardo seems the all-time favorite butt of this sort of activity, but there are a surfeit of instances of it for Quesnay and Smith as well. As with all other apologetic research agendas in economics, it has become a bit of an academic industry: search for the marginally renowned and as-yet unformalized economist and apply the recipe.

What is wrong with this harmless bit of storytelling? After all, the classical economists are dead and in their graves. Further, the sober and secular arm of the profession thinks it all a tempest in a teapot, since what matters in the hard-nosed world of economics in the paycheck, and not the *Weltanschaung*. The case of Maupertuis is sometimes mentioned in this respect (Samuelson 1972). His Principle of Least Action was not just a mathematical regularity in his opinion; it was simultaneously evidence for the existence of a benevolent and wise Supreme Being who efficiently minimized all effort. Subsequent physicists found that they could make use of Maupertuis's principle without bothering about questions of Divine Order. Don't neoclassical economists essentially act the same way? In particular, aren't these notions of theoretical progress just a lot of irrelevant excess metaphysical baggage?

Perhaps back in the era of Popper (an era that does evoke a certain modicum of nostalgia among neoclassicals) this stance appeared persuasive, but in the world after Kuhn, Feyerabend, Barnes, Bloor, and Rorty, it does seem a little dowdy and timeworn. The explosion of research in the history of science has taught us quite a bit about how intellectual disciplines work, and one of its primary lessons has been that the potted history of a discipline generated for internal consumption plays an important role as a heuristic in dictating legitimate research methods and topics, as well as fostering a camaraderie of shared perceptions (Graham, Lepenies, and Weingart 1983). Perceptions of progress do matter and are worth fighting over. In the context of a disciplinary matrix, the intellectual history of that discipline assumes a heightened significance; attempts to change the disciplinary reading of the history indicate deeper conflicts over the appropriate topics and methods of research. From this point of view, the neoclassical predilection to recast earlier economists in the mold of their own mathematical formalism is a profound hermeneutical tactic, a move to shift the grounds of the argument over progress onto their own turf.

There are a number of possible responses to this gambit, none of which is guaranteed to score points. One response is simply to denounce all retrospective mathematical models, but that does seem a no-win proposition when one takes into consideration the increased mathematicization of the discipline since World War II. A second response is to try to best the neoclassicals at their own game, in the sense of developing alternative mathematical models of important precursors that support research programs opposed to the neoclassical school. This, for instance, seems to have been the motivation behind Sraffa (1960) and Pasinetti (1973). Much can be said in favor of this gambit, but it does have the drawback that the quarrel appears to degenerate to one over the indifferent acceptability of alternative sets of "assumptions" (the F-twist), and it tends to ignore the larger issues of the impact of the formalization upon the theoretical substance and methodological orientation of the original texts. A third response is to attempt a hermeneutical reading of neoclassical mathematical restatements of important earlier texts, trying to evaluate their success relative to the object text and relative to the (generally unspoken) intentions of the author in rewriting the history of economic thought.

We shall attempt the third mode of response here. To focus our attention on the tensions inherent in the general practice of mathematical restatement, we shall choose to concentrate on the most criticized and most interpreted text in the entire history of economic thought, Marx's *Capital*. Marx is very important for the self-image and self-esteem of the neoclassicals, and not only because the other half of the world's population claims his text as their primary political inspiration. Marx's *Capital* represents the most advanced development of the classical system of economic theory prior to its demise in the West, and in order to provide a satisfying narrative of the progress of the discipline, that demise must be justified along some very stylized lines. This process was begun by Wicksteed and Bohm-Bawerk, but got seriously under way only when neoclassicals started to restate Marx mathematically, using neoclassical terminology and techniques (Samuelson 1957, 1971), (Georgescu-Roegen 1960). Such crude and openly unsympathetic bids to settle Marx's hash once and for all were not adequate to the underlying motivations of the exercise, which dictated walking a fine line between excessive elevation of Marx's achievements (although some elevation was called for to justify the attention bestowed) and excessive deprecation of Marx's "mathematical errors" (although, again, these had to be substantial to justify the primary message, which was the substantial progress achieved by neoclassicism after Marx).

The first neoclassical economist to aim at this fine balance was Michio Morishima in *Marx's Economics* (1973). It was his avowed intention to "recognize the greatness of Marx from the viewpoint of modern advanced economic theory and, by so doing, to contribute to the development of our science"(M, 5).[1] Now, this notion of a contribution to science is a bit vague. Does it contribute to the development of modern cosmology to praise the mistaken yet fascinating systems of Kepler and Ptolemy? Morishima is actually quite open about the object of his exercise, which is to hasten the day when "the division between valid Marxian economics and orthodox theory has been removed." There have been numerous commentaries and glosses upon Morishima's work, but it seems to the present author that all have missed this, the real point of the work, and consequently they have also passed lightly over many of the mathematical infelicities and theoretical incongruities of his book.

What follows is not another plaintive cry that yet another someone didn't get Marx right, since a hermeneutic perspective teaches that texts are open to contradictory yet legitimate readings. Instead, it is a meditation upon a certain overweening attitude among neoclassical economists that mathematical models are sufficient to brush aside all other considerations and crush competitor research programs under the wheels of their analytical engines. This may be effective from a sociological point of view, but it is simply false from the vantage point of the logic of assessment.

The Labor Theory of Value a Dead Dog?

The first thing that strikes the reader of *Marx's Economics* is that, in return for a substantial investment in mathematical manipulation, there is very little Marxian theory left unscathed by the end of the book. On page 103 we are informed, "Apart from ideological reasons, values are necessary in Marxian economics, not because they are the first approximation of prices, but because they are more fundamental than prices and enable us to get rid of circularity." This is a profound possibility (compare Mirowski 1986 and Krause 1982), but Morishima then appears to debase this insight by seeing it as only a problem in the theory of aggregation. The notion of a value theory as a prior prerequisite of a coherent theory of price, which was clearly the notion expressed by Marx in the first six chapters of volume 1 of *Capital,* has gone by the boards without comment or rationale. The reason it is ignored is not one of a lack of susceptibility to mathematical formalization, or even a case of external criticism, say, to the effect that it was a metaphysical residuum of Marx's unfortunate weakness for Hegelian wordplay. There is for Morishima only one criterion for whether some Marxian concept gets his mathematical attention, and it is stated at the end of the book: "one of the conclusions of this book is that Marx's economics can acquire citizenship in contemporary economic theory by detaching it from its root, the labor theory of value, and grafting it onto the Von Neumann stock so as to produce the Marx–Von Neumann flower" (M, 194).

If we may be permitted to mix metaphors with the same exhilarating freedom as Morishima, Marx may not be a citizen of the neoclassical nation, but he does not need a passport from Morishima to reside in the land of economics or even to smuggle in some agricultural produce. As for the flora of the land of the neoclassicals, horticulturalists for some time now have been trying to breed away the yeasty bitter juices of classical economics in their cassavas, but every effort seems to result in a root that's not very nourishing (although admittedly pretty) and a flower that is sterile (although undeniably convex). I suspect that Morishima is aware of this, and some later writings (see Morishima 1984) confirm the suspicion. Nevertheless, this has not deterred Morishima from riding roughshod over both Marx and Walras in order to foster the impression of one nation, one theory, one genetic heritage.[2]

Why should we want to entertain seriously the Marx–Von Neumann hybrid? In the context of *Marx's Economics,* I suppose there are two justifications: first, to demonstrate the expendability of the labor theory of value, and second, to reveal what new insights might be derived from such a model. Just on the evidence of pages devoted to each, Morishima is much more concerned with the first than the second. Let us then occupy ourselves in this section with Morishima's reasons for his Marx minus the labor theory, and postpone to the next section some consideration of the novel exercises that he promises.

Reason One

It is evident that consistency is not assured when the age structure of fixed capital is no longer stationary. There will not be universal consistency between "the replacement of the wear and tear portion of the value in the form of money" and "the replacement of fixed capital in kind" unless we get rid of the neoclassical [sic] method of depreciation and obey the Von Neumann golden rule in the valuation of capital costs. [M, 173]

While this reason for the rejection of what Marx actually said is somewhat arcane, it is a good place to start because it is fraught with the pitfalls of any attempt to make Marx look bad solely with mathematics. First, to set the stage: Morishima wishes to advocate the adoption of the Von Neumann method of capital accounting, where a one-period-older machine is treated as if it were an economically distinct commodity relative to a newer machine of the same physical identity. Marx does advocate a different method, using straightline bookkeeping methods, which Morishima inexplicably misrepresents as being "neoclassical." For most of the book Morishima just blasts ahead with the Von Neumann method, but relatively late in the book (M, 170–78) he feels the need to confront what Marx actually wrote. Rather than discuss Marx's reasons for such a choice, Morishima decides he will quickly model Marx's alternative and swiftly reveal its internal inconsistencies.

He proceeds as follows. First he defines the current input matrix A_I as composed of individual elements $a_{ij} = (k_{ij}/\tau_{ij})$, letting k_{ij} be the "stock of capital good i" required for the production of one unit of capital good j, and τ_{ij} be the effective lifetime of k_{ij} when used in the production of good j. The matrix A_{II} is defined for the wage and luxury good sectors in the same manner. Note that the entries of A_I are intended to represent *flows* of input per unit time period. Morishima then goes on to write the following cost-price equations:

$$p_I = (1+\pi)(p_I A_I + wL_I) \tag{1}$$

$$p_{II} = (1+\pi)(p_I A_{II} + wL_{II}) \tag{2}$$

where p_I denotes the price vector of capital goods, p_{II} the price vector of wage and luxury goods, π is the uniform rate of profit, w the given wage, and L the vector of labor requirements in production. The first bit of negligence in the area of textual exegesis is that equations (1) and (2) have the capitalists figuring their profits on flow costs of inputs rather than on stocks. This is an extremely awkward manner of incorporating the notion of fixed capital into mathematical analysis, and in any event Marx never made any such claim in volumes 2 and 3. But more to the point, it is inconceivable that Morishima can now teach Marx any lessons concerning "the replacement of fixed capital in kind." But there is more, so let us persevere.

On pages 171–173 a few more relatively innocuous assumptions are floated, and then the following relationship is deduced:

$$p_I A_I x_I(t) + p_I A_{II} x_{II}(t) = p_I R(t + 1) \tag{3}$$

where $x(t)$ is the vector of output levels for the respective sectors and $R(t)$ is the vector of input replacements at time t. Now, says Morishima, imagine that all capital goods last just two periods, and all of those available in period t are new. No producer needs any machines in period $t + 1$, hence $p_I R(t + 1) = 0$; but there is value set aside in period $t + 1$ for replacement—that is,

$$\sum_{i=I}^{II} p_I A_i x_i(t) > 0.$$

Hence the objection that value is not equal to replacement in kind. This is the sum total of Morishima's first indictment: the assumptions of *this* model imply an equilibrium condition that will obtain only with a certain pattern of the decay and replacement of stocks, one that exhibits a stationary age structure.

Here are a veritable concatenation of incongruities, so many that it makes one dizzy trying to sort them out. First, the model misrepresents Marx at the simplest possible level in miscalculating profits on flows alone. Second, the basic issue is that depreciation may not equal replacement investment because replacement is often bunched and depreciation is sometimes continuous, although this really is a question of money and accounting, which by no stretch of the imagination are given due consideration anywhere in Morishima's book. Third, the treatment of time is questionable, to say the least. Morishima draws various conclusions in words about the age structure of capital stocks, even though those specific temporal configurations are not seriously modeled.

To make this clearer, let us construct a model in parallel to that of Morishima, confining ourselves only to a state of simple reproduction with no fixed capital. Employing Morishima's notation, we shall now adopt equations (1) and (2) (this time consistently, since there is no divergence of stocks from flows by construction) and assume that the entire output of department II is consumed by the workers:

$$x_{II}(t) = C(t + 1) \tag{4}$$

$$x_I(t) = R(t + 1) \tag{5}$$

$$wL_I x_I(t) + wL_{II} x_{II}(t) = C(t + 1) \tag{6}$$

Substituting and simplifying, we arrive at:

$$p_I A_I x_I(t) + p_I A_{II} x_{II}(t) = P_I R(t + 1)$$

which is identical to equation (3). The fact of the matter is that equation (3) is a flow and not a stock condition and holds even in the case of simple reproduction. It has no real implications for the age structure of physical stocks, says nothing about balanced growth, certainly is incapable of being used to discuss accounting conceptions of depreciation, and assumes away most of Marx's profound concerns with respect to turnover in volume 2. Appeals concerning "money," "fixed capital," and "depreciation" are thoroughly unavailing, and juxtapose an aura of high logical rigor with the practice of low semantic comedy.

Fourth, to complain about Marx's recourse to the stationary state really must be seen as a case of the pot calling the kettle black when it comes to neoclassical theory. It is not even clear that anything exists that might be called a legitimate nonsteady state theory of capital within the neoclassical paradigm. The existence of a nonstationary capital stock implies a process of growth incompatible with the Von Neumann equilibrium path, and therefore Morishima's research program should have been to inquire whether the Von Neumann method of capital accounting materially helps or hinders such analysis. What has not been sufficiently appreciated is that the Von Neumann balanced growth ray is the closest analogue to a one-good economy in the economist's armamentarium, and therefore any analysis that commits itself to that format will discover that it is not capable of even phrasing questions concerning nonstationary capital stocks, because the formalism has effectively ruled them out of court. There still remains the question of the relative attractions of the Von Neumann method of capital accounting, even on the balanced growth ray. We postpone consideration of that issue until Reason Five below.

Reason Two

"In literary terms, Marx assumed that the rate of accumulation of capitalists of department one was an exogenous factor, to which that of the capitalists of department two was adjusted" (M, 145). Morishima objects to Marx's assumption as unrealistic (more pot black-calling?), suggesting that Marx chose it because he could conjure no other adequate way of distributing investment between sectors so that rates of profit could be equalized while the system converged to a state of balanced growth (M, 122). Morishima pro-

poses that we must tie the rate of accumulation to a demand-supply framework to explain it satisfactorily (M, 157). Two classes of reservations might
be broached at this point: Does this tactic indeed constitute a consistent explanation? and Does this tactic constitute an explanation that could be coherent in
any conceivable Marxian tradition?

The answer to the first reservation is that Morishima chooses an exceptionally awkward method of introducing macroeconomic demand into his model.
He postulates a two-equation dynamic input-output system, where the output
of department I must cover the flow material input requirements in the next
period (but there is no fixed capital, and therefore no long-term investment),
while the output of department II must meet the following requirement (M,
147):

$$x_{II}(t) = \omega B[L_I x_I(t + 1) + L_{II} x_{II}(t + 1)] + F(t) \tag{7}$$

where B is a column vector of the workers' subsistence wage bundle, and ω is
the fraction of B earned during one hour's labor.

In this formulation, "Capitalists' demands for wage and luxury goods $F(t)$
must be fulfilled at every point in time." Now, in what sense is this an
improvement over Marx's assumption about the investment behavior of capitalists in department II? Instead of mechanical investment behavior, we have
mechanical consumption behavior; recall that equation (7) is a *macroeconomic*
condition. Indeed, we can turn Morishima's complaint back upon his own
model (M, 146): Why does the general law of capitalist consumption demand
forcibly assert itself like a law of Nature, in spite of the fact that all the
members of society are ignorant of it (excepting, of course, the neoclassical
growth theorists)? Surely this is not at all an adequate representation of the
conventional mechanism of supply and demand, nor of the macroeconomic
concept of effective demand. Perhaps there is some implied idea of a capitalist power relationship over the consumption of goods, but it does seem even
more farfetched to think of a capitalist consumption basket as socially determined. If a power relationship is what Morishima intended, then it is but a
poor caricature of the Marxian concept of exploitation, which is not based on
the vagaries of consumption but an argument concerning the entire mode of
production.

Regardless of the overall question of the superiority of Morishima's alternative, there are also some technical problems. Again he has a certain devil-
may-care attitude evident in his treatment of temporal processes. Morishima
describes his model *in words* as asserting that "wages are paid before work
and there is no consumption lag" (M, 147). But there is not enough detailed
specification in equation (7) to justify any behavioral interpretation, and in
fact, the only aspect of equation (7) of any importance for the model is the
arbitrary specification that labor consumption requirements are out of phase
with capitalist consumption requirements. In this context, complaining about

a lead or lag here and there may seem picky and a little trivial, but it is one of the curses of mathematical expression that what at first seems trivial may later turn out to have been decisive. In this particular instance, a thoroughly unmotivated assumption about the phasing of consumption requirements becomes the driving force of a difference equation that is used later in the book to illustrate the stability of the growth path and, in Morishima's strained interpretation, evaluate the Marxian notion of the inherent instability of capitalist accumulation. [3]

In order to see what difference a little difference in the timing of consumption can make to a difference equation, let us temporarily drop capitalist consumption as a distinct category from equation (7), and rearrange the result:

$$x_{II}(t) - \omega BL_{II} x_{II}(t + 1) = \omega BL_I x_I(t + 1) \tag{8}$$

This is a simple first order difference equation whose solution can be expressed as an exponential function of the labor consumption bundle and the growth rate of the output of department I. Recalling that this is only a minor alteration of Morishima's equation (7), one can now state in words that this solution describes a situation in which the rate of accumulation of department I is given exogenously, and the capitalists of department II blithely adjust their investment behavior to it. This is one possible behavioral interpretation that may be imposed upon equation (8), but it is certainly not the only one possible. Remember it is taken from Morishima, where it was justified by some imprecise remarks about when workers got their wages. Morishima, blinded by the mathematics, does not see that what is sauce for the goose is sauce for the gander.

Further, the arbitrary lagging of differential consumption patterns is no way to get at the issues of time-phased production and sales that so preoccupied Marx in volume 2. Confusion has plagued macroeconomic theory because analysts insist on postulating that production and consumption of the same goods occur within the same analytical time period (Kennedy 1969; Bleany 1976). Morishima must have had some awareness of this issue, since he quietly drops the simultaneity assumption later in the book, but does so with different notation to cover his tracks (M, 171, equation 4).

A final word on the second reservation. Is there anything to be gained from incorporating utilitarian—or, more to the point, energetics metaphors'— formalisms into Marxian economic theory? I will restrain myself from chapter and verse quotations,[4] and try to pose the problem in a manner that avoids the old chestnut "What would have Marx thought of neoclassical economics?" The issue is that the metaphorical inspiration and therefore the respective logical structures of Marxian and neoclassical economic theory are divergent, and therefore incompatible. I do not mean to claim that it is impossible to write down a utility function and call yourself a Marxist; John Roemer, for one, has made a career of it, and Oskar Lange did it from time to time. The problem as I see it is that Marx's world revolved around the primacy of production in all areas of life, but the physics metaphor that provides the core of neoclassical price theory is inherently irreconcilable with any classical notion of production. Now, analysts can ignore this incompatibility, or try to suppress it, but history seems to teach that the problem never really goes away.

Reason Three

[The existence of alternative technologies] violates the uniqueness of the value system because when there are alternative processes it is possible for the same sorts of commodities to be produced simultaneously by different processes and therefore to have different values. Moreover, when a process is mixed with another equally profitable process the values may depend upon the proportions in which these processes are mixed; and the proportions may easily fluctuate since the processes are indifferent in profitability. [M, 189]

The objection in the first sentence would seem to miss the mark, since modern Marxian analyses generally assume the technique actually in use is itself the product of a search for the optimum technique, given an expected global rate of profit; it is possible to interpret Marx's concept of "socially necessary labor time" in such a light. Morishima himself has demonstrated the convergence properties of one such algorithm in chapter 4 of his *Equilibrium, Stability and Growth* (1964).

The second sentence does present a formidable problem for the labor theory of value *within the class of models that Morishima advocates*. In the jargon of the capital theory debates, it is one aspect of the problem of switch points between techniques. It should be noted that the same weaknesses arise in the neoclassical theory of capital under the same conditions; the neoclassical response to date has been to insist that the problem is an empirical one—whatever that can mean in a theoretical dispute—and to continue using the capital concept whenever convenient. Now, Marxian theory can wave no mathematical wand to make the non-uniqueness of labor values at switch points go away, but I do believe it has the option of a more serious response to the problem than has so far been exhibited by the neoclassicals. The initial point of the response starts from the fact that neoclassical price theory is predicated upon the physics of the field, and therefore has committed itself to the abolition of hysteresis from any and all explanations: for the neoclassical economist, it is illegitimate to premise any explanation upon dependence on the actual historical date. This time-independence is built into the mathematics through the artifice of conservation principles, as explained above in Chapter 5. Marxian theory, on the other hand, embraces the principle of hysteresis, as evidenced by its connection to historical materialism, the specificity of theory relative to the mode of production, and so forth. The upshot is that a Marxian economist would be willing to entertain a historical solution to a mathematical problem, and that could be one response to Morishima. Labor values at switch points could be conceptualized as a weighted average of the outputs of the plural processes at a particular point in time, and these weights in turn could be the resultants of the historical evolution of the industry. Clearly this is not an "elegant" solution from the viewpoint of a mathematician, and Morishima would probably not admit it to the class of mathematical models he would be willing to entertain. But nonetheless it is a legitimate possibility within the realm of Marxian economic theory. There is more to a school of thought than its isolated algebraic models.

Reason Four

Morishima derives one possible solution to the transformation problem in a dynamic growth model where $\pi = e/(k + 1)$, e being the rate of exploitation and k the value composition of capital for the entire economy. The precondition for this transformation to succeed is that there be no distinctly capitalist consumption; that is, $F(t) = 0$ in our equation (7). From this condition Morishima concludes that "s_c [the savings propensity of the capitalists] is considered being equal to one, at least approximately. Therefore Marx's model of reproduction is reduced to the Von Neumann model" (M, 155). Back under Reason One and Reason Two we had occasion to demonstrate in detail why Morishima's model is not Marx's model. Yet one solution to the transformation problem in Morishima's model, that shares an assumption that is critical to the structure of Von Neumann models, is supposed to be sufficient to demonstrate that Marx is "reduced" to Von Neumann? This is not even an argument.

Reason Five

"The introduction of joint production, alternative processes or heterogeneous labor will conflict with the above four requirements" for labor values to serve as weights for the purposes of value aggregation. These four requirements are: nonnegativity, uniqueness, independence from market phenomena, and the establishment of a uniform rate of exploitation (M, 181).

The problem of alternative processes has been discussed above under Reason Three. The question of the heterogeneity of labor has been dealt with at length in Bowles and Gintis (1977) and needs no further elaboration here. One ought to note that only Morishima, and not Marxists in general, harbors qualms concerning relinquishing the assumption of a uniform rate of exploitation.

The issue of joint production does deserve serious consideration, if only because it has been inexplicably bound up with the issue of the acceptance of the Von Neumann method (VNM) of capital accounting by most of the well-known Marxian economists, such as Steedman, Schefold, Roemer, and

Pasinetti. The argument in favor of the necessity of joint production usually goes as follows: all production processes take time, which implies the ubiquity of fixed capital. The only way legitimately to account for fixed capital is with the VNM, and therefore the joint products are the norm, not a special case. The challenge for Marxian economics is that, once VNM is allowed, all sorts of problems arise with labor values: negative labor values become possible, and any capital-theoretic paradox can be found in the Marxian system.

It is important to understand that this is a theoretical and not an empirical issue. No one would "know" a joint production process, even if it bit them on the foot. "Joint production" is an analytical construct that must be linked to economic phenomena through the use of auxiliary hypotheses and definitions, such as the delineation of the appropriate boundaries of a production process, a precise specification as to what constitutes the product, a specification of the appropriate level of aggregation and appropriate time unit, and so forth. To make this point as sharply as possible, let me make the following claim: if I were to reject VNM and arbitrarily shrink the analytical time unit to an infinitesimal interval, I can effectively *define away* the appearance of joint production in any model of the economy. Take, for instance, Sraffa's own example of mutton and wool (1960, 63). Since the lamb, no matter how meek, cannot be shorn and rendered into chops simultaneously, the mental act of shrinking the analytical time unit cleaves what had initially appeared to be a true joint production process in twain: process one produces woolless sheep, and process two is the production of lamb chops by means of commodities, one of which is shorn sheep.

So, the real problem is not the empirical prevalence of joint production; it is instead the issue of whether VNM makes sense as an analytical technique within the context of Marxian economics. I do not believe it does so for four reasons.

First is the issue of the time unit. Morishima's cavalier treatment of temporal processes is reflected in the lack of discussion of the appropriate time unit in VNM accounts. The unit chosen is not an insignificant matter, because it defines the number of "commodities" in the production sphere: the shorter the unit, the more n-period older machines there are to keep track of. There is an analytical rule for defining the relevant time unit, although I have not seen it discussed by any of the VNM partisans. The basic VNM time unit should be the shortest physical lifetime of any input in any production process in the entire economy: the reason for this stricture is that the "fixity" of capital must be defined against the most "circulating" of all physical commodities. It therefore goes without saying that the natural time unit for VNM accounts is a remarkably short duration, perhaps approaching our original infinitesimal. This result has three disturbing implications. (a) An infinitesimal time unit means input and output matrices of infinite dimensionality. Needless to say, this is analytically unwieldy. (b) This artificial proliferation of the number of "commodities" increases the burden on the labor theory of value without a commensurate increase in novel analytical propositions. (c) The VNM accounting scheme *assumes* that all commodities are reevaluated by the market at least as frequently as once per infinitesimal time unit. There is something ironic about Marxists finding themselves dependent upon a conception of market efficiency that even the most extreme defender of capitalism would not dream of proposing.

Second, the concept of "prices" as well as that of commodities assumes an awkward and counterintuitive meaning in VNM accounts. One important implication of treating an n-period old machine as a distinct commodity is that it then possesses a distinct price. Most partisans of VNM from Sraffa (1960, 64) onward have not interpreted these prices as the resultants of actual realized trades; this is because in VNM a machine is also identified by its location in a particular production process. By definition, the possibility of trade is thus severely limited for most "machines" to trades within the same industry. Given the incongruity of equilibrium prices without trades, VNM partisans call these prices "book values" or "accounting prices" in order to acknowledge their tenuous existence. If these equilibrium prices had some correspondence to the book values of assets in firms' accounts, then one could interpret the pattern of machine prices over the course of its physical lifetime as representative of the depreciation charges on the machine. This claim is rendered nugatory, however, by the fact that prices of old machines are often negative in VNM accounts, and indeed, negative prices cannot be ruled out by any economically meaningful assumptions. Given the cul-de-sac that this literature has wandered into, it seems plausible to suggest that the endogenous market determination of depreciation is not at all an imperative of Marxian theory (although a case could be made that it is a neoclassical imperative), and that the imposition of depreciation as part of firm accounting practices is a theoretically preferred solution as well as a description of actual empirical practice.

Third, as we have observed, in VNM accounts the physical lifetime of every good must be specified prior to the analysis, in order to identify both the analytical time unit and the number of "commodities" to be analyzed. In practice, all VNM theorists assume that this information is unique, and a given physical datum. But what can be the meaning of a unique exogenous physical lifetime of an input if one allows the option of maintenance? There is no escape from this dilemma: either the VNM accounts must have truck with intractable infinite matrices, or else relinquish claims that depreciation is determined endogenously.

Fourth, the question of the dimensions of the input and output matrices is the ultimate mathematical Achilles heel of VNM fixed capital. Every VNM partisan, with the possible exception of van Schaik (1976) and Pasinetti (1980), merely assumes that the matrices are square: that is, the number of production processes are exactly equal to the number of "commodities," and that both are finite in number. Table 10.1 reveals that the assumption of

Table 10.1. The Maximum Dimension of a Von Neuman Input Matrix

If matrix contains	Then maximum order is	
	Rows	Columns
Finished goods only	f	$f + s$
Plus: capital goods of identical lifespans	$k + f$	$k + f + s$
Plus: capital goods of differing lifespans	$kp(f + k)$	$[(k!)(p!)(k + f)] + s$
Plus: optional maintenance on fixed capital	$[(vp)!]kp(f + k)$	$\{[(k!)(p!)(k + f)] \cdot [(vp)!]\} + s$
Plus: capital goods which are true joint products	$[(vp)!]kp(f + k)$	$s + \{[(k - j)!] \cdot [p!] \cdot [(vp)!] \cdot [k - j + f]\}$

$s\ =\ $ Number of goods produced by unassisted labor.
$f\ =\ $ Number of "final goods"
$k\ =\ $ Number of "capital goods"
$p\ =\ $ Number of time periods, as defined by the duration in production of the longest-lived capital good divided by the duration in production of the shortest-lived capital good.
$v\ =\ $ Number of kinds of maintenance that can be performed on capital goods.
$j\ =\ $ Number of jointly produced capital goods.

Note: The rows of the input matrix are generally taken to denote "commodities," whereas the columns represent "processes." The dimensions given in this table are *maximum* sizes because each assumes that all capital goods are used in all processes. Obviously, the dimensions of any actual economy will be *arbitrarily* smaller than the table entries.

square matrices (number rows = number columns) is the special (and unlikely) case in VNM accounts. The reason for this, in simple terms, is that there are many more permutations of time patterns of inputs than there are of commodities themselves, once we leave the matchbook world of a single machine of relatively short lifespan. In complete generality, VNM technologies would never be represented by square matrices, contrary to the impressions promulgated by example in VNM texts (Steedman 1977; Morganstern and Thompson 1976). Again, this has profound consequences for the economic theory, since all VNM theorists—Morishima included—depend heavily upon either the Frobenius theorems for square indecomposable matrices, or theorems that hinge upon the ability to invert the input or output matrices.

To make it appear as if all of economic theory were just leading up to VNM accounts, Morishima sheds a few crocodile tears over Marx's "hard struggles with algebra, differential calculus and numerical examples" (M, 166); collates a few quotes from volume 2 of *Capital* that are more or less irrelevant for the justification of the VNM method of capital accounting; and insists that "It is almost certain that he could not have solved the mathematical problems of joint production, if he had got the idea of treating capital goods left over for production in the future as by-products of the current production process" (M, 167).

It is a safe bet that Marx would not have stumbled on the fixed point theorem that Von Neumann used to prove existence in the 1920s, given that it was discovered after Marx's death. It is almost as safe a bet that Marx would never have treated fixed capital as a joint product, because it leads to so many incoherencies and intractable problems, problems which Morishima, with all his vaunted mathematical advantages over Marx, is equally unable to resolve. It is misleading to give the impression that Von Neumann capital accounting cuts any Gordian knots in capital theory, and it is just as misleading to foster the impression that there are no alternative methods to deal with the same problems. For what it is worth, there has been an attempt to treat fixed capital as a separate matrix of stock requirements, initiated by Lange and developed by Brody (1970), which at least has the virtue from the vantage of Marxian economics that it is closer to Marx's schemes in volume 2. It is an indication of his disregard for presenting Marxian economics as a viable alternative that Morishima actually cites Brody (M, 167), but without giving any mention of the fact that his book contains a legitimate alternative method of capital accounting.

Reason Six

"If the rate of exploitation is not a maximum, it is clear that Marx's theory will collapse unless we have a theory which can satisfactorily explain the prevailing rate of exploitation" (M, 159). Again, the problem is not the mathematics per se, it is the inability to notice that concepts of explanation can vary drastically across rival research programs. Morishima's ideal situation would be a separate behavioral equation to which could be applied some optimization methods and which would result in a unique determinate rate of exploitation. He does not understand that it is neoclassical theory that dictates that all explanation must assume the format of constrained extrema over conserved fields. Marxist theory is based on another metaphor, that of a Cartesian substance in motion. The two metaphors are irreconcilable: Cartesian motion is not the same as energetic motion. There is no negative heuristic in Marxian thought that says, "Thou shalt not appeal to historically contingent processes in your explanations."

Reason Seven

In an actual economy, however, capitalists are not aware of the scientific law of reproduction; capitalist decisions are made, as are traders' decisions about exchange, not in terms of value but in terms of prices. Why does the "general law of capitalist accumulation" forcibly assert itself like a law of Nature, in spite of the fact that all the members of society are ignorant of it?" [M, 146]

Finally, we arrive at the real reason why Morishima dislikes the Marxian system and rejects its theoretical claims. His objection can be summarized thus: it does not propound laws as Morishima understands laws, and it does not conform to methodological individualism. Of course, we did not need to slog through all the mathematics to understand this objection. Neoclassical theory is bowdlerized nineteenth-century physics, and as such it wholeheartedly embraces the mid-nineteenth-century conception of deterministic law. Marx, of course, was an inheritor of the Hegelian tradition, as every volume written about Marx (except that of Morishima) explains in painful detail. If one is bound and determined to construct an economic theory that mimics physical laws (although not *modern* physical laws; see Farjoun and Machover 1983), then there is no escaping it—Marxian theory is going to be a big letdown.

Further, if one insists upon the requirement of methodological individualism, then one is bound to reject most of existing social theory, including much that Morishima favors. For example, why does the law of the marginal propensity to consume forcibly assert itself like a law of Nature, in spite of the fact that all the members of society are ignorant of it? Or, and more pointed, if all the members of society are cognizant of the laws of the economy, why do we have economists? Once one grasps hold of this stick to beat a theory, it can always be turned on the flagellator. Indeed, Boland (1986) has argued that Walrasian general equilibrium does not adequately conform to the dictates of methodological individualism.

The Empty Toolbox

If ends and not means are what really impress economists, then Morishima should be able to make a compelling case for his Marx–Von Neumann hybrid by showing us what we may do with it, regardless of any negative comments about rivals grounded in the labor theory of value. Sadly enough, this strategy is neglected in *Marx's Economics*. We are tendered only a few hints of the types of analysis we might perform; they are sketchy and in substance display a singular lack of novelty.

For instance, in his chapter on extended reproduction, we are instructed how to "graft the modern theory of the trade cycle" (M, 126) onto the proposed hybrid. What we are in fact presented with is a reduced-form linear difference equation that will display cyclical behavior for one of two economic reasons: the disproportionality of production between sectors as determined by the technical coefficients, and the choice of capitalists to consume a proportion of the surplus not commensurate with the optimum balanced growth rate. As in neoclassical economics in general, Morishima posits the only exogenous (causal) factors to be technology and tastes. It is ironic that this brand of cycle theory is dubbed "modern," since it was repudiated by econometric model builders around that same time (Hickman 1972). Further, Samuelson long ago pointed out that any linear model of the business cycle depended crucially upon the improbable knife-edge configuration of characteristic roots to keep it cycling; otherwise the model would blow up or contract to nothing in a very short time. Neither of those situations described an economy anyone was familiar with. Hicks's subsequent "floors and ceilings" was a not-very-successful attempt to make the mathematics conform a little more closely to the phenomena (Hicks 1950); in the interim most of these models have been quietly dropped.[5] It seems irrational for Marxian economics to emulate a dead end pioneered by its rival research program.

Although this issue of linear difference equations may seem a bit arcane, it is actually quite damaging in the context of Morishima's "positive" suggestions, since he exhibits a predilection for conflating the roots of difference equations with Marx's concerns over fluctuations in the reserve army of the unemployed and his long-run tendency for the rate of profit to fall. Although an entire chapter is devoted to this topic, it does not take a barrage of linear algebra to figure out what is going to happen to a laboring population growing at a fixed exponential rate if national product cycles for technological reasons and fixed proportionate labor requirements are assumed. In some crude sense this captures the Marxian notion that labor must dance to the syncopated expansion of capital, but it is not a very interesting "theory." Things mechanically grind along in much the same manner in Morishima's treatment of a change in the composition of capital (M, 137 et seq.). For ease of mathematical manipulation, "technical change" is defined as an increase in some required material inputs a_{ij} accompanied by an offsetting decrease in the labor requirement l_i, such that the resulting labor value of the commodity stays constant. It becomes immediately apparent that this is not technical progress as much as it is some Marxian equivalent of a neoclassical isoquant. It is interesting but not enlightening that the rate of profit falls along such an isoquant, but unfortunately it has nothing to do with Marx's thesis that the social and technical dynamism of capital accumulation would lead inadvertently and inexorably to a declining rate of profit.

Morishima's "Fundamental Marxian Theorem" (which asserts that exploitation of laborers by capitalists is necessary and sufficient for the existence of a set of prices and wages yielding positive profits) and his solutions to the dynamic transformation problem, while admittedly the most original and substantial achievements of the entire book, do not qualify as positive achievements, since Morishima has maintained that the labor theory of value should be abandoned. Who can be exploited if all trades and transactions are contracted without coercion in a market freely responsive to an individual's demand schedules? And what smacks more of scholasticism than transforming prices into useless labor values?

For all these reasons I think we can conclude that *Marx's Economics* is ultimately a futile exercise born of a self-fulfilling picture of progress in economic theory. It is a book written to prove a point; the real point is that the book need never have been written.

Notes

1. Henceforth, "M" will indicate page references to Morishima 1973.

2. In some respects the critical essay by Jaffe (1983) attempts a parallel hermeneutical reading of Morishima on Walras to what this paper attempts for Morishima on Marx.

3. In fact, Luxemburg's complaint against Tugan-Baranovski that his reproduction schemes allowed only for crises of disproportionality is equally germane here.

4. Except for one: "The quantity of commodities created in masses by capitalist production depends on the scale of production and on the need for constantly expanding this production, and not on any predestined circle of supply and demand, on wants that have to be satisfied." (Marx 1973, vol. 2, 75) Alas, one quotation, or even one hundred quotations, do not in and of themselves constitute a sympathetic reading.

5. In his haste to make Marx respectable—that is, like Hicks—Morishima again interprets the mathematics in a manner inimicable to common sense. On pages 126–27 he derives a second-order difference equation in national income, and then suggests that it is in principle the same as one found in Hicks. The fact that two radically different models can result in very similar reduced-form equations does not mean that one theory has been reduced to the other; they can still have differential theoretical content and be competing theories.

Part IV
Historical Studies in Institutionalist Economics

11

Adam Smith, Empiricism, and the Rate of Profit in Eighteenth-Century England

Adam Smith and Empiricism

There exists a recent trend in discussions of the philosophy of science which has, even more recently, made itself felt in some work in the history of economic thought. This philosophical trend, associated with the names of Kuhn, Toulmin, Feyerabend, and Lakatos, has brought into philosophy a heightened concern with the social processes of science within its historical milieu. This influence has been made manifest in the history of economic thought as less ado about strict textual exegesis and greater interest in the mores and practices of economic scientists.[1] For various reasons, this vein of work has concentrated on recent economists and their activities. The present article is an attempt to extend this tradition farther back in time and to examine methodological processes at the inception of economics.

The question we wish to pose here is this: What was the relation between early classical economics and empiricism? Or more pointedly, how dependable is Adam Smith as an informant concerning the eighteenth-century English economy? We do not mean to question the accuracy of each individual anecdote and tidbit of trivia in the *Wealth of Nations* (henceforth, *WON*)—a Herculean task in any event, since so much of *WON* is taken up with such trifles as the expense of the civil establishment of Nova Scotia and Georgia, the study of the Greek language in Spanish universities, and the question of whether the republic of Hamburg derived "considerable" revenue from the profits of a public wine cellar and apothecary shop. Neither, on the other hand, do we mean to pose such a question as, Was Adam Smith aware of the Industrial Revolution?[2] since it is patently impossible for Smith to have been aware of the shape of an intellectual construct fabricated a century after his own work. The question we wish to pose is, What was the role of empiricism for Adam Smith *within the context of his own science?* This point must be stressed at the outset, since the strain of philosophy of science from which we trace our present influence holds that the identification of "facts" is not independent of the theory and the activities of the scientist; and further, that much misinterpretation and misrepresentation of "outdated" science stems from the temptation to read today's terms into yesterday's texts. Observations take on the aura of "facts" when identified as significant or important by the body of scientists; otherwise, they are merely part of the inconsequential observation of everyday life. The empiricism that concerns us here links the theoretical construct and the structured observation in a single exposition. This definition will justify our present disregard of the many anecdotes and detours in *WON*. In their place, we shall concentrate on theoretical terms crucial to Smith's science, regardless of their relative standing in the hierarchy of facts of the twentieth-century economist.[3]

What, then is the preeminent "fact" in the theoretical structure of *WON?* G. S. L. Tucker, in his astute survey of English economic thought in the eighteenth and nineteenth centuries, makes the case that the rise of economics as a distinct discipline was marked by the elevation of the rate of profit from a position of relative obscurity in the pamphlet literature of the day to the very forefront of concern as the premier economic indicator of classical economics.[4] Previous to *WON*, political writers were occupied with the question of the determinant of the rate of interest on loans, their only concern with the rate of profit having to do with vague hypotheses relating interest to the average rate of return on investment in physical objects. With the advent of *WON*, the conception of the main economic problem itself changed, and questions about the determinants of interest receded into the wings. Smith had insisted that "it is the stock that is employed for the sake of profits which puts in motion the greater part of the useful labor in every society. The plans and projects of the employers of stock regulate and direct all the most important operations of labor, and profit is the end proposed by all these plans and projects."[5] If the rate of profit regulated the most important operations of labor—that is, regulated the economy itself—then it would seem that the most strenuous exertions of political economists would be devoted to the examination and explanation of that particular quantum.

Smith, as befitted the newfound significance of the rate of profit, set apart a whole book of *WON* for the consideration of the "Nature, Accumulation and Employment of Stock," following a separate chapter on "The Profits of Stock." In those contexts he made a number of empirical statements, chief among which were these: (a) "in the same society or neighborhood, the average and ordinary rates of profit in the different employments of stock should be more nearly upon a level than the pecuniary wages of different sorts of labor" (*WON*, 111); (b) "a good moderate, reasonable profit; terms which I apprehend mean no more than a common or usual profit" could be estimated by a rough rule of thumb at twice the prevailing interest rate (*WON*, 97); (c) "since the establishment of the act of navigation, the ordinary rate of British profit has fallen considerably" (*WON*, 565); (d) the profit rate of the East India Company was probably close to the "highest ordinary rate" (*WON*, 97); (e) "the diminution of profit is the natural effect of [a nation's] prosperity, or of a greater stock being employed in it than before" (*WON*, 91).

Obviously, these statements are not all on a par in significance. Statements (b) and (d) are almost purely contemporaneous description, once the theoretical context provides an operative definition of a 'common or ordinary rate of profit' (although this is not an insignificant problem, as we shall discover shortly). Statement (c) adds the complication of historical description, while statements (a) and (e) are predictions which follow from Smith's theoretical structure.

Clearly, Smith made some empirical statements which were linked in fundamental ways to his theoretical program. This pedestrian point needs to be made because of the repletion of rhapsody and requiem sung at the altar of Smith the methodologist. These paeans and elegies range from outrageous hyperbole—"No book was ever written in which theory was more constantly brought to the test of fact"[6]—to endowment with folksy canniness—"He was at home in facts. He enjoyed ferreting them out, and giving them their proper weights. They suited his shrewd common sense"[7]—to qualified praise—"he piled up facts to prove his point, e.g., the long digression on the value of silver, the statistics of wheat prices, wage rates and profits. . . . The important point, methodologically, is that he used such facts as he had; he believed that his conclusions were valid inferences from his data; he attempted to check his theories by factual observation. He was scientific for his day"[8]—to an extreme skepticism—"Smith's ideas were not subjected to a testing program of falsification; indeed, unlike Ricardo, Smith offered very few unambiguous predictions which would invite attempts at falsification."[9]

All of these passages presume implicitly or explicitly some contemporary (if not actually modern) notion of scientific methodology. Section II below will temporarily accept one such notion and apply it in testing Smith's statements about profits, using modern criteria. Section III employs our results to question the propriety of standing Smith up against modern measuring sticks and to contemplate the meaning of the choice of Smith as the founder of modern economics.

The Construction of an Index of
the Eighteenth-Century Rate of Profit in England

To perform our task, it remains for us to reproduce Smith's definition of the "common or ordinary rate of profit." Profit, for Smith is a return to a class who own and employ stock; interest is but a derivative return which is extracted from profit. Other than this, there is surprisingly little in the way of definition that might guide us toward the appropriate empirical sources. Smith does say:

> Profit is so very fluctuating that the person who carries on a particular trade cannot always tell you himself what is the average of his annual profit. . . . To ascertain what is the average profit of all the different trades carried on in a great kingdom,

must be much more difficult; and to judge what it may have been formerly, or in remote periods of time, with any degree of precision, must be altogether impossible.[10]

Smith is engaging in a little hyperbole himself here, as we can judge from his already quoted empirical statements. But upon reflection, his excuse for avoiding further precise definition of profit seems rather odd, in that fluctuation of the rate of profit may complicate its estimation *ex ante;* but it does not by itself present any obstacles *ex post.* Further, if the actual rate of profit was hidden from the participants' view, as Smith here maintains, it is difficult to comprehend how the classical notion of competition, in which investors shift resources from lesser to more profitable employments, could possibly function. This contradiction appears to be an example of Smith's lack of logical consistency: a quality often commented upon by others.[11]

In lieu of any explicit definition of the rate of profit in *WON,* we must take our cue instead from indirect evidence. Empirical statement (b) above is prefaced by the comment "Double interest is in Great Britain reckoned what the *merchants* call a good, moderate, reasonable profit" (my italics). One can only interpret this statement as defining the rate of profit in terms of what the merchant or businessman said it was: that is, the rate of profit embodied in the business accounts, subject to the proviso that all interest paid to the owners of the business's stock be included in the profit concept. There is an appreciable amount of evidence that Smith was in close contact with the merchants and industrialists of Glasgow prior to the composition of *WON;*[12] these occasions would have provided the sources of his empirical generalizations.

Many contemporary economic historians would view eighteenth-century accounting records with a jaundiced eye, at best. Most of their objections to taking those journal and ledger accounts seriously could be summarized broadly by the complaint that they were hopelessly haphazard in their execution, and further, they show no clear understanding of the concept of capital.[13] This objection is scrutinized elsewhere in detail by the present author[14] and therefore will not be examined here. For our present purposes, it is sufficient to note that such objections are here irrelevant: we do not wish to replicate some modern notion of capital and the rate of profit, but simply report information in records kept by the eighteenth-century actors *in the form in which they preserved them.* It would have been that rate of profit which Smith discussed with the Glasgow merchants, and that rate which would have served as grist for the mill of his "empiricism."

Guided by this principle, I have collected a number of eighteenth-century time series of profit rates. There are seventeen firms in this sample. Eleven of these time series came from previously published sources, while six were extracted from archival sources by the author. The criteria for the selection of a series were that the available data extend for at least twenty years; that the firm be a "going concern" (and therefore not immediately approaching bankruptcy); and that enough supplemental information exists that there might be some external check on the financial records. These relatively weak criteria excluded about three times as many firms as were finally included in this sample. The names of the firms, the dates of their records, their geographic location, product character and the main sources used are summarized in Table 11.1.

Table 11.1 Firms Included in the Profit Index

Concern	Dates of inclusion	Product or service	Geographical location	Source
London Assurance	1728–1826	insurance	London	SALI
Million Bank	1728–1782	investment trust	London	PRO C/114/10, ii
Scotch Mines	1755–1811	lead mining	Leadhills Scotland	GL/12033
Sun Fire	1729–1826	insurance	London	GL/11963 11933, 15042
East India Co.	1728–1779	trade	London	IOR:L/AG/18/ 2/1, L/AG/1/ 1/16–24
Westminister Fire	1761–1794	insurance	London	CWPL/343/83– 85
Whitbread	1762–1794	brewing	London	Matthias, p. 553
Carron Co.	1770–1826	mining & metal fab.	Prestonpans Scotland	Campbell, pp. 330–332
Hull Docks Co.	1775–1805	transport	Kingston-on-Hull	Jackson, p. 426
Drummonds	1777–1826	banking	London	Bolitho & Peel, pp. 212–213
Spencer Stanhope Partnership	1728–1762	iron forge	S. Yorkshire	Raistrick & Allen, pp. 179, 184
Fordell Colliery	1772–1789 1800–1812	mining	Scotland	Duckham, pp. 147, 197
Marshall Partners	1805–1826	flax spinning	Leeds	Rimmer, pp. 319–321
Clark	1805–1825	woolen trade	Wiltshire	Beckinsale, p. xxxi
Coalbrookdale	1739–45, 1799–1826	metal fabrication	Lancs.	Raistrick, pp. 278, 298
Bridgewater Trust	1806–1826	canal, transport	Lancs.	Mather, pp. 358–9
Cowpe, Oldknow, Siddon & Co.	1790–1813	cotton spinning	Notts.	Pigott, p. 89

Table 11.1—continued.

SOURCES:
SALI: Sun Alliance & Life Insurance, private muniments.
PRO: Public Record Office.
GL: Guildhall Library muniments.
IOR: India Office Records Library.
CWPL: City of Westminister Public Library.
Matthias: *The Brewing Industry in England, 1700–1830* (Cambridge, 1959)
Campbell: *Carron Company* (Edinburgh, 1961)
Jackson: *Hull in the Eighteenth Century* (Oxford, 1972).
Bolitho & Peel: *The Drummonds of Charing Cross* (London, 1967)
Duckham: *History of Scottish Coal* (Newton Abbott, 1970)
Rimmer: *Marshall of Leeds* (Cambridge, 1960)
Beckinsale: "Trowbridge Woolen Industry," *Wiltshire Arch. & Nat. Hist. Transactions,* 1951
Raistrick: *Dynasty of Iron Founders* (London, 1953)..
Raistrick & Allen: "The South Yorkshire Ironmasters," *Economic History Review,* May 1939.
Mather: *After the Canal Duke* (Oxford, 1970).
Pigott: *Hollins* (Nottingham, 1949).

As far as possible, profits were defined as inclusive of interest paid to owners, but exclusive of interest paid on outside debt. The denominator of the profit rate is defined as the nominal capital of the concern, as entered in the balance sheet.[15] In one instance, that of the Sun Fire Assurance, profit is taken from a closing account called the Office Account; in all other cases it comes from an explicit profit-and-loss account.[16] All dividends paid out of accounts were restored to the final profit tally. Obviously, in the cases of the published series, where information is lacking there is no way of assuring that the above definitions were employed by the relevant author; but wherever the components of firm accounts were also published, the appropriate corrections have been calculated by the author.

To evaluate these data, we must first pause to consider the classical Smithian notion of the rate of profit, which differs appreciably from modern conceptions.[17] The classical long-period conception of the rate of profit was a quantum that was a center of gravity toward which subsets of the economy were constantly moving. While it is true that the more integrated the economy, the less dispersion the classicists would expect about that rate, it was not necessarily true that greater integration would have meant greater correlation between the subsets of firms. This is one possible interpretation of Smith's statement (a) above. An example of a more modern concept of integration would be provided by contemporary studies that examine the cross-spectra of time series of wheat prices or exchange rates for different geographical areas: greater coherence squared and less phase shift over time are interpreted as evidence of the spread of efficient market structures.[18] Since Smithian economics did not view the profit rate as the "price" of capital in the same way that neoclassical economics does, it would not predict that an effectively operating market would necessarily entail rapid and high correlations of profit rates between individual sectors of the economy. On the other hand, the long-period rate of profit in Smithian economics was a single number, and when the determinants of that rate changed, it was expected that the whole distribution of individual rates would follow in train. Therefore, a "center of gravity" model of the profit rate would predict a certain amount of positive correlation between firms in any sample from an integrated market.

To test this interpretation of Smith's statement (a), the same period correlation matrix of the sampled firms' rates of profit series is displayed in Table 11.2. If there were fewer than ten overlapping annual data points between any two time series, a zero is entered in the appropriate cell. (For example, the Million Bank and the Bridgewater Canal Trust had no overlapping data points.) If the correlation coefficient, either positive or negative, was significant at the two-tailed 10 percent level of the t-test, a plus or minus is entered in the appropriate cell. Blank cells represent insignificant correlations. Under the null hypothesis of no significant correlations in the sample, one would expect (.05 {(mu 84 =) 4 negative and 4 positive correlations, given that of the 136 possible correlations, 52 had fewer than 10 shared data points, leaving 84 potential correlations. In fact, of the potential 84 cells, there were 14 significant positive correlations (16.6%) and three significant negative correlations (3.5%). The profit rate of the London Assurance Company was significantly positively correlated with the largest number of other series (5), which three firms had no same-period positive correlations: Scotch Mines, the Bridgewater Canal Trust, and the Clark Proprietorship.

Same-period correlation is not the only way that given firms or sectors may move toward the center of gravity; there may also be leads and lags. A statistically complete description would be provided by cross-spectral analysis, but none of our data series is long enough to approach the statistical requirements of spectral analysis. Yet we may further approximate a dynamic test by lagging each series one year relative to every other series, and then calculating correlation coefficients. These results are reported in matrix format in Table 11.3, using the same notation as in table 11.2. The horizontal list of series is lagged one period relative to the vertical list. Thus, the diagonal presents the correlation between a series and its own lagged values, while off-diagonal rows represent lagged correlations. Out of 272 non-diagonal cells, 103 have fewer than 10 data points in common. Of the remaining 169 cells, 25 have significant positive correlations, and 7 have significant negative correlations. Under the null hypothesis of no significant correlation in the aggregate, one would expect 8(= .05 × 169) significant negative correlations and 8 significant positive correlations. Thus in both tables, the number of *positive* correlations rejects the null hypothesis of no significant correlation in the aggregate.

The Clark Proprietorship and the East India Company are the only concerns not positively correlated with any other firm's profit rate in Table 11.3. Combining this result with the information in Table 11.2, it seems that only

Table 11.2 Same Period Correlation Matrix

	London Assr.	Million Bank	Scotch Mines	Whitbread	Carron	Sun Fire	Spencer	Westminister	East India	Hull Dock	Drummond	Cosco	Fordell	Marshall	Clark	Coalbrook	Bridgewater	Number of cols. +	Number of rows +
London Assr.	#																	5	
Million Bank		#																2	
Scotch Mines			#																
Whitbread		+	−	#														1	1
Carron					#													1	
Sun Fire	+	+	−			#												1	1
Spencer	+				0	0	#												1
Westminister						+	0	#											1
East India	+								#										1
Hull Dock	+	0				0		0		#									
Drummond				+			0		0		#							2	1
Cosco						−				0	+	#						1	1
Fordell	+					0				+	0		#					1	2
Marshall						0				0	+	+	+	#					3
Clark						0				0	0	0			#			1	
Coalbrook		0				0				0	0	0			+	#			
Bridgewater	0	0	0				0	0	0	0	0				0	0	#		1

[a] Keyed by number—see column 1.

Table 11.3 One-period Lag Correlation Matrix

	London Assr.	Million Bank	Scotch Mines	Whitbread	Carron	Sun Fire	Spencer	Westminster	East India	Hull Dock	Drummond	Cosco	Fordell	Marshall	Clark	Coalbrook	Bridgewater	Other firm + corr. Lead	Other firm + corr. Lag
London Assr.		+			+	+	+	+		o	o	o	o	o	o	o	+	1	3
Million Bank				+			o			.				o	o	o	o	3	2
Scotch Mines					+	+	o					o	+	o	o			1	1
Whitbread			o		o		o	o			+	−	o				o		1
Carron				o						o	o			o	o	o	+	2	2
Sun Fire	+	+			o		+	−			o	o	o	o	o	o	+	3	2
Spencer	+		+			+	o			o	o	+	o			o	o	1	1
Westminster	+				+			o	o	+		o	+	o	o	o	o		1
East India							o		o			+		−			o		
Hull Dock	+	+	o	o		+	o	o	o	+			+	o	o	o		4	1
Drummond				+	o		o	o	o	o		o	o	o	o	+	o	1	2
Cosco		o	o	o			o	o	o	o		o	o	+		−	o		1
Fordell		o	o	o			o	o	o	o			o	−				5	3
Marshall		o		o			o		o	o		o	o	+		+		1	1
Clark		o		o			o		o	o									
Coalbrook		o					o		o								+	1	1
Bridgewater		o		o	+	+	o	o	o		+	o						1	3

a Keyed by number—see column 1.

the Clark Proprietorship has no positive correlation with any other firm in this sample. It is germane in this respect to note that Clark has by far the smallest capital stock in our sample for thirteen of its twenty-one years of inclusion, and is also unusual because it is the only firm whose records cover the initial starting-up period of growth. On the whole, the material presented in Tables 11.2 and 11.3 is evidence of a fair amount of integration in firms' rates of profit in the eighteenth and early nineteenth centuries. This result is significant for two reasons: (a) because Smith *may* have been justified in theorizing about a central tendency in the profit rate; and (b) because the concept of a central tendency in the rate of profit motivates our next step: using the sample of individual rates to estimate the center of gravity of the rate of profit in this period.

Given this goal, the problem arises of the appropriate estimator. In the Smithian system, the long-period profit rate is an aggregate equilibrium configuration. In this instance, each quantum of profit and capital would need to be evaluated at the appropriate "natural" prices and weighted by proportions of total equilibrium output. This type of information is not available and is not theoretically well defined in any event. As an alternative, various weighting schemes could be devised, the most obvious of which is to weight the profit rates by the size of their nominal capitals, producing an index that would be equivalent to the sum of all profits divided by the sum of all capitals. The problem with this particular scheme is that it places inordinate emphasis on the East India Company, with its exceptionally large capital of more than three million pounds, whereas the capitals of the other concerns range from a thousand to nine hundred thousand pounds. Since we possess no other a priori evidence as to the proper weighting scheme, the best guide is a flat prior: that is, to take the unweighted mean of the information embodied in the sample. Hence, our estimator of the aggregate of profit is the sum of the individual firm profit rates divided by the number of firms in the sample at time t. The product of these calculations is called "mean profit." [19]

Because the composition of the sample is changing over time, the differing means of profit rates of firms that enter and exit the sample will cause fluctuations in the index that are independent of any of the fluctuations in individual series. If we are interested in gauging fluctuations, we can adjust for this effect by dividing each of the series by their means, and then sum the results and divide them by the number of firms in the sample at time t. This adjusted index, called 'adjusted profit' is displayed together with the first index in Table 11.4.

The "mean profit" is denominated in actual percentage units of profit rate. We see that for this sample, the average profit rate varies mostly between 9 percent and 18 percent (the grand mean for the whole period is 13 percent) and seems to be rising over the course of the later eighteenth and early nineteenth centuries. This index is useful for an indication of trend, because the "adjusted profit" index, while not detrended, has been rotated somewhat in a clockwise direction by the mean adjustment calculation.

Table 11.4 Profit Indices 1728–1826

Year	Adjusted Profit	Mean Profit	Number of Firms
1728	.275	.65	4
1729	−.376	−2.24	5
1730	.765	6.20	5
1731	−.011	.78	5
1732	1.384	10.68	5
1733	2.187	16.20	5
1734	.955	7.64	5
1735	.705	6.16	5
1736	1.447	11.72	5
1737	.565	5.10	5
1738	1.467	11.06	5
1739	.873	7.48	6
1740	.731	6.38	6
1741	.966	8.21	6
1742	.870	5.58	5
1743	.702	6.50	6
1744	.650	8.10	6
1745	1.128	9.26	6
1746	.983	10.90	5
1747	.645	6.04	5
1748	1.002	11.48	5
1749	.530	5.64	5
1750	.902	9.72	5
1751	.942	11.14	5
1752	1.246	8.12	5
1753	.796	9.98	5
1754	1.250	13.58	5
1755	.982	10.96	6
1756	.919	10.48	6
1757	.669	9.75	6
1758	1.509	14.41	6
1759	1.128	11.53	6
1760	1.102	11.95	6
1761	.935	9.44	7
1762	.869	9.29	8
1763	1.164	11.28	7
1764	1.114	14.01	7
1765	1.050	11.22	7
1766	1.158	13.56	7
1767	1.180	12.41	7
1768	1.136	13.75	7
1769	.902	9.50	7
1770	1.204	15.70	8
1771	1.151	14.48	7
1772	.789	11.82	8
1773	.973	11.25	9
1774	.907	12.66	9
1775	1.077	12.16	10

Table 11.4—continued.

Year	Adjusted Profit	Mean Profit	Number of Firms
1776	1.063	14.31	10
1777	.965	14.09	11
1778	.772	11.78	11
1779	.594	8.14	11
1780	.645	12.22	10
1781	.726	9.00	9
1782	1.256	17.61	10
1783	.668	8.50	9
1784	.802	11.24	9
1785	.428	6.35	9
1786	.842	12.73	9
1787	.853	12.34	9
1788	1.222	15.70	9
1789	1.056	15.38	9
1790	.995	13.73	9
1791	1.263	17.56	9
1792	.825	15.86	9
1793	.617	9.42	9
1794	.859	8.04	9
1795	.828	14.81	7
1796	.907	16.05	7
1797	.916	16.11	7
1798	1.097	19.90	7
1799	1.297	18.96	8
1800	1.153	15.52	9
1801	1.688	24.17	9
1802	1.184	14.95	8
1803	1.526	21.18	8
1804	1.319	19.48	8
1805	1.453	21.12	11
1806	1.211	17.33	11
1807	1.252	20.70	11
1808	1.127	15.84	11
1809	1.215	16.66	11
1810	.766	19.00	10
1811	.977	14.79	10
1812	.924	16.98	10
1813	.850	13.94	9
1814	1.228	20.95	8
1815	.967	16.17	8
1816	.911	18.02	8
1817	1.215	20.53	8
1818	.926	17.12	8
1819	1.700	19.50	8
1820	1.161	20.55	8
1821	1.040	15.98	8
1822	1.089	17.45	8
1823	1.015	15.32	8

Table 11.4—continued.

Year	Adjusted Profit	Mean Profit	Number of Firms
1824	1.235	18.61	8
1825	2.025	40.10	8
1826	.920	12.35	7

We are now equipped to judge Smith's statements (b) through (e) concerning the behavior of the rate of profit by modern empirical standards, with the caution that our sample size is, of necessity, quite small. In statement (b), Smith suggests a rule of thumb by which to gauge the rate of profit in his time, which was twice the prevailing rate of interest. Smith clearly meant this as description, and not explanation. In his spirit of description, and *not* that of model estimation, the following least squares regression was fitted:

$$\text{Profit index} = \underset{(1.836)}{3.1536} + \underset{(.6355)}{2.0168} \text{ yield 3\%} \quad \begin{array}{l} R^2 = .128 \\ \text{DE} = 1.84 \end{array}$$

first-order autocorrelation parameter = .25
years of sample period: 1731 to 1801

Standard errors of coefficients are in parentheses. The yields on 3 percent government funds were taken from Ashton.[20] Examining the equation, our time series seems to corroborate Smith's dictum that the rate of profit was roughly double interest, if we are allowed to amend Smith's statement to read twice interest plus a constant.

Smith's statement (c) maintains that the trend in the profit rate had been unambiguously downward since the Navigation Acts in the later seventeenth century. While surviving business accounts from the late seventeenth and early eighteenth centuries are not abundant enough to make such a long-term comparison, our tentative evidence from the 8 years prior to the publication of *WON* does not support Smith's contention. Again, in the spirit of description, we fit the following least-squares trend to the profit index from 1728 to 1775:[21]

$$\text{Profit index} = \underset{(.74)}{5.348} + \underset{(.03)}{.175} \text{ time} \qquad R^2 = .418$$

Standard errors are again in parentheses. Far from falling, the trend is significantly positive over the sample period. One might object that the actual trend of the rate of profit might not be adequately captured by this index, because there is the possibility that more high-profit firms entered the sample in the latter part of the period, thus artificially raising the trend. While this objection has some validity, an examination of the constitutent individual profit-rate series generally reveals a flat or upward trend over the period. Given the limitations of our information, Smith seems to be mistaken here.

Smith's statement (d) suggests that the profit rate of the East India Company was nearly the highest experienced in the England of his time. We can begin to evaluate this statement by examining the average profit rates of the firms in our sample in the years immediately prior to the publication of WON.[22] These rates are displayed in Table 11.5.

While the average rate of profit of the East India Company is dwarfed by that of Whitbread's and Sun Fire, we must caution the reader that the latter two concerns were probably anomalous relative to the rest of eighteenth-century experience: Sun Fire, because the form and structure of its business accounts were very different from all of the other records that the author has examined; and Whitbread's because of the inclusion in profits of the large sums of money extracted from the business in the form of owners' withdrawals. (The profit rate for the same period exclusive of withdrawals was 13.3%.) Another consideration relevant in judging Smith's statement (d) is the fact that the profit rate in the accounts of the East India Company diminished appreciably in variance in the second half of the eighteenth century. Before that time the company's profit rate would swing from a large positive rate in one year to a negative rate in the next, largely due to problems stemming from the demands of record keeping in such a large and far-flung operation. During the intermittent battles for the control of the company, the large positive rates of profit would be hinted at in the pamphlet literature, while the negative rates would be ignored. Smith would have been acquainted with these pamphlet debates and was probably influenced by these casual remarks.

Finally, let us evaluate Smith's preoccupation with the future falling rate of profit. Examination of the movement of the profit index over the course of the period belies any simple notion of an empirically falling rate of profit. Although our sample is much too small to make any definitive global state-

Table 11.5 Average Rates of Profit, 1758–1776

Concern	Average percent rate of profit	Number of years of data
Sun Fire	37.4	19
Whitbread's (incl. private withdrawals)	22.3	7
East India Co.	14.2	19
Scotch Mines Co.	10.5	17
Carron Co.	7.3	7
Million Bank	6.5	19
Westminster Fire	5.3	15
London Assurance	4.3	19

ment, we can say that the profit rates of some of the largest firms of the period did not deteriorate over long stretches of time, and many flourishing concerns showed a pronounced rise.

One possible explanation for Smith's conviction that the rate of profit had fallen in the face of the contrary evidence was the implied relation between his statement (b) and statement (c). As we have seen, his twice-interest rule had some justification as an estimate of contemporary profit rates; and Smith, avoiding any direct empiricism, probably just extended the rule into the past. Since it was a well-known fact that rates of interest had fallen (and Smith traces their fall from the time of Henry VIII), it would follow by his logic that profit rates must have fallen in tandem.

This explanation does not seem to justify his extrapolation of this trend into the future, however, since interest rates begin to rise once more at the end of this period. One other characteristic of Smith's system may account for the *prediction* of a falling rate of profit. G. S. L. Tucker notes in his study of the classical economists that Smith often meant two distinct quanta when he referred to the "rate of profit": one, a ratio of flow profits to capital stock invested in the process; and the other, a ratio of flow profits to flow costs, or flow profits to flow sales.[23]   It is a commonplace that the stock/flow distinction was not wielded with any great subtlety in classical economics: for example, Ricardo's "corn model" was an analytical way of bypassing the pitfalls of accounting for stocks in economic thinking, as was his assumption of uniform constant turnover. This lack of attention to stock/flow distinctions could possibly have extended into their casual empiricism regarding the rate of profit. There is some fragmentary evidence that profit *margins* (ratio of flow profits to flow sales) were quite high in the eighteenth century, much higher than the margins of contemporary experience.[24] Over time, as competition increased in any particular industry, profit margins do seem to have been reduced. If it was the case that profit margins fell in response to competition, and Smith confused the profit rate with the profit margin in his casual empiricism, this would explain his prediction of a falling rate of profit. Moreover, Smith's explanation of the falling rate—increased competition arising as the result of the accumulation of capital—would have been, in fact, the explanation given by businessmen of a perceived regularity in their profit margins. This conjecture gains some credibility from the fact that Smith probably derived most of his empirical information from conversations with men of business.

Smith as the Founder of a Paradigm

In the light of the results of the preceding section, we may now reconsider Smith the methodologist. Smith was somewhat reliable as a reporter on events linked to his theory that were contemporary with the composition of

WON. When it came to history, he was on less solid ground, and his theoretical prediction did not fare well at all. Further, Smith mixes empirical reports of some validity—statements (a) and (b)—with observations of little quality—statements (c) and (d)—and with predictions—statement (e)—all with little or no differentiation as to the relative merit or standing of each observation. As W. P. D. Wightman has written, "What puzzles the modern reader is the willingness of men of intellectual power, as were Smith and D'Alembert, to leave him in doubt as to where the 'fact' ended and the fiction began. . . . where evidence was lacking they supplied a 'likely story.' "[25] This was not quite the same as doing the best with such facts as he had, since that would at least entail specifying the definition and relative quality of the facts, something Smith makes no pretense of doing. Therefore, by modern standards, Smith is at best an indifferent empiricist.

But this may be the crux of the problem with the quotations concerning Smith's empirical bent in the first section above: they all presume "modern" notions of scientific justification. Smith's notions of science were very different from those today held dear—something that should not surprise us. In *WON* (501) he wrote, "I have no great faith in political arithmetic," and it also seems our notion of a "test" held no great attraction for him. One student of his work notes that "it is a striking feature of Smith's system of science that he more frequently refers to his own standard of judgment as aesthetic than as strictly rational, and that as his final criteria of truth he is willing to accept neither the rational test of consistency nor the empirical standard of correspondence with the observed facts."[26] Smith adopted this position because he objected to the empiricism of Bacon, Hobbes, and Locke on the grounds that they neglected the "secondary qualities" of experience, which included color, sound, taste, and smell. These "secondary qualities" were the components of "beauty," which in turn evoked "wonder," "surprise," and "admiration" in the breast of the beholder. Since Smith believed that the latter triad of emotions were the fundamental motive forces in scientific inquiry, he was inclined toward the view that empiricism—that is, empiricism in the modern sense of quantification and a skeptical posture towards the "facts"—was a stifling influence upon the progress of scientific inquiry.[27] Thus, for Smith, science had more of the character of what we think of as artistic representation.

It should be clear from all of this that Smith was *not* "methodologically comprehensive,"[28] as some twentieth-century economists would have it; but he followed his own standards of discourse, which bear little resemblance to our standards. In that case, in what sense did Smith "succeed"? His work in *The Moral Sentiments,* the essays on astronomy and language, and *WON* were all meant to be part of an interrelated and coherent system of moral philosophy; unfortunately, this grand design was never realized. Smith did not aim at founding a unique discipline of political economy; that came afterwards, and was the conscious intent of others. Smith's book more than met the test of the market, in that it sold quite well; but judging from his other works, Smith probably would not deem this as substantial justification for his ideas. Why, then, is Smith persistently identified as the founder of "political economy" or "economics"?

It cannot be because he originated either the method or the mode of discourse: as we have seen, he is but an indifferent "empiricist" in the modern sense; he cared little about substantiating the predictions he had made; and as we have intimated and others have observed,[29] logical consistency was neither his forte nor his concern.

If there is a reason for his elevation, it would have to be the one summarized by T. H. Hutchison: "The justification for the concept of a Smithian 'revolution' must be based on the generalization in WON of the notion of a 'natural' effective self-adjusting mechanism as being usually at work throughout competitive economies or markets."[30]

The work of Thomas Kuhn suggests that the identification of "famous" scientists as part of a shared lineage of a science performs a pedagogic purpose: to inculcate in tyro practitioners the goals and values of that science. If this be the case, what can we infer about the values of a discipline which persistently identifies Smith as its founder? We cannot infer, I think, that Smithian methods or logics are meant to be held in high esteem, a "paradigm" for present practices. (This is so, no matter how much twentieth-century commentators try to endow Smith with the qualities of empiricism or a logical system after the fact.) Instead, it seems that the predominant value of our science is this faith in the "natural" mechanism of the market and a "natural progress" in the economic affairs of the race. It is this "vision" of Smith that overcomes any other subsidiary failings in scientific values in the view of Western economists and places him in the hallowed position he occupies in the history of economic thought.

Notes

1. For some recent examples, see S. Latsis (1976) and D. Landon, "Resistance to Evidence in Development Economics," *Haifa University Discussion Papers* 7 (Feb. 1976).

2. See R. Koebner (1959) and R. M. Hartwell (1978).

3. Preliminary comments on this article force me to stress this point with greater sharpness. In no way is this essay concerned with what I personally believe constitutes empiricism; rather, it deals with (a) one conventional notion of empiricism as hypothesis testing, usually in some sort of numerical framework, and its relation to (b) Adam Smith's specification and employment of certain salient "facts" *from his own point of view.* Anyone with an interest in the history and philosophy of science associated with the names of Kuhn, Feyerabend, and the others is well aware that the very concept of empiricism is undergoing profound revision at present. For a summary of this discussion, see the articles collected in Harold Morick (1972). To repeat, I am concerned with recent perceptions of Smith's methodology.

4. G. S. L. Tucker (1960, chs. 4 and 5).

5. Adam Smith (1937, 249).

6. J. S. Nicholson, "Introductory Essay," in *The Wealth of Nations,* ed. J. S. Nicholson (London, 1895), 6.

7. A. L. MacFie (1967, 13).

8. H. J. Bitterman (1940, 505).

9. D. P. O'Brien (1976, 141).

10. Smith, *WON,* 87. Although Smith often writes "the profits of stock" as in this passage, he appears from the context to mean the rate of profit, and not the absolute mass of profits. In this regard, see Tucker (1960, 59).

11. "Judged by standards of analytical competence, Smith is not the greatest of the 18th century economists." See Mark Blaug (1978, 65); and also E. von Böhm-Bawerk (1959, 49).

12. See, for example, J. Rae (1965, 90–92); and W. Scott (1934, 506–8).

13. See S. Pollard, "Capital Accounting in the Industrial Revolution," in F. Crouzet (1972); G. Lee (1975); and R. Grassby (1969. Grassby's article is not useful for our present purposes for a number of reasons. First, he persists in *not* taking the contemporary accounts at their own word, but feels he must alter those accounts to fit some modern notion of capital. Second, as he admits (731 n.9), "No attempt has been made here systematically to collect evidence of profit rates for the eighteenth century." Third, not once does he report either time series or the data underlying his generalizations, but only impressionistically cites "average" rates. Finally, he insists (724) that he is interested only in profits invested solely in the commodity trade, while we are interested in the classical nature of a general rate of profit.

14. P. Mirowski, "Some Parables in the Theory and History of Fixed and Circulating Capital." Paper presented to the 1981 Cliometrics Conference, University of Iowa.

15. Questions of the "appropriate" of "inappropriate" valuation of assets in the cases of individual companies are largely irrelevant in this context, since we are not interested in any modern notion of accounting or capital, but simply in reporting business records as they were kept. The denominator is simply the net worth reported in business accounts.

16. In keeping with the spirit of respect for contemporary accounting practices, the time patterns of profit realization were preserved, with a single exception. The Million Bank, one of the firms in our sample, made a decision in the midst of its career that is not preserved in our summary. The bank chose to depreciate its holdings of government annuities in an unusually abrupt manner—a bit of erratic behavior that can be explained in the context of the bank's history. In 1741–42 a number of its stockholders began to be concerned that the annuities constituting the bulk of the bank's assets would expire in less than fifty years, and that the government had ceased issuing new annuities; thus they argued that the bank should expand its investment horizons. For various reasons the opinion prevailed that the original charter had permitted investment only in annuities; thereafter the financial operations of the bank entered a period of benign neglect. The annuities were depreciated as an afterthought, since all parties concerned realized that the decisions of 1741–42 tacitly implied that the bank was to self-destruct in parallel with the annuities. For our present purposes, the importance of the "going concern" assumption outweighs our distaste for altering surviving records. Therefore, the author has calculated the rate of profit that would have existed for the Million Bank if the annuities had remained unchanged in its asset structure. This involved recalculation of profit for the years 1764, 1765, 1773, 1774, 1776, 1778, 1779, and 1781.

17. Compare Pierangelo Garegnani (1976) and M. Milgate (1979, 1–10).

18. For example, see R. Eagly and V. Smith (1976).

19. It is sometimes stated that the mean of a series of ratios is better calculated by taking the geometric rather than the arithmetic mean. We have not chosen this option for three reasons: (a) in such a small sample, all data points are valuable, and the geometric mean would exclude negative values; (b) the usual reason for preferring a geometric mean is the somewhat dubious advantage that the reciprocal of the mean is always equal to the mean of the reciprocals of the data points, a criterion that is irrelevant for our purposes; and (c) when Smith refers to an average rate of profit, he is clearly not thinking of a geometric mean.

20. T. S. Ashton (1959, 187). The regression as reported is corrected for auto-correlation in the residuals.

21. The reader will notice that this equation neither reports the Durbin-Watson statistic nor attempts to correct for autocorrelation in the residuals. This is not an oversight but a conscious step, because conventional methods of correcting for auto-correlation have the side effect of altering the trend in the variables concerned: the proper method of fitting trends is thus still a matter of econometric contention. An example may serve to indicate the problem. William Nordhaus, in a paper titled "The Falling Share of Profits" (*Brookings Papers* 1974, 1) suggested the rate of profit in the postwar United States was falling. A trend-line regression fit to his data gives a significant negative coefficient; thus one would conclude the rate of profit was falling. In a rejoinder, Martin Feldstein and Lawrence Summers (1977, 1) fit a trend regression to essentially the same data, but correct the regression for autocorrelation in the residuals and find that the negative trend coefficient is no longer significant. In fact the reported result is ambiguous, since correcting for autocorrelation involves differencing the time series; and it is well known that differencing the time series either alters or removes trends (see G. Box and G. Jenkins 1976, ch. 4). The point of econometric contention is whether fitting a trend-line regression should be regarded as being statist-ically the same as estimation of an underlying deterministic equation.

22. The profit rates for the East India Company employed here are not the same as the ones reported in K. N. Chaudhuri (1978, 438–40). The reason for this is that Chaudhuri calculates profit by reconstructing all the subsidiary accounts and then cal-culating a rate of profit according to a modern definition, whereas the series employed here simply takes the East India Company's profit-and-loss account at face value, in keeping with our policy of respecting the integrity of the existing accounts.

23. Tucker (1960, 59).

24. This evidence may be found in P. Mirowski (1985, ch. 4).

25. W. P. D. Wightman, "Adam Smith and the History of Ideas," in A. S. Skinner (1975, 54).

26. H. F. Thompson (1965, 219).

27. Compare ibid. and A. S. Skinner (1972).

28. T. W. Hutchison (1978, 9).

29. See note 11 above.

30. Hutchison (1978, 24).

12

What Do Markets Do?

Market Efficacy and the Economic Historian

Everyone acquainted with Economics I knows that the benchmark of successful market operation in neoclassical economics is "efficiency." "Efficiency"
can be construed as a relative term, depending upon the vantage point of the
observer. To avoid any whiff of relativism, neoclassical theory posits a generic goal of the economy called "utility": a goal separable from the means by
which the goal is achieved. This separability of means from ends is
guaranteed by the stipulation that utility must be a variable of state, and thus
suited to the mechanical manipulation of variational principles (that is, maximization) and conservation principles. Historically, this explanatory format,
with its attendant mathematical formalism, was appropriated lock, stock, and
barrel from nineteenth-century physics, by invoking a metaphorical similarity
between "utility" and "energy."

While this research program has had its successes, its ability to isolate and
manipulate utility has never approached the facility and fecundity of the
energy concept in physics. The reasons for this failure have been many and
varied, and have been the subject of a voluminous literature in economic
theory.[1] The pros and cons of this debate are not our present concern. Here
we only wish to cite the well-known (if not openly acknowledged) fact that
there is no effective theoretical or empirical standard with which to gauge utility, and therefore, there has been *no* successful demonstration that any market
has ever functioned so as to maximize utility. The bottom line is that the
definition of the successful operation of the market as the maximization of
utility has been a dead end. Further elaboration of that hypothesis has always
ended in an empirical deadlock or a meaningless tautology.

I would like to argue that, for practical purposes, many neoclassical
economists have acknowledged this fact, since they have frequently opted to
circumvent the entire apparatus of utility by constructing other, more narrow,
definitions of what it would mean to say that a market "worked." Those who
have blazed this trail rapidly became aware of the tangled profusion of possi-

Apologies to Marglin (1974) for the title. I would like to thank James Riley and
Larry Neal for helpful comments.

ble and potential determinants of market outcomes. For instance, market prices might be thought to function most generally as vehicles of information, but further research in game theory has begun to reveal that such a conception is simultaneously too restrictive, and yet hopelessly complicated. That path is further muddied by the plausible inference that the purposes served by the market are as varied and multiform as the commodities themselves; for many, the specter of relativism appears to lurk in that direction.[2]

Economists, being plucky and resourceful souls, have not let the dearth of well-marked trails immobilize them. Some neoclassical theorists have sought to avoid all these problems by concentrating upon one commodity that, by its very nature, exists for a single purpose. A generic financial asset, it is claimed, abstracts from all the messy characteristics of physical commodities, and is purchased for the express purpose of laying claim to a stream of monetary returns. Since both the market outcome and the unit of the commodity are expressed in the same terms (that is, money) and are apparently well defined, the entire conundrum of the identification of market fundamentals has been bypassed, so to speak. An efficient market in financial assets should relate the money return to the money price of the asset in a direct, accessible, and comprehensible fashion. The conviction that the market for financial assets is more transparent than that for other commodities has led to the explosion of literature in financial economics on "efficient markets theory."

Of course, this is only a stylized caricature of what has happened in financial economics; there is much more to financial theory than the bald assertion that returns drive prices in an adequately functioning market. Nevertheless, this narrowing of the definition of what a market does has been one of the most fruitful new departures in the economics of the postwar period, in the sense that it has resulted in the suggestion of a number of ways to structure tests of market efficiency. One such class of tests starts with the proposition that an efficient market maximizes money returns, and reinterprets it to imply that in an efficient market no more money could be made from a mechanical prediction and investment scheme based upon regularities in past prices. Other classes of tests are more committed to the specification of the underlying causal processes that relate money returns to money prices. In the former class, a representative test might examine a time series of share prices in order to discover whether it was entirely random, or white noise (see Neal 1984). In the latter case, further theoretical structure must be imposed to specify how prices are related to returns in an efficient manner. For obvious reasons, the former class of tests have come to be known as "weak tests" of efficiency, while the latter class are referred to as "strong tests" (First 1977; Keane 1983).

Most versions of strong tests of market efficiency are based upon neoclassical capital theory, which suggests that the present price of an asset in an efficient market is one that is equated to the present value of the future stream of money returns. This portrayal of the market as an enforcer of the present value relation constitutes the theme of this chapter, or at least the theme for the right hand. The left hand will concurrently provide the accompaniment, which consists of the refrain that the real question behind all of the jargon is "What do markets do?" In the best traditions of twentieth-century music, we shall lose the theme for the right hand for a few moments, only to discover it again in the second section. With the indulgence of the audience, I will bang out a few more left-handed chords, because the historical intermezzo is critical in asking what markets do.

A very important aspect of the question "What do markets do?" renders it slippery and hard to pin down. Implicitly, the question has to be imbedded in an historical context, but one searches in vain to find someone who phrases it legitimately as "What do markets do *now?*" The neglect of historical specificity can be traced back to the fact that neoclassical economic theory is characteristically ahistorical and timeless, in the sense that its variables of state must be independent of their temporal location: this is the analytical significance of energy in physics, and its analogue utility in economics. This indifference to temporal location is clearly embedded, for instance, in present-value theory. The present-value formula is not time-dependent; and moreover, the stream of money returns can extend into the infinite future, which must necessarily imply that the market will continue to function in the "same" manner into the indefinite future. An important but little noted corollary of neoclassical economic theory is that there is no expectation of any marked trend in market efficiency over time. Hence, once it is settled what markets do, they are presumed to have done the same things, no matter where or when.

This presumption of the immortality of market functions has served as a subtext throughout the literature of economic history. Debates over the question of whether prices served to clear markets in the ancient world, or whether Victorian Britain failed, or whether American slave prices could be accounted for by human capital theory, or whether feudal agriculture was organized in such as way as to diversify risk, are all in fact variations upon a single theme: Can all defunct economic structures be explained as if they were protean manifestations of a single abstract form of market organization, and if so, did those markets work? [3]

The program to implement the neoclassical explanation of the market in these variegated historical contexts has not gone without hesitation and cognitive dissonance in some quarters. After all, the mythos of the timeless and eternal operation of the market does tend to collide with the Western faith in progress and improvement. Further, the study of history does seem a somewhat idosyncratic pursuit if the past really is not substantially different from the present. The response to the dissonance has been to repress the problem: many economists deride the study of history as an antiquarian pastime, while, on their own part, neoclassically trained economic historians defend their activities on the grounds that old numbers are not necessarily of worse quality and reliability than their modern counterparts, and anyway there are a lot more of them, abundant grist for mills of econometrics (McCloskey 1976). These squabbles over status grow out of the fact that the economic historian can always potentially embarrass the neoclassical economist by reminding him that his "general theory" might not be applicable to all temporal locations; whereas the neoclassical economist can always discomfit the economic historian by reminding him that everyone knows the market has improved over time, suggesting thereby that no one expects to learn much from earlier inchoate economic formations.

The sticking point of this sorry impasse is that the historians have neglected the opportunity to exploit this issue to their own advantage. Instead of straining to make neoclassical theory fit, it would seem to be the forté of the historian to inquire into the sort of situations that would challenge the ahistorical aspects of the theory, providing a critical perspective that could not be maintained in the hurly-burly of modern policy discussions. Historians are more congenitally disposed to be taxonomists than theorists, but this might be a valuable activity in the face of a theory that denies temporal diversity.

The purpose of this chapter, therefore, is to try to restate the question of market efficiency in as careful a manner as possible, and in such a way as to render it a tractable historical question. For the reasons indicated above, we will choose a particularly narrow construction of what a market does: the present value theory of asset pricing, predicated upon neoclassical capital theory. To this theory we shall bring abundant evidence from a market exhibiting remarkable stability over a long period of time: the eighteenth-century London joint-stock share market. This market has the added attraction that it has recently been the object of intensive scrutiny by economic historians (Cope 1978; Dickson 1967; Mirowski 1981; Neal 1984, 1985a). But before we come to the actual evidence, we shall discover that we need to be even more precise about what it means to say that a market does or does not work.

Shiller Tests and Present Values

It is a commonplace in the history of science that there is no such thing as an *experimentum crucis*, and no test is as simple as it seems. The present value theory of market operation appears at first glance to be very precise, in that we can write down an exact quantitative expression for the price of a given financial asset at time t:

$$P_t = \sum_{n=1}^{\infty} \frac{d_{t+n}}{(1 + \rho)^n} \tag{1}$$

Here d is the dividend per share at time $t + n$, and ρ is the discount rate. In equation (1), the discount rate is assumed to be constant during the stream of returns. As everyone familiar with present value calculations knows, the apparent precision of equation (1) is deceptive. The intuitive insight that motivates the entire theory of present values is that the price of a share should be equated to the money returns it generates, suitably adjusted for the distribution of those returns through time: but therein lies the rub. Only in a world where the future is indistinguishable from the present in every respect could such future market events be related to a contemporary market event in such a colorless and mechanical fashion (Bausor 1986).

Anything can happen with the passage of time, anything from smooth exponential economic growth to utter breakdown of the world market economy. (The twentieth century lives, however uncomfortably, with the real possibility of apocalypse.) The response to this objection in the neoclassical camp is to acknowledge that some things might change over time, combined with a denial (or a refusal to consider) that certain other drastic changes might take place (Mirowski 1985, 121–26). For instance, in present value theory, it is allowed that the rate of discount might change. It is also allowed that the estimation of dividends in period $t + n$ at period t might not be precise, but rather that dividend $t + n$ is drawn from some stable stochastic distribution, whose parameters might themselves be a function of the information set $\Phi(t)$ at time t. Taking into account these alterations, we would then rewrite equation (1) as:

$$p_t = \sum_{n=1}^{\infty} \frac{E\{d_{t+n} \,|\, \Phi(t)\}}{(1 + R_n^t)} \tag{2}$$

Haste should not cause one to overlook the sort of changes that are prohibited by the method encapsulated in equation (2). It does incorporate a certain peculiar notion of risk, but not of true uncertainty, which contradicts the assumption of stable probability distributions (Hicks 1979; Bausor 1982). In general, any catastrophic disaster is ruled out of court (Blatt 1979). Quite significantly, it also places certain restrictions upon the expectational process itself, which we discuss below under the rubric of "ergodicity" (Davidson 1982). As we have already indicated, these prohibitions are not arbitrary nor easily relinquished: in neoclassical theory, the market as an institution cannot operate differently over time. In other words, the hard core of neoclassical theory is timeless and ahistorical.

Even though many potential types of change are ruled out in equation (2), it should be obvious that there is more than sufficient freedom to vary both the forms of the probability distributions and the pattern of the discount rates in order to arrive at any desired pattern of p_t's. As long as the present value theory remains at this level of discourse, it is in danger of being true tautologically, since it can be used post hoc to justify any market outcome. To give this hypothesis some teeth, and hence to assert that an efficient market sets asset prices equal to present values in such a manner that some price movements are prohibited, further structure must be imposed upon equation (2).

The next step was taken by a number of financial theorists, most notably by Robert Shiller in his now infamous article, "Do Stock Prices Move Too Much to Be Justified by Subsequent Changes in Dividends?" (1981). Shiller added two innovations to equation (2) in order to turn it into a theory of efficient market operation. The first, which he admitted was provisional, was to assume that the one-period discount rate r was constant over time. The second was to define an "ex post rational price," here identified as $\hat{z}^*_t$, as the price that would have been observed at time t if the market really did know the future stream of all actual dividends d^*.

$$\hat{z}^*_t = \sum_{n=1}^{\infty} \frac{d^*_{t+n}}{(1 + r)^n} \tag{3}$$

One could think of the ex post price $\hat{z}^*$ as a realization of a random variable p^* defined over all possible sets of states of the economy and dividend outcomes. The *actual observed price* at time t is therefore the expected value of the distribution of p^*_t conditional upon the information available at time t, or:

$$p_t = E\{p^*_t | \Phi(t)\} \tag{4}$$

The next step is to assume that the realizations of drawings from all possible ex post rational prices correspond to the expected value of those prices, plus any unpredictable disturbances:

$$\hat{p}^*_t = E\{p^*_t | \Phi(t)\} + \eta_t = p_t + \eta_t.$$

At this stage, further conditions are imposed. The error terms η_t are assumed to be orthogonal to the actual observed prices p_t: this is the "rational expectations" assumption that there is no "unused" information left over once the market sets the price. Also, the variances of all processes are assumed to be finite. Employing the lemma that all variances are strictly positive, and that the variance of the sum of orthogonal variables is the sum of their variances, Shiller arrived at the first of his variance-bound tests:

$$Var(\hat{p}^*_t) = Var(p_t) + Var(\eta_t)$$

or

$$Var(\hat{p}^*_t) \geqslant Var(p_t). \tag{5}$$

In effect, inequality (5) argues that the variance of the conditional expectation of draws from the distribution of ex post rational prices should be less than or equal to the variance of a draw from an unconditional distribution of all possible realizations of all possible economies at time t. Since we can't observe the distribution of all possible economies, and in fact can observe only one realization, there is still one more rather major assumption necessary to implement an *empirical* variance bounds test of the type of inequality (5). Shiller had to assume that the unconditional distribution of ex post rational prices across all potential economies at a point in time should be identical to the conditional distribution of a time series of realized ex post rational prices, or:

$$Var(\hat{p}^*_t) = Var(z^*_t).$$

Of all the assumptions involved in Shiller's procedure—and we have seen there are quite a few—this is the one that has drawn the most objections (LeRoy 1984; Kleidon 1983). We shall accumulate a handlist and guide to all of the objections below; it should suffice for the moment to identify this critical step as the assumption of *ergodicity*. Explicitly invoking the parallel with physics, the assumption of ergodicity means that the time average (or in this case, the second moment) of a process is assumed equal to its ensemble average at a single point in time (Prigogine 1980, 33–38; Lebowitz and Penrose 1973).

Keeping in mind the various steps, Shiller then interpreted inequality (5) as a variance bounds test of the present value relationship in history. He proceeded to calculate the ex post rational price series for the Dow Jones and Standard & Poor share indices for 1928–1979 and 1871–1979, respectively, using equation (3) and the actual dividends; and then calculated the estimated variances of the ex post rational series and the actual price series, in order to discover whether inequality (5) obtained. At this stage it is important to note that Shiller admitted that equation (1) could not be tested in isolation, and that all that could be empirically implemented was a test of the joint hypothesis of a combination of all of the above hypotheses. Acknowledging this, for the sake of convenience we shall refer to inequality (5) and its attendant joint hypotheses as "test A."

Because the basic insight of variance bounds tests of the present value relationship is that the distribution of actual dividends should restrict the distribution of actual prices, Shiller (1981a) also attempted to derive a more direct version of the test. To do so, he had to impose even further assumptions, most notably that the time series of actual prices and actual dividends be jointly covariance stationary. His result, which we shall refer to as "test B," is much less intuitively accessible, lacking the (relatively) simple interpretative structure of the previous test. Test B also assumes the format of an inequality restriction, but one in terms of first differences of the actual prices, namely:

$$Var(\Delta p) \leqslant Var\{(d)/(\sqrt{2r})\} \tag{6}$$

At the risk of some confusion, we will propose a third test procedure, which is only a minor variation upon Shiller's original insight. The actual historical realizations of $\hat{z}^*_t$ $(= \hat{p}^*_t)$ and p_t contain much more useful information than can be gleaned from a sparce report of the variance bounds (5) and (6). The pattern of the divergence of actual prices from ex post rational prices over time, that is, $p_t - \hat{p}^*_t$, should be very close to white noise if the market effectively incorporates fully all information about profitability into the share prices. In the event that it fails to do so—that is, the market is not efficient—examination of the divergence should reveal any patterns of market behavior which might themselves demand further explanation. For instance, do actual prices consistently overshoot or undershoot their ex post rational price? Are the divergences serially correlated? Any and all of these phenomena would raise the possibility that other forces drive market prices, or that equating present values does not exhaust the list of what markets do.

While a simple time series plot of the divergence is a good way to begin this search, this test can be expressed more formally through the use of time series methods, such as autoregressive moving average models (Box and Jenkins 1976). If such mechanical models can explain a high proportion of the variance of the divergence, then one could imagine that some market participants could have made money by predicting it, and hence unexploited gains were to be realized from the neoclassical point of view. We shall refer to this attempt to model the divergence between actual and ex post rational prices as "test C."

Shiller's proposed tests of the present value relationship have provoked quite a storm of controversy amid the ranks of financial economists. Both Shiller (1981) and LeRoy and Porter (1981) found that the variance-bound restrictions of tests A and B were violated in most cases using recent American share prices and dividend data; that the extent of the violations were often "flagrant" (to use their terminology), to the extent that the estimated variance of the actual share prices was many multiples of the variance of the ex post rational series. To quote LeRoy and Porter: "in our view, the fact that asset prices appear to fluctuate more than is consistent with most financial models in current use should be regarded as a major challenge to those models" (1981, 559).

And, indeed, it was rapidly regarded as a major challenge to the decades of literature dedicated to the demonstration of the untrammeled efficiency of the market in financial assets. It should come as no surprise that the immediate reaction was to explore all the conditions under which Shiller tests would be reversed: that is, models were proposed that displayed the result that actual prices would fluctuate with more volatility than the ex post rational prices.

Those familiar with the philosophy of science will recognize this sequence of events as yet another instance of the Duhem-Quine thesis, which states that no hypothesis can be definitively empirically falsified, owing to the fact that every test must confront a cluster of auxiliary hypotheses that themselves cannot entirely be separated out and subjected to independent test (Harding 1976). Any subset of the profusion of hypotheses required to get us from expression (1) to expressions (5) and (6) can be called into question and criticized, and further auxiliary hypotheses can be brought into play to neutralize Shiller's results.

The Duhem-Quine thesis may prove distressing, especially to some cliometricians, given that their rise to dominance in economic history was a blitzkrieg under the banner of rigorous scientistic falsificationism. I do not know how many unreconstructed Popperians are still lurking out there. For our present purposes we shall not spurn this "innocuous falsificationism," but rather view it as part and parcel of the process of normal scientific inquiry. The invocation of auxiliary hypotheses in response to an empirical test that threatens a widely held theory (here the present value hypothesis and the belief in efficient markets) may be progressive if those auxiliary hypotheses add new empirical content to the existing theory, and (NB) do not contradict it in other respects. Upon these grounds we shall briefly assess the various criticisms of Shiller's variance bounds tests.

The following are the primary classes of objections to Shiller's tests.

1. Nonconstant Discount Rate

We shall maintain that this is the only objection, of all the various objections to date, that has served to lead to further fruitful empirical hypotheses. Indeed, Shiller (1981) himself entertained the possibility of nonconstant discount rates, making the interesting observation that the implied series r_t, which would equate observed and ex post rational share prices, should also be observed in the movements of the present value series of other assets. In other papers, he then examined independent evidence on land prices, housing prices, and long-term bond prices, and concluded that no two of these series exhibited similar movements of discount rates.[4]

Other criticisms of constant discount rate assumptions, such as that of Grossman and Shiller (1981), rely upon the theory that nonconstant discount rates can be accounted for by a utility function of a specific functional form that incorporates a risk aversion parameter. Since this involves a retreat to an unobservable utility function to define market efficiency, we consider this a retrograde development. Recall from the first section above that the entire purpose of this market efficiency literature was to circumvent the tautology of utility-defined efficiency.

2. Incorrectly Specified Returns

Kleidon (1983) suggests that the stream of money returns that drives share prices should not be taken to be the dividends paid, precisely because managers try to smooth the time pattern of dividends relative to earnings. He instead proposes that the relevant stream of returns be the net earnings as

defined in the accounts of the firm. While this is an interesting idea, it is not
a progressive auxiliary hypothesis from the neoclassical viewpoint, for two
reasons. First, it begins indiscriminately to confuse the information set $\Phi(t)$
with the actual moneyflows d_t that accrue to the owner of the asset. Second,
it is dissonant with the general neoclassical predisposition to disparage company accounts as unreliable and not representative of "real" economic variables (see Mirowski 1985, 173–201).

3. Ergodicity

Both Leroy (1984) and Kleidon (1983) give numerical examples where
different plausible assumptions about the processes driving dividends will
result in nonergodic probability distributions, which would in turn imply
situations where the variance of ex post rational prices would be *less* than that
of actual prices: that is, inequality (5) would be reversed. While their examples do appear quite plausible in isolation, these critics do not seem to realize
that to relinquish ergodicity in the determinants of asset returns would not
only undermine the Shiller tests, but would also bar any employment of the
rational expectations hypothesis (Davidson 1982), render fallacious almost the
entire finance literature and, as if that were not enough, ultimately render
incoherent the core of neoclassical economic theory. Lest the reader think
this claim too histrionic and extravagant, we quote an unimpeachable source,
Paul Samuelson:

> [The neoclassical economist] naturally tended to think of models in which things
> settle down to a unique position independently of initial conditions. Technically
> speaking, we theorists hoped not to introduce *hysteresis* phenomena into our model,
> as the Bible does when it says "We pass this way only once" and, in so saying,
> takes the subject out of the realm of science and into the realm of genuine history.
> [Samuelson 1970, 184–85]

This, of course, is precisely the main issue, as mooted in the first section
above. The scientific pretensions of neoclassical theory demand that its explanations be ahistorical and independent of temporal location. For critics of
Shiller tests to suggest that some plausible cases in the world do exhibit
nonergodicity is certainly true, but it is self-defeating, if their object is to
defend the neoclassical notion of market efficiency. Because it throws out the
baby with the bathwater, this is not a progressive auxiliary hypothesis from
the vantage point of neoclassical economics.

4. Small Sample Bias

Flavin (1983) reports that small samples may bias variance bounds tests
toward rejection. This is a potentially progressive auxiliary hypothesis, since
independent evidence can be invoked in its evaluation.

5. Nonstationarity

Kleidon (1983), Leroy (1984), and many others have pointed out that, if the underlying time series are not stationary (that is, all moments of their distributions are not independent of time), then the variance bounds tests are invalid. Again, this is unquestionably true, but it is not a progressive auxiliary hypothesis, for exactly the same reason discussed under the nonergodicity objection. If pervasive nonstationarity were admitted, then most statistical models of neoclassical relations would be consigned to the rubbish heap.

6. Securities Held for Reasons Other than Their Money Returns

This objection to the Shiller tests is often raised in casual conversations; indeed, we shall seriously entertain it below. It should be acknowledged, however, that the admission of this hypothesis undermines the entire research program described above in the first section. Recall that the main reason that the whole issue of market efficiency has centered upon financial markets was that the definition of the purpose of market operation was purportedly more clearly and narrowly identifiable. What this objection does is demote financial markets to the status of the markets for other commodities; henceforth it is no longer transparent what those markets do. In this sense, from the neoclassical point of view, it is a retreat. (On the other hand, from our point of view, it might be considered the starting point of a rival conceptualization of what markets do.)

In summary, there are quite a few objections to the Shiller tests in the literature, but taking them all equally seriously would result in a pyrrhic victory for efficient markets, since it would be tantamount to killing the patient to cure the disease. I personally think it is instructive that such drastic critiques in the finance literature were not raised in the context of earlier models, when it appeared everything was going swimmingly in the neoclassical camp, but were invoked only as desperate measures when a core tenet of the neoclassical world view was under attack. If markets did not appear to be efficient under some well-defined empirical definition, then the very raison d'être of neoclassical economics was in question.

Objections (1), (3), (5), and (6) should be of particular interest to economic historians, because they illustrate a general thesis broached above in the first section. In effect, when their stories about the efficiency of market operation started running into trouble, neoclassical economic theorists opted to invoke the qualification that market functions do possess a temporal dependence; that is, history matters in a fundamental way. The economic historian has two options in response. In the first, the cliometrician will realize that this impugns his belief that the market operates in all places and times in exactly the same manner, and he can simply hunker down and hope that someone else will rapidly demonstrate that the Shiller tests were spurious due to some arcane technical issue. In the second case, a more open-minded economic historian could choose to highlight the inconsistencies, researching whether historical change in market functions is more the norm rather than the anomaly. In this particular instance of variance bounds tests, the historian has the advantage that only very long runs of data are expected to give legitimate results, due to objection (4). Hence, the historical mode of inquiry is more suitable than others for adequately posing the question "What do markets do?"

Shiller Tests and Eighteenth-Century London Share Prices

Many considerations exist to suggest that, if indeed the market operates the way that neoclassical present value theory says that it should, some historical contexts would be more favorable to its operation than others. Although it may initially appear paradoxical, if not downright perverse, I will argue that it is at least as likely, and plausibly more likely, that one should observe the neoclassical present value relation in eighteenth-century London share markets; that is, if the present value relation has *ever* been the dominant determinant of asset prices.

The first reason follows directly from the discussion above. Neoclassical theory has as a core premise that there is no expected trend in the efficiency of the market as an institution. The second reason involves equations (1) and (2) above. These equations presume that there is a direct and unencumbered connection between share prices and money dividends. One of the common complaints of the twentieth-century finance literature is that, in fact, this is not the case. For instance, differential taxation of dividends and capital gains, transfer taxes, investment controls, and other governmental constraints that neoclassicism finds so objectionable should be taken into account in any model, and quite often these influences mitigate or reverse the results of the simpler model. These considerations patently also apply to Shiller tests, although no one to my knowledge has yet raised these objections. A marked advantage of research into the present value relation in the eighteenth-century context is that it is remarkably free of such complications. The only direct taxation on the market for joint stock shares was the stamp tax on the transfers of shares at a fixed lump sum rate; it is generally agreed that the amount exacted was so small as to have negligible effects on the market (Dickson 1967, 462; Dowell 1888, v.II, 290–91). Since a lump sum tax is conventionally the least "distorting" form of government intervention in neoclassical theory, from that point of view this situation is the next best thing to no government intervention at all. Other taxes, such as income taxes, capital gains taxes, and so forth, did not exist during the period considered below.

The third consideration is that the information set $\Phi(t)$ in equation (2) includes not only information about the vicissitudes of the particular firm, but also information concerning the course of macroeconomic events. In twentieth-century terms, this information should include a theory of macroeconomic fluctuations, as well as the corresponding set of potential determinants of market fluctuations. In many instances, dissatisfaction with assumptions of ergodicity in Shiller tests are prompted by the belief that it is these sorts of structural macroeconomic changes that are important. An advantage of the eighteenth-century share markets is that (a) inasmuch as the actors can be said to possess a macroeconomic theory, it was much simpler, and did not change appreciably over the course of the century; and (b), until the 1780s, macroeconomic fluctuations were relatively muted and government policy was relatively stable (Mirowski 1985). Thus, if the ergodic assumption was ever justified, it was most justified in the eighteenth century.

The fourth reason the eighteenth century is attractive is that the most legitimate format of the Shiller tests is one employing a very long time series of prices and dividends of a generic identical asset, under as stable market circumstances as possible.[5] Such an ideal stability requires an inordinate number of circumstances: no splits, no mergers or takeovers, no buyouts; and strangely enough, even growth creates problems here, since it would by definition lead to nonstationary prices and dividends. Ideally, it also requires completely regularized reporting of prices and dividends at regular time intervals, in a market where rules and practices are relatively fixed over the interval. Curiously enough, the eighteenth-century London share market approaches this idea much more closely than does that of the twentieth century. As it so happens, modern studies often have to detrend their data series to approximate stationarity: yet the data series described below were already nearly stationary over the sample period, therefore allowing us to avoid issues of the appropriate methods of detrending, and so on.

Finally, inflation might disrupt some aspects of the present value calculation. While no historical period was entirely free of changes in the price level, eighteenth-century England (with the exception of the first and last decades) experienced lower trend inflation (or deflation) rates than either the nineteenth or twentieth centuries.

Just because there are certain specific reasons why the eighteenth-century share market might be a more appropriate arena in which to test the present value relation, one should not get the impression that the eighteenth century was some kind of Golden Age of the market, or that there are not reasons to counsel caution when using eighteenth-century data. For instance, it should be a matter of concern whether the actors in the eighteenth-century London share market were capable of performing the calculation of equation (1), much less equation (2). It does seem that the rudiments of present value theory were available in the eighteenth century. Tables of reference for compound interest calculations date back to the sixteenth century (Chatfield 1977, 181), and the price of land was commonly expressed in terms of the number of years' discounted rents.

Another common caveat is that the English share market really began to function continuously only in the 1690s, which might lead one to suspect that the eighteenth century is too early to expect the existence of a well-established market institution, capable of performance of all the functions associated with enforcing the present value relationship. Given the ubiquitous lags in transportation and communications, how is it possible to put the eighteenth-century market on the same footing with that of the twentieth century? A very interesting result of the recent research into eighteenth century financial markets is that, with respect to issues of information transfer and geographical integration, the London and Amsterdam markets were quite modern in appearance. The financial press was much more extensive and comprehensive than had previously been believed (Neal 1985c), and price movements appear to have been highly integrated between the two markets (Neal 1985a; Eagly and Smith 1976). Most of the institutional prerequisites were in place in London by the first decade of the eighteenth century (Mirowski 1981).

This surprising and unexpected modernity has frequently been misinterpreted as evidence that those markets were *efficient,* whereas the existing evidence can support the only inference that these markets "resemble" modern ones. The question of efficiency must be separated from questions of integration or resemblance, since the former are predicated upon an explicit theory of what a market does, while the latter is not. This potential disjunction of structure and function can be illustrated by the history of the eighteenth-century London share market (Mirowski 1981). Although there was an active and well-developed market in the shares of the few large semipublic joint stock companies—the Bank of England, the East India Company, the Million Bank—by 1710, it is well known that, outside of the period of the South Sea Bubble, private British companies did not resort to issuing public shares to raise funds.[6] The curious juxtaposition of a market that seemingly worked and yet was not utilized by existing firms raises a further question: Will actors always use a market if it is accessible and fully operative? The eighteenth-century London share market responded contrary to theoretical expectations, in that, by most measures of operation—shares listed, trading volume, runs of constant prices—its functioning declined from a peak at the beginning of the century to a trough at midcentury, only to recover by late in the century (Dickson 1967, 466; Carter, 1975).

These estimates of share turnover suggest that, far from improving incrementally over the century, the London share market declined from an early frenzy of operation to a period of quiescence in midcentury. This evidence would appear to argue against the notion that the share market was so rudimentary and underdeveloped as not to be capable of performing the necessary functions requisite for the enforcement of present value relations; however, it does warn us that the market was becoming thinner over time, and that this may have some effect upon our test results.

The Test Results

To assess the effectiveness of the present value relation, we developed a consistent time series of share prices and dividend payouts at fixed quarterly intervals. The preeminent source for share prices in eighteenth-century London is *The Course of the Exchange,* a semiweekly price list that maintained its format unchanged from 1698 to 1811 (Mirowski 1981; Neal 1985c). Because dividends were generally paid semiannually in the eighteenth century, with the dates of payment changed sporadically, it was decided that quarterly share prices were the most appropriate time frame for studying the present value relation. One price report a week was recorded, generally that on Wednesday, and then quarterly averages were calculated. Dividend payments were also reported in the *Course of the Exchange,* and were supplemented by consultations of the histories of the Bank of England (Clapham 1945, vol. 1, 292), and the East India Company (Chaudhuri 1978, 439), as well as the surviving records of the Million Bank (Public Record office C/114/10). Particular care was taken to include calls made upon stock as negative dividends, since Shiller tests are based upon a buy-and-hold strategy, rather than the special case of an hypothetical original subscriber to the stock.

Next, following the methodology of Shiller (1981), both the share prices and the dividends were divided by the Schumpeter-Gilboy producer price index, which was interpolated from annual data in Mitchell and Deane (1962, 468). The ex post rational present value of the share was calculated recursively, using the formula

$$p^*_t = [p^*_{t-1} + d_t]/(1 + \bar{r})$$

where $\bar{r}$ is the mean of the long-term rate of interest over the century, set equal to 0.89 percent at a quarterly rate, or 3.56 percent at an annual rate (See Weiller and Mirowski 1983). The endpoint chosen to start the recursive calculation was the actual price of the share in the last quarter of the sample period: this is tantamount to an assumption that the last price was itself the correct present value of all future dividends outside the sample period. This procedure was then repeated for each share price after it had been exponentially detrended, but since the series was already near stationary, the detrending made very little difference in the results.

The Bank of England sample runs from its charter renewal in 1708 until just prior to the suspension of cash payments in 1797. The East India Company sample runs from 1709.2, which marked the unification of the Old and

New India companies, until 1775, by which date it was widely recognized that the company was no longer simply a trading body, but was also openly assuming the functions and powers of a government in India (Sutherland 1952; Watson 1960, 172). The Million Bank sample runs from 1708 to 1749. The choice of endpoint was governed by the decision of the directors of the bank in 1742–43 to allow the annuities that comprised nearly all the assets of the firm to depreciate away without any new investment.

Plots of the divergences between actual quarterly prices and ex post present values for the Bank of England, the East India Company, and the Million Bank in figures 12.1, 12.2, and 12.3 reveal that they are not random in nature, but reasonably systematic and, indeed, relatively smooth, with the major exception of the period of the South Sea Bubble, 1720.1 to 1721.1. When the divergences are below zero, it means that actual prices were below ex post present values, which can be broadly interpreted as periods of "pessimism"; the converse situations can be interpreted as periods of "optimism."

For all three joint stock companies, the divergences are negative from 1708 until 1718–19; they abruptly turn positive and then subsequently turn abruptly negative in the South Sea Bubble, and recover in 1731–32; after this point each share divergence tends to move more independently of the others. Comparison of each of the plots suggests that, in general, each joint stock share's divergence of actual price from ex post present value is similar to that of the others', and this impression is borne out by the fact that the simple correlation coefficient for the period 1709 to 1749 between the Million Bank divergence

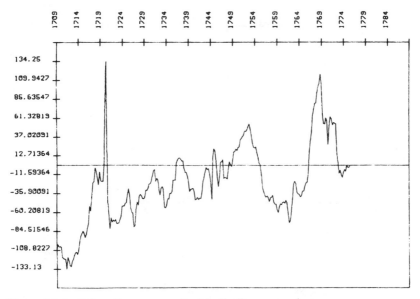

Figure 12.1. Price divergences, East India Company shares.

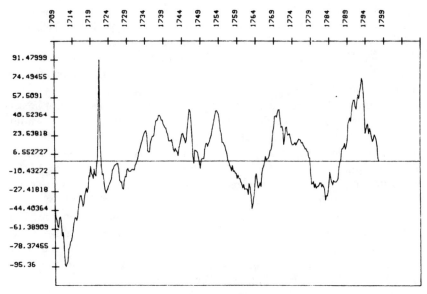

Figure 12.2. Price divergences, Bank of England shares.

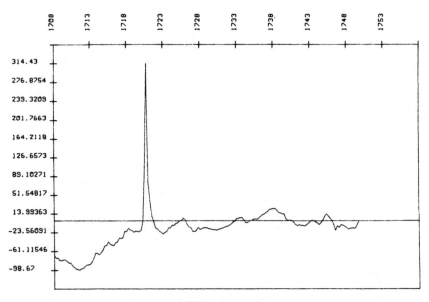

Figure 12.3. Price divergences, Million Bank shares.

and that of the Bank of England is 0.838; while that between the Million Bank and the East India Company is 0.793.

The fact that the divergences of actual historical share prices from their ex post rational present values were smooth, systematic, and highly correlated across different companies suggests that the present value theory is not a sufficient explanation of the process of the formation of share prices: it does not seem to capture what markets *did*. This intuition can be more formally expressed by being cast in the format of Shiller's variance bounds tests.

The results of tests A and B, for both original and detrended data series, are reported in Table 12.1. The first thing one notices is that the original series were very near stationary, because the process of detrending prices and dividends made little difference to the variance calculations, and did not affect the results of the variance bounds tests. Second, all the variance bounds were violated, with the exception of the case of test B for the Bank of England.

As one can observe from Table 12.1, the estimated variances for the Bank of England are much closer to those implied by neoclassical present value theory than either those of the Million Bank or the East India Company. The overall pattern, however, does suggest that the present value theory is an inadequate explanation of the process of the determination of asset prices. There is also an interesting sidelight to our results. Although direct compari-

Table 12.1 Shiller Test Results

Firm	Detrend	$\hat{\sigma}(p) \leqslant \hat{\sigma}(\hat{p}^*)$		Test A
Bank of England				
1708.1	yes	24.20	20.26	fails
1796.4	no	23.99	19.81	fails
East India Company				
1709.2	yes	44.36	35.94	fails
1775.4	no	40.17	22.69	fails
Million Bank				
1708.1	yes	36.37	13.13	fails
1749.3	no	35.92	12.41	fails
Firm	Detrend	$\hat{\sigma}(\Delta p) \leqslant \hat{\sigma}(d)/\sqrt{2r}$		Test B
Bank of England				
1708.1	yes	10.04	11.92	passes
1796.4	no	9.94	11.82	passes
East India Company				
1709.2	yes	20.46	14.95	fails
1775.4	no	16.87	12.79	fails
Million Bank				
1708.1	yes	26.92	11.20	fails
1749.3	no	26.39	11.00	fails

son between Shiller's actual numerical results for the twentieth century and ours for the eighteenth are not strictly legitimate, owing to differences in data format, time unit, and so forth, a broad impressionistic summary would note that Shiller's test A is often violated in the twentieth century by very large multiples of the ex post rational variance. For example, Shiller (1981, 431) finds the variance bound to be violated by multiples of five to thirteen times the ex post rational variance. Our test A never rejects at a multiple of three times the variance, and the rejection rarely reaches twice the variance in the eighteenth century. In this very narrow and loose sense, the eighteenth-century share market was "closer" to the present value relationship than the twentieth-century market. Surely this is an incongruous inversion of the usual stories told concerning the improvement of capital markets over time.

On the suspicion that the South Sea Bubble might have played a critical role in our rejection of the neoclassical variance bounds. The longest series—the Bank of England share prices—was split into two subsamples, 1708.1 to 1749.4 and 1750.1 to 1796.4. As expected, *all* estimates fell in the second subsample relative to the earlier period; the market was clearly less active in the later eighteenth century. Nonetheless, the variance bounds test results were identical to those reported for the pooled sample: test A was violated in both subsamples, and test B was not violated in either subsample. This might be interpreted as suggesting that the fundamental determinants of the price of Bank of England shares did not change over the course of the century, either in the presence or absence of the South Sea Bubble. We are confronted with the paradox of a market becoming thinner over time, yet which behaves in much the same manner with regard to asset pricing.

To complete our analysis, we now invoke test C, which specifically asks whether the divergences of actual share prices from present values had a substantial systematic component. This is of interest for two reasons: it is a further test of market "efficiency," and it is also an indicator of the types of phenomena an alternative theory of asset pricing would have to explain. We have chosen to formalize the notion of systematic divergence by attempting to fit ARMA models to the divergences plotted in Figures 12.1, 12.2, and 12.3. For the sake of comparison, various AR and ARMA models were fitted to the divergences of the Bank of England and the East India Company for an identical time period, 1708.1 to 1774.3. A similar procedure was applied to the shorter series of the Million Bank, 1708.1 to 1749.3. The models that provided the best fits are reported below in table 12.2

As the other tests and our commentary have already stressed, the substantial stability of the divergences from the present value relation is mirrored in the high degree of variance that can be explained using ARMA models: 93 percent of the variance in the cases of the Bank of England and the East India Company, and 62 percent of the variance in the case of the Million Bank. While the form of the best·fit varies dramatically between any two share prices—an AR(2) for the Bank, an AR(1) for the Million Bank, and a baroque

Table 12.2 Time Series Models of Divergences

Bank of England
DIVBANK = .212 + 1.118 DIVBANK(-1) $-$ .164 DIVBANK(-2)
period = 1708.1 $-$ 1774.3 R^2 = .93

East India Company
DIVIND = 1.192 DIVIND(-1) $-$ .353 DIVIND(-2) +
.122 DIVIND(-3) + .06 error(-1)
period = 1708.1 $-$ 1774.3 R^2 = .93

Million Bank
DIVMIL = -2.79 + .786 DIVMIL(-1)
period = 1708.1 $-$ 1749.3 R^2 = .62

ARMA(3,1) for the East India Company—steady state solutions reveal that a rule-of-thumb investment strategy that was based on the principle that any sharp change of actual price from expected present value would persist in the next quarter would have made money. In other words, from a neoclassical point of view, the market was not "efficient." Test C shows that an eighteenth-century English investor who looked only to his dividends for market signals would be at a significant disadvantage relative to the active market speculator.

Given that this was the case, where did the active speculator look for his market signals? In other words, what drove asset prices?

What Asset Markets Did Do

At this point, the above question could be satisfactorily answered only through an extended discussion of alternative theories of what markets do, but this would not be the most appropriate venue for such a discussion. (See, however, Ong 1981; Levine 1980.) Nonetheless, a brief assessment of what the results of the Shiller tests imply for market operation is in order. Shiller himself has tended to interpret the persistent violation of the variance bounds as evidence of "fads" or waves of irrational behavior that periodically sweep the market. This portrayal of the theoretical alternatives as being either neoclassical present value theory or nothing at all is profoundly mistaken in our view; it has certainly helped to foster the impression that the violation of variance bounds is merely a "technical" issue, destined to be solved upon the bringing to bear of greater mathematical ingenuity. We merely wish to point out that there *is* a third possibility—namely that the Shiller tests indicate that the neoclassical ideal of an ahistorical theory of market functions independent of temporal location should be relinquished.

In this view, financial markets do not merely equate asset prices to the future income streams associated with the asset. Ong (1981) has suggested that product pricing behavior exists to serve a number of different functions, some of an ergodic character and some temporally specific. We might suppose that there also exists a hierarchy of market functions in an asset market, some supratemporal and some historically specific. If these functions were relatively independent (and hence additive), one might resolve an asset price into its equalization function (relating ideal prices to ideal returns), its structural function (relating observed prices to rule changes in market structure), its semiotic function (relating price to conscious attempts to signal to other market participants), and its prepotency function (relating observed prices to shifts in power relations, either in the form of "market power," or in a more direct sense, such as takeover bids). Only the first of these functions might be ergodic, in that it would operate in the same manner in all temporal locations. Contrary to Samuelson, such a theory would openly embrace hysteresis as a legitimate principle of explanation. This, after all, is what historians do.

A brief illustration of this alternative analysis, using the historical data developed in this chapter, may serve to provide indications of how this alternative analysis might work. Consider once again Figures 12.1, 12.2, and 12.3. While actual prices clearly did not track ex post rational present values, neither did they appear to be totally unrelated to returns. To a first approximation, one might aver that even eighteenth-century markets did perform some kind of equalization function, albeit only over very long stretches of time and with considerable inertia. Assuming that this equalization function was additive, one could subtract out the ex post rational present value, as we have indeed done, and assert that the other market functions must be invoked to explain the divergence theoretically. These other functions are not ergodic, and therefore cannot generally be expressed as time-independent functional relations. In other words, an historical narrative is required to account for the divergence.

Let us examine one brief illustration of such a theoretical account. Consider the divergence of the prices of East India Company shares in the 1760s and 1770s. While this divergence is generally more pronounced than that of the Bank of England shares during the same period, the divergence from 1766 to 1769 stands out as being exceptional. There is a sharp rise from negative "pessimistic" values to extreme "optimism," and then a contraction to a lower positive plateau in 1770. In the same period the Bank of England stock rises to an optimistic (but lower) plateau, without the ensuing contraction. The difference in price behavior can be explained by the institutional and historically contingent fact that a fixed level of share ownership was required for voting privileges at the General Court of the East India Company, and multiple votes by individuals with large holdings were prohibited. This induced the splitting of large holdings by "selling" blocks of shares to others who would vote in sympathy with the original holder, especially in the period after 1766. Thenceforth, the increasing penetration of the company into Indian political disputes precipitated an acrimonious battle between Clive and Lawrence

Sulivan for leadership of the directors of the company, to the extent of attracting both covert and overt intervention in the share market by the government (Sutherland 1952, 141–91). Thus the issue of corporate control and prerogative loomed larger in the minds of speculators than the capitalization of expected returns. This incident is an illustration of the prepotency function of the market.

It is clear that this sort of reconceptualization of what markets do would drastically alter the question of whether markets are "efficient," or if they "improve" over time. Neoclassical theory, caught in the sway of physics, posited a timeless standard of excellence as a benchmark. Unfortunately, no actual historical market has ever lived up to this standard, nor, we venture to hazard, will there ever be any solid evidence for the absolute improvement of markets. (Recall that integration must not be confused with efficiency.) Our proposed alternative, which might be dubbed "institutionalism" for lack of a better name, asserts that market operation is always contingent upon an historically shifting set of market functions, and therefore "efficiency" can never be anything more than relative. More bluntly, there is no strict separation between theory and history. The dream of man as automaton, subject to a Laplacean equation encompassing all human activity, dies hard.

One last word on the significance of these results. Shiller tests reveal that there has been no strict monotonic relationship between effective rates of return and the value of "capital," an hypothesis ubiquitously assumed in neoclassical theory. From a particular vantage point, this is an answer and a challenge to all those who have asserted that the Cambridge capital controversy (Harcourt 1972) was a tempest in a teapot because it produced no empirical research program, as well as to those who have maintained that the controversy should be settled by empirical work (Blaug 1974; 1980, ch. 10). The market for corporate shares, which Walras (1969, 84) asserted was the very epitome of his theory of the determination of all prices, does not conform to the neoclassical paradigm. This failure was predicted by the Cambridge, England, theoretical critics; it is now supported by historical empiricism.

Notes

1. For a refutation of the commonly held opinion that utility is "unnecessary," see Wong (1978).

2. This literature began with Lancaster (1966). For a discussion of its demise, see Mirowski (1986).

3. See, for instance, the controversy between Mayhew, Neals, Tandy, and Silver in the March 1985 *Journal of Economic History* (127-137); economic historians will recognize the other controversies as associated with the names of Donald McCloskey, Robert Fogel, and Stanley Engerman.

4. Further evidence that time-varying liquidity premia do not reverse the result are presented in Amsler (1984).

5. Shiller and others frequently use share price *indices,* which raise all sorts of objections having to do with the added complications of index numbers. If he had used prices for individual firms, he would have run into the problems of mergers, and so forth.

6. The exceptional cases were the canal companies in the 1780s. See Mirowski (1985, 248–49)

Bibliography

Agassi, Joseph. 1971. *Faraday as a Natural Philosopher.* Chicago: University of Chicago Press.

———. 1981. *Science and Society.* Boston: Reidel.

Akerman, Johan. 1957. *Structures et Cycles Economiques.* Paris: Presses Universitaires de France.

Alchian, Armen. 1950. "Uncertainty, Evolution and Economic Theory." *Journal of Political Economy* 58 (June).

Amsler, Christine. 1984. "Term Structure, Variance Bounds and Time-Varying Liquidity Premia." *Economics Letters* 16.

Andersen, Torben. 1984. "Some Implications of the Efficient Markets Hypothesis." *Journal of Post Keynesian Economics* 6 (Winter).

Anderson, B. L., and Cottrell, P. 1974. *Money and Banking in England.* London: David & Charles.

Antonelli, Giovanni. 1886. *Sulla Theoria Mathematica della Economia Politica.* Trans. in John Chipman, Leonic Hurwicz, and Hugo Sonnenschein, eds., *Preferences, Utility and Demand.* New York: Harcourt Brace Jovanovich.

Apel, Karl. 1981. *Charles S. Peirce: From Pragmatism to Pragmaticsm.* Amherst: University of Massachusetts Press.

Aristotle. 1961. *The Poetics.* New York: Hill & Wang.

Arrow, Kenneth, and Hahn, Frank. 1971. *General Competitive Analysis.* San Francisco: Holden-Day.

Ashton, T. S. 1959. *Economic Fluctuations in England, 1700–1800.* Oxford: Oxford University Press.

Aumann, Robert. 1964. "Markets with a Continuum of Traders." *Econometrica* 32.

———. 1981. "Survey of Repeated Games," In Aumann et al., eds., *Essays in Game Theory and Mathematical Economics in Honor of Oskar Morganstern.* Mannheim: Bibliographisches Institut.

Auspitz, Richard, and Lieben, R. 1889. *Untersuchungen über die Theorie des Preises.* Leipzig: Duncker and Humblot.

Ayres, Clarence. 1962. *The Theory of Economic Progress.* 2nd ed. New York: Schocken Books.

Bachrach, Michael. 1977. *Economics and the Theory of Games.* Boulder: Westview Press.

Barkai, Haim. 1959. "Ricardo on Factor Prices and Income Distribution in a Growing Economy." *Economica* 26 (August).

Barnes, Barry, and Shapin, Stephen, eds. 1979. *Natural Order.* Beverly Hills: Sage Publications.

Barnes, Julian. 1985. *Flaubert's Parrot.* New York: Alfred A. Knopf.

Barro, Robert, and Grossman, Herschel. 1976. *Money, Employment and Inflation*. New York: Cambridge University Press.

Bausor, Randall. 1982–83. "Time and the Structure of Economic Analysis." *Journal of Post Keynesian Economics* 5 (Winter).

———. 1986. "Time and Equilibrium." In Philip Mirowski, ed., *The Reconstruction of Economic Theory*. Hingham, Mass.: Kluwer-Nijhoff.

Becker, Gary. 1976. "Altruism, Egoism and Genetic Fitness." *Journal of Economic Literature* 14 (September).

Bernal, J. D. 1970. *Science and Industry in the Nineteenth Century*. 2nd ed. Bloomington: Indiana University Press.

Bernstein, Richard. 1966. *John Dewey*. New York: Washington Square.

———. 1983. *Beyond Objectivism and Relativism*. Philadelphia: University of Pennsylvania Press.

Bharadwaj, Krishna. 1978. "The Subversion of Classical Analysis: Alfred Marshall's Early Writings on Value." *Cambridge Journal of Economics* 2 (September).

Bitterman, H. J. 1940. "Smith's Empiricism and the Law of Nature." *Journal of Political Economy* 48.

Black, R. D. C.; Coats, A. R.; and Goodwin, C., eds. 1973. *The Marginal Revolution in Economics*. Durham: Duke University Press.

Blatt, John. 1979. "The Utility of Being Hanged on the Gallows." *Journal of Post Keynesian Economics* 2.

Blaug, Mark. 1974. *The Cambridge Revolution: Success or Failure?* London: Institute for Economic Affairs.

———. 1978. *Economic Theory in Retrospect*. 3rd ed. Cambridge: Cambridge University Press.

———. 1980. *The Methodology of Economics*. Cambridge: Cambridge University Press.

Bleaney, Michael. 1976. *Underconsumption Theories*. London: Lawrence & Wishart.

Bloor, David. 1976. *Knowledge and Social Imagery*. Boston: Routledge & Kegan Paul.

———. 1982. "Durkheim and Mauss Revisited." *Studies in the History and Philosophy of Science* 13 (December).

Böhm-Bawerk, Eugen von. 1959. *Capital and Interest*. 3 vols. South Holland, Ill.: Libertarian Press.

Boland, Lawrence. 1979. "Knowledge and the Role of Institutions in Economic Theory." *Journal of Economic Issues* 13 (December).

———. 1981. "On the Futility of Criticizing the Neoclassical Maximizing Hypothesis." *American Economic Review* 71 (December).

———. 1982. *The Foundations of Economic Method*. Winchester, Mass.: Allen & Unwin.

———. 1982. *Methodology for a New Microeconomics*. Winchester: Allen & Unwin.

Bolitho, Hector, and Peel, Derek. 1967. *The Drummonds of Charing Cross*. London: George Allen & Unwin.

Boninsegni, Pasquale. 1902. "I Fondamenti dell' Economia Pura." *Giornale degli Economisti* 29 (February).

Bos, Hendrik. 1980. "Mathematics and Rational Mechanics." In G. Rousseau and R. Porter, eds., *The Ferment of Knowledge*. Cambridge: Cambridge University Press.

Bowles, Samuel, and Gintis, Herbert. 1977. "The Marxian Theory of Value and Heterogeneous Labor." *Cambridge Journal of Economics* 1 (June).

Bowley, Marion. 1973. *Studies in the History of Economic Thought Before 1870*. London: Macmillan.

Box, George, and Jenkins, G. 1976. *Time Series Analysis*. San Francisco: Holden Day.

Brannigan, A. 1981. *The Social Basis of Scientific Discoveries.* Cambridge: Cambridge University Press.

Brems, Hans. 1986. *Pioneering Economic Theory.* Baltimore: Johns Hopkins University Press.

Brody, Andras. 1970. *Proportions, Prices and Planning.* London: North Holland.

Brown, S. C., ed. 1979. *Philosophical Disputes in the Social Sciences.* Atlantic Highlands, N. J.: Humanities Press.

Bukharin, Nikolai. 1927. *Economic Theory of the Leisure Class.* New York: International Publishers.

Cahn, S., ed. 1977. *New Studies on the Philosophy of John Dewey.* Hanover: University Press of New England.

Campbell, R. S. 1961. *Carron Company.* Edinburgh: Oliver & Boyd.

Cannon, Susan Faye. 1978. *Science in Culture.* New York: Dawson.

Cardwell, D. S. L. 1971. *From Watt to Clausius.* Ithaca: Cornell University Press.

Carswell, John. 1960. *The South Sea Bubble.* London: Cresset.

Carter, Alice. 1975. *Getting, Spending and Investing in Early Modern Times.* Assen: Van Gorcum.

Cass, David, and Shell, Karl. 1976. *The Hamiltonian Approach to Dynamic Economics.* New York: Academic Press.

_____. 1983. "Do Sunspots Matter?" *Journal of Political Economy* 91 (April).

Chatfield, Michael. 1977. *A History of Accounting Thought.* Huntington, N. Y.: Krieger.

Chaudhuri, K. N. 1978. *The Trading World of Asia and the East India Company.* Cambridge: Cambridge University Press.

Checkland, Sidney. 1951a. "The Advent of Academic Economics in England." *Manchester School* 19 (January).

_____. 1951b. "Economic Opinion in England as Jevons Found It." *Manchester School* 19 (September)

Cheung, Stephen. 1968. "Private Property Rights and Sharecropping." *Journal of Political Economy* 76 (December).

_____. 1969. "Transactions Costs, Risk Aversion, and the Choice of Contractual Arrangements." *Journal of Law and Economics* 12 (April).

Chipman, John. 1976. "An Episode in the Early Development of the Ordinal Utility Theory: Pareto's Letters to Hermann Laurent." *Cahiers Vilfredo Pareto* 37.

Chipman, John; Hurwicz, Leonid; Richter, Marcel; and Sonnenschein, Hugo. 1971. *Preferences, Utility and Demand.* New York: Harcourt Brace Jovanovich.

Clapham, John. 1945. *The Bank of England.* 2 vols. Cambridge: Cambridge University Press.

Clower, Robert. 1965. "The Keynesian Counterrevolution." In Frank Hahn and F. Brechling, eds., *The Theory of Interest Rates.* London: Macmillan. Also 1970 in Clower, ed., *Monetary Theory.* Baltimore: Penguin.

_____. 1967. "A Reconsideraton of the Microfoundations of Monetary Theory." *Western Economic Journal* 6 (December).

Colvin, Phyllis. 1977. "Ontological and Epistemological Commitments in the Social Sciences." In E. Mendelsohn, P. Weingart, and R. Whitely, eds., *The Social Production of Scientific Knowledge.* Boston: Reidel.

Commons, John R. 1934. *Institutional Economics.* New York: Macmillan.

Cope, S. R. 1978. "The Stock Exchange Revisited." *Economica* 45 (February).

Crouzet, Francois, ed. 1972. *Capital Formation in the Industrial Revolution.* London: Methuen.

Crowe, Michael. 1967. *A History of Vector Analysis.* Notre Dame: University of Notre Dame Press.

Crum, William. 1953. *The Age Structure of the Corporate System.* Berkeley: University of California Press.

D'Abro, A. 1951. *The Rise of the New Physics.* 2 vols. New York: Dover Publications.

Daly, Herman. 1980. "The Economic Thought of Frederick Soddy." *History of Political Economy* 12 (Spring).

Damme, E. van. 1981. "History-Dependent Equilibrium Points in Dynamic Games." In O. Moeschlin and D. Pallachke, eds., *Game Theory and Mathematical Economics.* Amsterdam: North Holland.

Davidson, Paul. 1982–83. "Rational Expectations: A Fallacious Foundation for Studying Crucial Decision-making Processes." *Journal of Post Keynesian Economics* 5 (Winter).

Deane, Phyllis. 1967. *The First Industrial Revolution.* Cambridge: Cambridge University Press.

Debreu, Gerard, and Scarf, Herbert. 1963. "A Limit Theorem of the Core of the Economy." *International Economic Review* 4.

Dennis, Ken. 1982. "Economic Theory and Mathematical Translation." *Journal of Economic Issues* 16 (September).

Dewey, John. 1931. *Philosophy and Civilization.* New York: Minton & Balch.

———. 1938. *Logic: The Theory of Inquiry.* New York: Henry Holt.

———. 1939. *John Dewey's Philosophy.* New York: Modern Library.

Dickson, P. G. M. 1967. *The Financial Revolution in England.* London: Macmillan.

Dobb, Maurice. 1937. *Political Economy and Capitalism.* London: Routledge.

Douglas, Mary. 1970. *Natural Symbols.* London: Barrie & Jenkins.

———. 1975. *Implicit Meanings.* London: Routledge & Kegan Paul.

———. 1982. *In the Active Voice.* London: Routledge & Kegan Paul.

Dowell, Stephen. 1888. *A History of Taxation and Taxes in England.* London: Longmans.

Drazen, Allan. 1980. "Recent Developments in Macroeconomic Disequilibrium Theory." *Econometrica* 48 (March).

Dubey, Pradeep, and Shubik, Martin. 1979. "Bankruptcy and Optimality in a Closed Trading Mass Economy Modelled as a Noncooperative Game." *Journal of Mathematical Economics* 6 (July).

———. 1980. "A Strategic Market Game with Price and Quantity Strategies." *Zeitscrift für Nationalökonomie* 40.

Duhem, Pierre. 1977. *The Aim and Structure of Physical Theory,* trans. P. Weiner. New York: Atheneum Publishers.

Dupuit, Jules. 1952. "On the Measurement of the Utility of Public Works." *International Economic Papers* 2.

Durkheim, Emile, and Mauss, Marcel. 1963. *Primitive Classification.* London: Cohen & West.

Dyer, Alan. 1986. "Veblen on Scientific Creativity." *Journal of Economic Issues* 20 (March).

Eagly, Robert. 1974. *The Structure of Classical Economic Theory.* New York: Oxford University Press.

Eagly, Robert, and Smith, V. K. 1976. "Domestic and International Integration of the London Money Market." *Journal of Economic History* 36 (March).

Edgeworth, Francis Ysidro. 1881. *Mathematical Psychics.* London: Routledge.

Edwards, Richard. 1975. "Stages in Corporate Stability and the Risks of Corporate Failure." *Journal of Economic History* 35 (June).

Eisele, Carolyn. 1957. "The Peirce-Newcomb Correspondence." *Proceedings of the American Philosophical Society* 101.

Farjoun, Emmanuel, and Machover, Moshe. 1983. *Laws of Chaos*. London: New Left Books.

Farmer, Mary. 1983. "Some Thoughts on the Past, Present and Future of the Rational Actor in Economics." Paper presented to History of Thought Conference, University of Manchester, September.

Feinstein, Charles. 1967. *Capitalism and Economic Growth*. Cambridge: Cambridge University Press.

Feldstein, Martin, and Summers, Lawrence. 1977. "Is the Rate of Profit Falling?" *Brookings Papers on Economic Activity,* no. 1.

Feynman, Richard. 1965. *The Character of Physical Law*. Cambridge: MIT Press.

———. 1985. *Surely You're Joking, Mr. Feynman*. New York: Simon & Schuster.

Field, Alexander. 1979. "On the Explanation of Rules Using Rational Choice Models." *Journal of Economic Issues* 13 (March).

———. 1984. "Microeconomics, Norms and Rationality." *Economic Development and Cultural Change* 32 (July).

Firth, Michael. 1977. *The Valuation of Shares and Efficient Markets Theory*. London: Macmillan.

Fisher, Irving. 1892. *Mathematical Investigations in the Theory of Value and Prices*. Transactions of the Connecticut Academy, vol. 9. Reprinted New Haven: Yale University Press, 1926.

Flavin, Marjorie. 1983. "Excess Volatility in the Financial Markets." *Journal of Political Economy* 91 (December).

France, Peter. 1965. *Racine's Rhetoric*. Oxford: Clarendon Press.

Friedman, James. 1977. *Oligopoly and the Theory of Games*. New York: Elsevier–North Holland.

Friedman, Milton. 1953. *Essays in Positive Economics*. Chicago: University of Chicago Press.

Furubotn, Eric, and Pejovich, Svetozar. 1970. "Property Rights and the Behavior of the Firm in a Socialist State." *Zeitschrift für Nationalökonomie* 30 (Winter).

———. 1972. "Property Rights and Economic Theory: A Survey of the Recent Literature." *Journal of Economic Literature* 10 (December.

Fusfeld, Daniel. 1977. "The Development of Economic Institutions." *Journal of Economic Issues* 11 (December).

Garcie-Mata, Carlos, and Schaffner, Felix. 1934. "Solar and Economic Relationships." *Quarterly Journal of Economics* 49 (November).

Garegnani, Pierangelo. 1976. "On a Change in the Notion of Equilibrium." In M. Brown, K. Sato, and P. Zarembka, eds., *Essays in Modern Capital Theory*. Amsterdam: North Holland.

Garner, C. A. 1979. "Academic Publication, Market Signalling and Scientific Research Decisions." *Economic Inquiry* 17.

Gayer, Arthur; Rostow, W. W.; and Schwartz, Anna. 1953. *The Growth and Fluctuations of the British Economy*. Oxford: Oxford University Press.

Georgescu-Roegen, Nicholas. 1960. "Mathematical Proofs of the Breakdown of Capitalism." *Econometrica* 28 (April).

———. 1971. *The Entropy Law and the Economic Process*. Cambridge: Harvard University Press.

———. 1976. *Energy and Economic Myths.* New York: Pergamon Press.

Geweke, John. 1982. "Inference and Causality in Economic Time Series Models." In Zvi Griliches and Michael Intrilligator, eds., *Handbook of Econometrics.* Amsterdam: North Holland.

Geweke, John; Meese, R.: and Dent, W. 1982. "Comparing Alternative Tests of Causality in Temporal Systems." University of Wisconsin SSRI Workshop Paper no. 8212 (April).

Goldberg, Victor. 1974. "Institutional Change and the Quasi-Invisible Hand." *Journal of Law and Economics* 17 (October).

Goldstein, Herbert. 1950. *Classical Mechanics.* Reading, Mass.: Addison-Wesley.

Gorman, John. 1981. *Time Series Analysis.* New York: Cambridge University Press.

Graham, Loren; Lepenies, W.; and Weingart, P. 1983. *Functions and Uses of Disciplinary Histories.* Boston: Reidel.

Grandmont, Jean Michel. 1977. "Temporary General Equilibrium Theory." *Econometrica* 45 (April).

Grassby, Richard. 1969. "The Rate of Profit in Seventeenth Century England." *English History Review* 84 (October).

Grossman, Stephen, and Shiller, Robert. 1981. "The Determinants of the Variability of Stock Market Prices." *American Economic Review* 71 (May).

Guth, Alan. 1983. "Speculations on the Origin of Matter, Energy and the Entropy of the Universe." In Guth, K. Huang, and R. Jaffe, eds., *Asymptotic Realms of Physics.* Cambridge: MIT Press.

Hacking, Ian, ed. 1982. *Scientific Revolutions.* Oxford: Oxford University Press.

———. 1983. *Representing and Intervening.* New York: Cambridge University Press.

Hahn, Frank. 1978. "On Non-Walrasian Equilibria." *Review of Economic Studies* 45 (January).

———. 1980. "General Equilibrium Theory." *The Public Interest* 61.

Halévy, Elie. 1972. *The Growth of Philosophical Radicalism.* London: Faber & Faber.

Hands, D. Wade. 1985. "Karl Popper and Economic Method." *Economics and Philosophy* 1 (April).

Hankins, Thomas. 1980. *Sir William Rowan Hamilton.* Baltimore: Johns Hopkins University Press.

Harcourt, Geoffrey. 1972. *Some Cambridge Controversies in the Theory of Capital.* Cambridge: Cambridge University Press.

———. 1982. *The Social Science Imperialists.* Boston: Routledge & Kegan Paul.

Harding, Sandra, ed. 1976. *Can Theories Be Refuted?* Boston: Reidel.

Harman, P. 1982. *Energy, Force and Matter.* Cambridge: Cambridge University Press.

Harsanyi, J. C. 1968. "Individualistic and Functionalistic Explanations." In Imre Lakatos and Alan Musgrave, eds. *Problems in the Philosophy of Science.* Amsterdam: North Holland.

———. 1977. *Rational Behavior and Bargaining Equilibrium in Games and Social Situations.* Cambridge: Cambridge University Press.

———. 1982. "Noncooperative Bargaining Models." In M. Deistler, E. Furst, and G. Schwodiauer, eds., *Games, Economic Dynamics and Time Series Analysis.* Vienna: Physica Verlag.

Hartwell, R. M. 1978. "Adam Smith and the Industrial Revolution." In F. Glahe, ed., *Adam Smith and the Wealth of Nations.* Boulder: Westview Press.

Hayek, Friedrich. 1979. *The Counterrevolution of Science.* Indianapolis: Liberty Press.

Heims, Steve. 1980. *John von Neumann and Norbert Wiener.* Cambridge: MIT Press.

Henderson, James, and Quandt, Richard. 1971. *Microeconomic Theory.* New York: McGraw-Hill.

Hesse, Mary. 1966. *Models and Analogies in Science.* Notre Dame: University of Notre Dame Press.

———. 1974. *The Structure of Scientific Inference.* Berkeley: University of California Press.

———. 1980. *Revolutions and Reconstruction in the Philosophy of Science.* Bloomington: Indiana University Press.

———. 1985. "Texts without Types and Lumps without Laws." *New Literary History* 17 (Autumn).

Hickman, Bert, ed. 1972. *Econometric Models of Cyclical Behavior.* New York: Columbia University Press.

Hicks, J. R. 1950. *A Contribution to the Theory of the Trade Cycle.* Oxford: Clarendon Press.

———. 1969. *A Theory of Economic History.* Oxford: Oxford University Press.

———. 1972. "Ricardo's Theory of Distribution." In M. Peston and B. Corry, eds., *Essays in Honour of Lord Robbins.* London: Weidenfeld & Nicolson.

———. 1973. *Capital and Time.* Oxford: Oxford University Press.

———. 1979. *Causality in Economics.* New York: Basic Books.

Hiebert, E. N. 1962. *The Historical Roots of the Principle of the Conservation of Energy.* Madison: State Historical Society of Wisconsin.

Hirshleifer, Jack. 1976. "Comment." *Journal of Law and Economics* 19 (August).

Hollis, Martin, and Nell, Edward. 1975. *Rational Economic Man.* Cambridge: Cambridge University Press.

Howey, R. S. 1960. *The Rise of the Marginal Utility School.* Lawrence: University of Kansas Press.

Hutchison, T. W. 1978. *On Revolutions and Progress in Economic Knowledge.* Cambridge: Cambridge University Press.

———. 1982. "The Politics and Philosophy in Jevons's Political Economy." *Manchester School* 50 (December).

Jackson, Gordon. 1972. *Hull in the Eighteenth Century.* Oxford: Oxford University Press.

Jaffe, William. 1983. *William Jaffe's Essays on Walras.* New York: Cambridge University Press.

Jahnke, H., and Otte, M., eds. 1981. *Epistemological and Social Problems of the Sciences in the Early Nineteenth Century.* Boston: Reidel.

Jevons, William Stanley. 1884. *Investigations in Currency and Finance.* London: Macmillan.

———. 1905a. *The Principles of Science.* 2nd ed. London: Macmillan.

———. 1905b. *The Principles of Economics.* London: Macmillan.

———. 1970. *The Theory of Political Economy,* ed. R. D. C. Black. Baltimore: Penguin.

———. 1972–81. *The Papers and Correspondence of W. S. Jevons,* ed. R. D. C. Black. 7 vols. London: Macmillan.

Johansen, Leif. 1982. "On the Status of the Nash Type of Noncooperative Equilibrium in Economic Theory." *Scandanavian Journal of Economics* 34.

———. 1983. "Mechanistic and Organistic Analogies in Economics." *Kyklos* 34.

Johnson, Mark, ed. 1981. *Philosophical Perspectives on Metaphor.* Minneapolis: University of Minnesota Press.

Kahl, R., ed. 1971. *Selected Writings of Hermann von Helmholtz.* Middletown: Wesleyan University Press.

Kauder, Emil. 1965. *A History of Marginal Utility Theory.* Princeton: Princeton University Press.

Keane, Simon. 1983. *Stock Market Efficiency.* Oxford: Philip Allan.

Kennedy, Charles. 1969. "Time, Interest and the Production Function." In J. N. Wolfe, ed., *Value, Capital and Growth.* Chicago: Aldine Publishing.

Keynes, John Maynard. 1963. *Essays in Biography.* New York: Harcourt Brace.

Kindleberger, Charles. 1978. *Manias, Panics and Crashes.* New York: Basic Books.

Klamer, Arjo. 1983. *Conversations with Economists.* Totowa, N. J.: Rowman & Allanheld.

Kleidon, Allan. 1983. "Variance Bounds Tests and Stock Price Valuation Models." Stanford University working paper.

Kline, Morris. 1972. *Mathematical Thought from Ancient to Modern Times.* New York: Oxford University Press.

———. 1980. *Mathematics: The Loss of Certainty.* New York: Oxford University Press.

Knight, Frank. 1956. *On the History and Methodology of Economics.* Chicago: University of Chicago Press.

———. 1965. *Risk, Uncertainty and Profit.* New York: Harper & Row.

Knorr-Cetina, Karin. 1981. *The Manufacture of Knowledge.* New York: Pergamon Press.

Knorr-Cetina, Karin, and Mulkay, Michael. 1983. *Science Observed: Perspectives on the Social Study of Science.* London: Sage Publicatons.

Koebner, R. 1959. "Adam Smith and the Industrial Revolution." *Economic History Review* 49 (April).

Koopmans, Tjalling. 1947. "Measurement Without Theory." *Review of Economics and Statistics* 29 (August).

———. 1957. *Three Essays on the State of Economic Science.* New York: McGraw-Hill.

Krantz, David; Luce, R.; Suppes, P.; and Tversky, A. 1971. *Foundations of Measurement.* New York: Academic Press.

Krause, Ulrich. 1982. *Money and Abstract Labor.* London: New Left Books.

Kregel, Jan. 1976. *The Theory of Capital.* London: Macmillan.

Krimsky, Sheldon. 1982. *Genetic Alchemy.* Cambridge: MIT Press.

Kuhn, Thomas. 1970. *The Structure of Scientific Revolutions.* Rev. ed. Chicago: University of Chicago Press.

———. 1977. *The Essential Tension.* Chicago: University of Chicago Press.

Lakatos, Imre. 1976. *Proofs and Refutations.* Cambridge: Cambridge University Press.

Lakatos, Imre, and Musgrave, Alan, eds. 1968. *Problems in the Philosophy of Science.* Amsterdam: North Holland.

Lakoff, George, and Johnson, Mark. 1980. "Conceptual Metaphor in Everyday Language." *Journal of Philosophy* 77.

Lancaster, Kelvin. 1966. "A New Approach to Consumer Theory." *Journal of Political Economy* 74 (April).

Lange, Oskar. 1970. "Some Observations on Input-Output Analysis." In his *Papers on Economics and Sociology.* New York: Pergamon Press.

Latour, Bruno, and Woolgar, Steven. 1979. *Laboratory Life.* Beverly Hills: Sage Publications.

Latsis, Spiro, ed. 1976. *Method and Appraisal in Economics.* Cambridge: Cambridge University Press.

Laudan, Larry. 1984. *Science and Values.* Berkeley: University of California Press.

Laundhardt, Wilhelm. 1885. *Mathematische Begrundung der Volkswirtschaftslehre*. Leipzig: Engelmann.

Laurent, Hermann. 1870. *Traité de Mécanique Rationelle*. Paris: Gauthier-Villars.

Lebowitz, Joel, and Penrose, Oliver. 1973. "Modern Ergodic Theory." *Physics Today* 26.

Lee, G. 1975. "The Concept of Profit in British Accounting, 1760–1900." *Business History Review* 49 (Spring).

Lee, Ronald. 1974. "The Formal Dynamics of Controlled Populations and the Echo, the Boom, and the Bust." *Demography* 11 (November).

Leijonhufvud, Axel. 1977. "The Costs and Consequences of Inflation." In G. Harcourt, ed., *The Microeconomic Foundations of Macroeconomics*. London: Macmillan.

Lepley, Ray, ed. 1949. *Value: A Cooperative Inquiry*. New York: Columbia University Press.

LeRoy, Stephen. 1984. "Efficiency and the Variability of Asset Prices." *American Economic Review* 74 (May).

Levi, Albert. 1974. *Philosophy as Social Expression*. Chicago: University of Chicago Press.

Levine, David. 1977. *Economic Studies: Contributions to the Critique of Economic Theory*. Boston: Routledge & Kegan Paul.

_____. 1980. "Aspects of the Classical Theory of Markets." *Australian Economic Papers* 19 (June).

_____. 1986. "The Reconceptualization of Classical Economics." In Philip Mirowski, ed., *The Reconstruction of Economic Theory*. Hingham, Mass.: Kluwer-Nijhoff.

Levinson, Arnold. 1978. "Wittgenstein and Logical Laws." In K. Fann, ed., *Ludwig Wittgenstein: The Man and His Philosophy*. New York: Humanities Press.

Liebhafsky, H. H. 1986. "Peirce on the Summum Bonum and the Unlimited Community." *Journal of Economic Issues* 20 (March).

Lisman, J. H. C. 1949. "Economics and Thermodynamics." *Econometrica* 17 (January).

Lowe, Adolf. 1951. "On the Mechanistic Approach in Economics." *Social Research* 18 (January).

Lucas, Robert. 1981. *Studies in Business Cycle Theory*. Cambridge: MIT Press.

MacFie, A. L. 1967. *The Individual in Society*. London: Spon.

Malinvaud, Edmond. 1977. *The Theory of Unemployment Reconsidered*. Oxford: Basil Blackwell.

Manley, G. 1953. "Mean Temperature of England, 1698–1952." *Quarterly Journal of the Royal Meteorological Society* 42.

Marglin, Steven. 1974. "What Do Bosses Do?" *Review of Radical Economy* 6 (Spring).

Marshall, Alfred. 1898. "Mechanical and Biological Analogies in Economics." In *Memorials of Alfred Marshall*, ed. A. C. Pigou. London: Macmillan; reprint 1925.

_____. 1920. *Principles of Economics*. 8th ed. London: Macmillan.

Marx, Karl, 1973. *Capital*. 3 vols. New York: Vintage Books.

Mather, R. 1970. *After the Canal Duke*. Oxford: Oxford University Press.

Mathias, Peter. 1959. *The Brewing Industry in England, 1700–1830*. Cambridge: Cambridge University Press.

_____. 1969. *The First Industrial Nation*. London: Methuen.

McCloskey, Donald. 1976. "Does the Past Have a Useful Economics?" *Journal of*

Economic Literature 14 (June).

———. 1983. "The Rhetoric of Economics." *Journal of Economic Literature* 21 (June).

———. 1985a. *The Rhetoric of Economics.* Madison: University of Wisconsin Press.

———. 1985b. "Sartorial Epistemology in Tatters." *Economics and Philosophy* 1 (April).

Menard, Claude. 1980. "Three Forms of Resistance to Statistics: Say, Cournot, Walras." *History of Political Economy* 17 (Winter).

———. 1983. "La Machine et le Coeur." In André Lichnerowicz, ed., *Analogies et Connaissance.* Paris: Dunod.

Menger, Carl. 1963. *Problems of Economics and Sociology,* trans. F. Nock. Urbana: University of Illinois Press.

———. 1981. *Principles of Economics,* trans. P. Dingwall and B. Hoselitz. New York: New York University Press.

Meyerson, Emile. 1962. *Identity and Reality.* New York: Dover Publications.

Milgate, Murray. 1979. "On the Origins of the Notion of Intertemporal Equilibrium." *Economica* 46 (February).

Mini, Piero. 1974. *Economics and Philosophy.* Gainesville: University of Florida Press.

Mirowski, Philip. 1981. "The Rise (and Retreat) of a Market." *Journal of Economic History* 41 (September).

———. 1985. *The Birth of the Business Cycle.* New York: Garland Publishing.

———, ed. 1986. *The Reconstruction of Economic Theory.* Hingham, Mass.: Kluwer-Nijhoff.

Mitchell, Brian, and Deane, Phyllis. 1962. *Abstract of British Historical Statistics.* Cambridge: Cambridge University Press.

Mitchell, Wesley Clair. 1937. *The Backward Art of Spending Money.* New York: Kelley. Reprint New York: McGraw-Hill, 1950.

———. 1941. *Business Cycles and Their Causes.* Berkeley: University of California Press.

———. 1953. "The Role of Money in Economic History." In F. C. Lane and J. C. Riemersma, eds., *Enterprise and Secular Change.* London: Allen & Unwin.

Morganstern, Oskar, and Schwödiauer, G. 1976. "Competition and Collusion in Bilateral Markets." *Zeitscrift für Nationalökonomie* 36.

Morganstern, Oskar, and Thompson, Gerald. 1976. *Mathematical Theory of Expanding and Contracting Economies.* Lexington: D. C. Heath.

Morgenbesser, Sidney, ed. 1977. *Dewey and His Critics.* New York: Journal of Philosophy Press.

Morick, Harold, ed. 1972. *Challenges to Empiricism.* Belmont, Calif.: Wadsworth Publishing.

Morishima, Michio. 1964. *Equilibrium, Stability and Growth.* Oxford: Oxford University Press.

———. 1973. *Marx's Economics.* Cambridge: Cambridge University Press.

———. 1977. *Walras' Economics.* Cambridge: Cambridge University Press.

———. 1984. "The Good and Bad Uses of Mathematics." In Peter Wiles and Guy Routh, eds., *Economics in Disarray.* Oxford: Basil Blackwell.

Mosley, Nicholas. 1983. *The Rules of the Game.* London: Fontana.

Neal, Larry. 1984. "Efficient Markets in the 18th Century?" In J. Atack, ed., *Proceedings of the Business History Conference.* Urbana: University of Illinois.

———. 1985a. "Integration of International Capital Markets." *Journal of Economic History* 45 (June).

_____. 1985b. "Integration and Efficiency of the London and Amsterdam Stock Markets in the Eighteenth Century." University of Illinois working paper.

_____. 1985c. "The Rise of a Financial Press: London and Amsterdam, 1681–1796." University of Illinois working paper.

Nelson, Richard, and Winter, Sidney. 1982. *An Evolutionary Theory of Economic Change.* Cambridge: Harvard University Press.

Nersessian, Nancy. 1984. *From Faraday to Einstein.* Dordrecht: Nijhoff.

North, Douglas. 1978. "Structure and Performance: The Task of Economic History." *Journal of Economic Literature* 16 (September).

North, Douglas, and Thomas, Robert. 1973. *The Rise of the Western World.* Cambridge: Cambridge University Press.

O'Brien, D. P. 1976. "The Longevity of Adam Smith's Vision." *Scottish Journal of Political Economy* 23 (June).

Olson, Harry. 1958. *Dynamical Analogies.* 2nd ed. New York: Van Nostrand.

Ong, Nai-Pew. 1981. "Target Pricing, Competition and Growth." *Journal of Post Keynesian Economics* 4 (Fall).

Ortony, Anthony, ed. 1979. *Metaphor and Thought.* Cambridge: Cambridge University Press.

Pareto, Vilfredo. 1935. *The Mind and Society.* New York: Dover.

_____. 1953a. "On the Economic Phenomenon." *International Economic Papers* 3.

_____. 1953b. "On the Economic Principle." *International Economic Papers* 3.

_____. 1971a. "Ophelimity in Nonclosed Cycles." In John Chipman et al., eds. *Preferences, Utility and Demand.* New York: Harcourt Brace Jovanovich.

_____. 1971b. *Manual of Political Economy.* New York: Kelley.

Pasinetti, Luigi. 1973. *Growth and Income Distribution.* Cambridge: Cambridge University Press.

_____. 1980. *Essays on the Theory of Joint Production.* New York: Columbia University Press.

Patinkin, Donald. 1956. *Money, Interest and Prices.* New York: Harper & Row.

Peirce, Charles Sanders. 1931–58. *Collected Papers.* 8 vols. Cambridge: Harvard University Press.

Pigott, Stanley. 1949. *Hollins.* Nottingham: Viyella.

Pikler, Andrew. 1955. "Utility Theories in Field Physics and Mathematical Economics." *British Journal for the Philosophy of Science* 5.

Polanyi, Karl. 1944. *The Great Transformation.* Boston: Beacon Press.

_____. 1968. *Primitive, Archaic and Modern Economies.* Garden City, N. Y.: Anchor Books.

Popper, Karl. 1957. *The Poverty of Historicism.* London: Routledge & Kegan Paul.

_____. 1965. *Conjectures and Refutations.* New York: Harper & Row.

Posner, Richard. 1977. *Economic Analysis of the Law.* 2nd. ed. Boston: Little, Brown.

Prigogine, Ilya. 1980. *From Being to Becoming.* New York: W. H. Freeman.

Putnam, Hilary. 1983. *Realism and Reason.* New York: Cambridge University Press.

Radnitzsky, Gerald. 1973. *Contemporary Schools of Metascience.* Chicago: Regnery Gateway.

Rae, John. 1965. *Life of Adam Smith.* New York: Kelley.

Raistrick, A., and Allen, R. 1939. "The South Yorkshire Ironmasters." *Economic History Review* 9.

Rapaport, Anatol. 1960. *Fights, Games and Debates.* Ann Arbor: University of Michigan Press.

_____. 1970. *N-Person Game Theory.* Ann Arbor: University of Michigan Press.

Reid, Joseph, Jr. 1977. "Understanding Political Events in the New Economic History." *Journal of Economic History* 37 (June).

Rescher, Nicholas. 1978. *Peirce's Philosophy of Science.* Notre Dame: University of Notre Dame Press.

Rimmer, W. 1960. *Marshall of Leeds.* Cambridge: Cambridge University Press.

Robbins, Lionel. 1952. *An Essay on the Nature and Significance of Economic Science.* London: Macmillan.

Roemer, John. 1978. "Neoclassicism, Marxism and Collective Action." *Journal of Economic Issues* 12 (March).

_____. 1981. *Analytical Foundations of Marxian Economics.* New York: Cambridge University Press.

_____. 1982. *A General Theory of Exploitation and Class.* Cambridge: Harvard University Press.

Rorty, Richard. 1979. *Philosophy and the Mirror of Nature.* Princeton: Princeton University Press.

_____. 1986. "The Contingency of Language." *London Review of Books* 3 (April 1).

Rorty, Richard; Schneewind, J.; and Skinner, Quentin, eds. 1984. *Philosophy in History.* Cambridge: Cambridge University Press.

Rosenberg, Alexander. 1979. "Can Economic Theory Explain Everything?" *Philosophy of the Social Sciences* 9 (December).

Rostow, W. W. 1978. *The World Economy.* Austin: University of Texas Press.

Sahlins, Marshall. 1976. *The Use and Abuse of Biology.* Ann Arbor: University of Michigan Press.

Samuels, Warren. 1978. "Information Systems, Preferences and the Economy in the JEI." *Journal of Economic Issues* 12 (March).

_____, ed. 1979. *The Economy as a System of Power.* New Brunswick: Transaction Books.

Samuelson, Paul. 1942. "Constancy of the Marginal Utility of Income." In Oskar Lange, F. McIntyre, and Theodore Yntema, eds., *Studies in Mathematical Economics and Econometrics.* Chicago: University of Chicago Press.

_____. 1950. "On the Problem of Integrability in Utility Theory." *Economica* 17 (November).

_____. 1952. "Economic Theory and Mathematics—An Appraisal" *American Economic Review* 42 (May).

_____. 1954. "Symposium on Mathematics in Economics." *Review of Economics and Statistics* 36 (November).

_____. 1957. "Wages and Interest: A Modern Dissection of Marxian Models." *American Economic Review* 47 (December).

_____. 1965. *Foundations of Economic Analysis.* New York: Atheneum.

_____. 1966. *The Collected Scientific Papers,* ed. Joseph Stiglitz. 2 vols. Cambridge: MIT Press.

_____. 1970. "Classical and Neoclassical Monetary Theory." In R. Clower, ed., *Monetary Theory.* Baltimore: Penguin.

_____. 1971. "Understanding the Marxian Notion of Exploitation." *Journal of Economic Literature* 9 (June).

_____. 1972. "Maximum Principles in Analytical Economics." *American Economic Review* 62 (June).

Scheffler, Israel. 1974. *Four Pragmatists.* New York: Humanities Press.

Schotter, Andrew. 1981. *The Economic Theory of Social Institutions.* Cambridge: Cambridge University Press.

_____. 1983. "Why Take a Game Theoretical Approach to Economics?" *Economie Appliquée* 36.

Schotter, Andrew, and Schwödiauer, G. 1980. "Economics and the Theory of Games: A Survey." *Journal of Economic Literature* 18 (June).

Schumpeter, Joseph. 1939. *Business Cycles.* New York: McGraw-Hill.

Scott, W. R. 1934. "Adam Smith and the Glasgow Merchants." *Economic Journal* 44.

_____. 1951. *The Constitution and Finance of English, Scottish and Irish Joint Stock Companies.* New York: Peter Smith.

Sebba, George. 1953. "The Development of the Concepts of Mechanism and Model in Physical Science and Economic Thought." *American Economic Review* 43 (March).

Shackle, G. L. S. 1967. *Time in Economics.* Amsterdam: North Holland.

_____. 1973. *Epistemics and Economics.* Cambridge: Cambridge University Press.

Shapin, Stephen. 1984. "Talking History: Reflections on Discourse Analysis." *Isis* 75 (March).

Sheehan, R., and Grieves, A. 1982. "Sunspots and Cycles: A Test of Causation." *Southern Economic Journal* 48 (January).

Shiller, Robert. 1981a. "Do Stock Prices Move Too Much to Be Justified by Subsequent Changes in Dividends?" *American Economic Review* 71 (June).

_____. 1981b. "The Use of Volatility Measures in Assessing Market Efficiency." *Journal of Finance* 36.

Shoemaker, Paul. 1982. "The Expected Utility Model." *Journal of Economic Literature* 20 (June).

Shubik, Martin. 1959. "Edgeworth Market Games." In Robert Luce and Albert Tucker, eds., *Contributions to the Theory of Games.* Princeton: Princeton University Press.

_____. 1972. "Commodity Money, Oligopoly, Credit and Bankruptcy in a General Equilibrium Model." *Economic Inquiry* 11 (March).

_____. 1974. "Money, Trust and Equilibrium Points in Games in Extensive Forms." *Zeitscrift für Nationalökonomie* 34.

_____. 1974a. "The General Equilibrium Model Is Incomplete and Not Adequate for the Reconciliation of Macro and Micro Theory." *Kyklos* 28 (Fall).

_____. 1975b. "Mathematical Models for a Theory of Money and Financial Institutions." In R. Day and T. Groves, eds., *Adaptive Economic Models.* New York: Academic Press.

_____. 1976. "A General Theory of Money and Financial Institutions." *Economie Appliquée* 29.

_____. 1981. "Perfect or Robust Noncooperative Equilibrium: A Search for the Philosopher's Stone?" In *Essays in Game Theory and Economics in Honor of Oskar Morganstern.* Mannheim: Bibliographisches Institut.

_____. 1982. *Game Theory in the Social Sciences.* Cambridge: MIT Press.

Shubik, Martin, and Wilson, Charles. 1977. "Optimal Bankruptcy Rule in a Trading Economy Using Fiat Money." *Zeitscrift für Nationalökonomie* 37.

Siddiqi, A. 1981. "Money and Prices in the Earlier Stages of Empire." *Indian Economic and Social History Review* 18 (July–December).

Simon, Herbert. 1979. "Rational Decision Making in Business Organizations." *American Economic Review* 69 (September).

_____. 1982. *Models of Bounded Rationality.* Cambridge: MIT Press.

Skinner, Andrew. 1972. "Adam Smith: Philosophy and Science." *Scottish Journal of Political Economy* 19.

_____. 1975. *Essays on Adam Smith.* Oxford: Oxford University Press.

Smith, Adam. 1937. *An Inquiry into the Nature and Causes of the Wealth of Nations.* New York: Modern Library.

Smyth, R. L. 1962. *Essays in Economic Method.* London: Duckworth.

Sohn-Rethel, Alfred. 1978. *Intellectual and Manual Labour.* London: Macmillan.

Sorokin, Pitrim. 1956. *Contemporary Sociological Theories.* New York: Harper & Row.

Sraffa, Piero. 1926. "The Laws of Returns Under Competitive Conditions." *Economic Journal* 36 (December).

———. 1960. *Production of Commodities by Means of Commodities.* Cambridge: Cambridge University Press.

St. Clair, David. 1980. "Schumpeter's Theory of Capitalist Development." *Economic Forum* 11 (Summer).

———. 1981. "The Motorization and Decline of Urban Public Transit." *Journal of Economic History* 41 (September).

Stark, W. 1944. *The History of Economics in Relation to Its Social Development.* London: Routledge & Kegan Paul.

Steedman, Ian. 1977. *Marx After Sraffa.* London: New Left Books.

Stetson, Harlan. 1937. *Sunspots and Their Effects.* New York: Whittlesey House.

Stigler, Stephen. 1982. "Jevons as Statistician." *Manchester School* 50 (December).

Suppe, Frederick. 1977. *The Structure of Scientific Theories.* Urbana: University of Illinois Press.

Sussmann, Martin. 1972. *Elementary General Thermodynamics.* Reading, Mass.: Addison-Wesley.

Sutherland, Lucy. 1952. *The East India Company in Eighteenth Century Politics.* Oxford: Oxford University Press.

Taylor, Charles. 1985. *Human Agency and Language.* Cambridge: Cambridge University Press.

Theobald, D. W. 1966. *The Concept of Energy.* London: Spon.

Thoben, H. 1982. "Mechanistic and Organistic Analogies in Economics Reconsidered." *Kyklos* 35.

Thompson, H. F. 1965. "Adam Smith's Philosophy of Science." *Quarterly Journal of Economics* 79.

Tiles, Mary. 1984. *Bachelard: Science and Objectivity.* Cambridge: Cambridge University Press.

Tucker, G. S. L. 1960. *Progress and Profits in British Economic Thought.* Cambridge: Cambridge University Press.

Tugan-Baranowsky, M. 1913. *Les Crises Industrielles en Angleterre.* Paris: Giard & Briere.

van Schaik, A. 1976. *Reproduction and Fixed Capital.* Tilberg: Tilberg University Press.

Veblen, Thorstein. 1914. *The Instinct of Workmanship.* New York: Huebsch.

———. 1919. *The Place of Science in Modern Civilization.* New York: Huebsch. Reprint New York: Capricorn, 1969.

———. 1921. *The Engineers and the Price System.* New York: Viking. Reprint 1934.

———. 1923. *Absentee Ownership.* New York: Huebsch.

———. 1932. *The Theory of Business Enterprise.* New York: Mentor.

———. 1933. *The Vested Interests and the Common Man.* New York: Viking Press.

———. 1934. *Essays in Our Changing Order.* New York: Viking Press.

Von Neumann, John, and Morganstern, Oskar. 1964. *The Theory of Games and Economic Behavior.* 3rd ed. New York: Wiley.

Walras, Leon. 1960. "Économique et Mécanique." *Metroeconomica* 12.

———. 1965. *Correspondence of Leon Walras and Related Papers,* ed. William Jaffe. 3 vols. Amsterdam: North Holland.

———. 1969. *Elements of Pure Economics,* trans. William Jaffee. New York: Kelley.

Watson, J. 1960. *The Reign of George III.* Oxford: Oxford University Press.

Weiller, Ken, and Mirowski, Philip. 1983. "The Term Structure of Interest Rates in the Eighteenth Century." Tufts University working paper.

Weintraub, E. Roy. 1979. *Microfoundations.* Cambridge: Cambridge University Press.

Weisskopf, Walter. 1979. "The Method Is the Ideology." *Journal of Economic Issues* 13 (September).

Westfall, Richard. 1980. *Never at Rest: A Biography of Issac Newton.* New York: Cambridge University Press.

Wicksell, Knut. 1938. *Lectures on Political Economy.* 2 vols. London: Routledge.

Wilbur, Charles, and Harrison, Robert. 1978. "The Methodological Basis of Institutional Economics." *Journal of Economic Issues* 12 (March).

Willett, H. C., and Prohaska, J. 1960. "Long-term Indices of Solar Activity." NSF Report 5931, MIT, Cambridge, Mass., September 30.

Williams, George C. 1966. *Adaptation and Natural Selection.* Princeton: Princeton University Press.

Winter, Sidney. 1964. "Economic Natural Selection and the Theory of the Firm." *Yale Economic Essays* 4.

Wittgenstein, Ludwig. 1976. *Lectures on the Foundations of Mathematics, Cambridge 1939,* ed. Cora Diamond. Ithaca: Cornell University Press.

———. 1978. *Remarks on the Foundations of Mathematics.* Rev. ed. London: MIT Press.

Wong, Stanley. 1978. *The Foundations of Paul Samuelson's Revealed Preference Theory.* Boston: Routledge & Kegan Paul.

Wright, Crispin. 1980. *Wittgenstein on the Foundations of Mathematics.* Cambridge: Harvard University Press; London: Duckworth.

Zawadski, W. 1914. *Les Mathématiques Appliquées a L'Economie Politique.* Paris: Marcel Riviere.

Index